DEVELOPING CULTURAL INTELLIGENCE AT WORK

CQ

Developing Cultural Intelligence at Work

P. CHRISTOPHER EARLEY

SOON ANG

JOO-SENG TAN

STANFORD BUSINESS BOOKS
An imprint of Stanford University Press
Stanford, California 2006

Stanford University Press
Stanford, California

Library of Congress Cataloging-in-Publication Data
Earley, P. Christopher.
   CQ: developing cultural intelligence at work / P. Christopher Earley,
Soon Ang, Joo-Seng Tan.
      p. cm.
   Includes bibliographical references and index.
   ISBN 0-8047-4313-4 (cloth : alk. paper)
   1. Diversity in the workplace. 2. Cross-cultural orientation. 3. Social intelligence. 4. Social
values—Cross-cultural studies. 5. Intercultural communication. 6. Management—Cross-cultural
studies. I. Title: Cultural intelligence at work. II. Ang, Soon. III. Tan, Joo-Seng. IV. Title.

HF5549.5.M5E17 2006
658.3'008—dc22

2005023670

Typeset by G&S Book Services in 10/13.5 Minion Roman

Original Printing 2006

Last figure below indicates year of this printing:
15   14   13   12   11   10   09   08   07   06

CONTENTS

PREFACE

Coming into the turbulent twenty-first century has confronted us all with the challenge of globalization. But rather than coming together, united by common business practices, companies struggle with national, regional, and local differences among their employees, shareholders, and customers. Our focus in this book is to provide a consistent and new way of thinking about these cultural differences from a personal standpoint.

In this book we introduce an idea we call "cultural intelligence" and discuss its implications for managing in diverse work environments. Simply stated, cultural intelligence refers to a manager's capability to adapt to new cultural environments. This adjustment may be necessary if a manager is transferred overseas, but it is just as likely to be relevant to someone who is moving from one region to another of his or her home country (e.g., from San Diego to Atlanta), changing business units within a large company (e.g., from Chevrolet trucks to Saturn), or moving across functional areas (e.g., from accounting to sales).

Culture is, simply defined, a group of people's worldview, or what Geert Hofstede calls the software of the mind. Dealing with people who have radically different views of the world around them requires cultural intelligence.

The basic idea that people have different facets of intelligence is not new; it dates back to the early 1900s in the field of psychology. What has remained hotly debated among scholars is the forms these facets might take and how they are acquired. Some people suggest that our basic intelligence is formed at a very early age and only changes marginally thereafter. Others go even further and suggest a strong genetic and inherited facet of intelligence. Our position is that while some of a person's intelligence may be "hardwired" at birth and through their early developmental experiences, there is still a great deal that a person can do to shape and refine his or her cultural intelligence. The focus of our book is to describe cultural intelligence and provide a self-assessment so that the reader may focus on weak areas and seek to improve them. Additionally, we describe the way to make use of cultural intelligence in a variety of business settings, including leadership roles, teams, and expatriate work assignments in general.

Our book was inspired by a number of influences that were both practical and academic. For example, we noticed in our work with various clients that some managers who were found by their subordinates to be highly effective within their own cultural setting would flounder during an overseas work assignment. In odd contrast, a manager who seemed misanthropic in his own culture sometimes blossomed overseas, for reasons unknown. This led us to consider that very different capabilities may be involved in working with other people in one's own culture than in new cultures. From an academic perspective, our work in this book builds upon that of a number of giants in the fields of business, psychology, and cross-cultural management, including Robert Sternberg, Howard Gardner, Daniel Goleman, and Harry Triandis, as well as of colleagues working on similar trends, including Lynn Offerman, David Thomas, and Kerr Inkson, among others. We are grateful as well to numerous colleagues who have worked on this topic and provided invaluable critiques and suggestions, including James Bailey, John Berry, Deepak Bhawuk, Richard Brislin, Chay Hoon Lee, Elaine Mosakowski, Kok Yee Ng, Randall Peterson, Klaus Templer, and Linn Van Dyne.

We are grateful to many individuals and to our universities for their support during the preparation of this book. The first author wishes to thank the Nanyang Business School for support through the Nanyang professorship he received during the writing of this book, as well as the Cycle and Carriage Chair at the National University of Singapore business school and an appointment at the London Business School. The second author wishes to acknowledge the valuable assistance of Anand Chandrasekar, Pam Steel, Klaus Templer, Harry Triandis, Linn Van Dyne, and Kok Yee Ng for sharing their experiences in working and interacting with people across cultures. The second author dedicates this book to S. D. G., "who maketh us same yet different." The third author wishes to thank Chris Earley and Soon Ang, whose indefatigable enthusiasm and energy made this enterprise possible.

P. C. E.

S. A.

J. S. T.

ABOUT THE AUTHORS

P. CHRISTOPHER EARLEY is the dean of the National University of Singapore Business School, Cycle and Carriage Professor, and on leave as a professor of organizational behavior at the London Business School. His interests include cross-cultural and international aspects of organizations such as the dynamics of multinational teams, negotiation and conflict, the role of face in organizations, and motivation across cultures. He is the author of ten books and numerous articles and book chapters, and his recent publications include "Cultural Intelligence" (with E. Mosakowski, *Harvard Business Review*), *Cultural Intelligence: Individual Interactions across Cultures* (with Ang Soon), *Multinational Work Teams: A New Perspective* (with Cristina Gibson), *Culture, Self-Identity, and Work* and *The Transplanted Executive: Managing in Different Cultures* (both with Miriam Erez), *Face, Harmony, and Social Structure: An Analysis of Behavior in Organizations*, and "Creating Hybrid Team Cultures: An Empirical Test of International Team Functioning" (with E. Mosakowski, *Academy of Management Journal*). He is the former editor of *Group and Organization Management* as well as the former associate editor of the *Academy of Management Review* and a member of several other editorial boards. He received his Ph.D. in industrial and organizational psychology from the University of Illinois, Urbana-Champaign. He has taught on the faculties of the University of Arizona, the University of Minnesota, and the University of California, Irvine, and he has taught executives and consulted for companies such as the Islamic Development Bank, General Motors, Unilever, British Aerospace, Mercury Asset Management, and Eli Lilly Pharmaceuticals, among others, in England, France, Germany, Hong Kong, Israel, the People's Republic of China, Singapore, South Korea, and Thailand, among others.

SOON ANG is Goh Tjoei Kok Chair Professor in Management and Executive Director of the Center for Cultural Intelligence (CCI) at the Nanyang Business School, Nanyang Technological University, Singapore. She is also the Director of the Human Resource Round Table (HARRT-Singapore), an affiliate of HARRT-UCLA. She received her Ph.D. from the Carlson School of Management with a supporting field in industrial and organizational psychology at the University of Minnesota. She is a multiple-award-winning researcher and world authority on cultural intelligence, talent management, and employment outsourcing. She has published numerous journal articles, won international best paper awards at the Academy of Management and others. She is the Senior Editor of *Information Systems Research, Journal of the Association of Information Systems*; an associate editor of *Management Science*, and on editorial boards of *Organization Science, Journal of Organizational Behavior, Management and Organization Research*, and others and won the Meritorious Reviewer Award from *Human Relations*. She has served as a principal research investigator, consultant, and advisor to the Singapore Airlines; Singapore Dispute Resolute Advisory Committee; the Ministry of Manpower, the Ministry of Defense; the Singapore Armed Forces Training Institute; the Overseas-Chinese Banking Corporation; Accenture; Pace Consulting; National Computer Systems; the International Labor Organization; the California Judicial and Administrative Courts Systems, and others. She established the world's first Center for Cultural Intelligence at Nanyang Business School to promote basic research and pedagogical innovations in cultural intelligence. Together with Professor Linn Van Dyne at Michigan State University, she has developed both short and long versions of a globally validated psychological tool for assessing cultural intelligence. The theory and measurement of cultural intelligence have been widely disseminated in top academic conferences in management and cross-cultural psychology, including meetings of the Academy of Management (AOM), the American Psychological Association, the Society for Industrial and Organizational Psychology (SIOP), and the International Academy of Intercultural Research (IAIR).

JOO-SENG TAN is associate professor of management at the Nanyang Business School, Nanyang Technological University, Singapore. He is the program director at the Center for Cultural Intelligence. He has been responsible for developing training and development programs on cultural intelligence. Tan's areas of expertise include cultural intelligence, cross-cultural organizational behavior, cross-cultural negotiation and conflict management, cross-cultural communication, and change management. He has authored several books and book chapters, and his research has been published in international journals and publications. Tan's more recent publications include "Developing and Training Cultural Intelligence" (in Earley and Ang, *Cultural Intelligence*; Stanford University Press), *Strategies for Effective Cross-Cultural Negotiation* (with Elizabeth Lim; McGraw-Hill), and *Organizational Behavior in Asia: Issues and Challenges* (with Chi Ching R. G.; McGraw-Hill). Tan has presented papers at top academic conferences and professional meetings in the United States, France, Sweden, Japan, Korea, China, Hong Kong, Malaysia, Australia, and New Zealand. Tan has extensive experience in consulting and executive development. DuPont Asia Pacific, Merial Asia Pacific, Singapore Airlines, SIA Engineering Company, Overseas-Chinese Banking Corporation, Great Eastern Life, and the Monetary Authority of Singapore are some of the organizations for which he has provided consulting and training services. He is a director-at-large for the Association for Business Communication. In 2005, Tan was a visiting research scholar at Cornell University's School of Hotel Administration.

DEVELOPING CULTURAL INTELLIGENCE AT WORK

INTRODUCTION: POSITIONING CULTURAL INTELLIGENCE IN THE GLOBAL ECONOMY

Imagine a world where you could just depend on yourself and your community for all that you need. In this imaginary world, you would never need to venture out of your community, society, or country. If you find it difficult to visualize such a world, it is because such a world does not exist in reality. The world we live in has experienced waves of dramatic, even disruptive changes since the advent of globalization. And globalization is here to stay, whether we like it or not. The concept of the "global village," first coined in the 1960s by the well-known media scholar Marshall McLuhan, is now a reality. People from distant and different cultures are now increasingly interconnected owing to advances in technology and telecommunications.

Globalization has rendered geographic boundaries porous, sometimes even insignificant. It has increased permeability of all kinds of borders — physical borders such as time and space, nation-states and economies, and industries and organizations, as well as less tangible borders such as cultural norms or assumptions about how "we" do things "here." Complex global matrix relationships and communication technology have moved borders and boundaries directly into the workplace today. Workforces in most countries are increasingly heterogeneous and diverse. Increased interdependence between nation-states leads to more encounters among people from different cultures. Viewed in this context, we can define globalization as a large-scale, interactive social process in which people increasingly interrelate, communicate, and work in an increasingly culturally diverse workplace, both within and outside the organization.

Consequently, it is urgent to build individual and organizational capacity to meet the social, relational, and communication needs thrown up by globalization.

Among the twenty-first-century skills frequently talked about are the ability to adapt constantly to different people from diverse cultures and the ability to manage the interconnectedness of today's world. Interactions in the global workplace require individuals to be sensitive to different cultures, capable of analyzing them as they are encountered, identifying what is required of people from other cultures, and engaging in appropriate interactions with them. To be able to do all this, individuals need to have cultural intelligence, a concept we will explain later in this chapter.

The sense of a shrinking world has heightened feelings of vulnerability, as people from different cultures and ideologies have to learn how to live with each other or pay a heavy price for the inability to understand and respect one another. In these difficult times of the aftermath of the September 11 tragedy, of horrendous conflicts between the Israelis and the Palestinians, and of a war on terrorism being conducted around the globe, it seems obvious that something needs to be done for people to understand one another better. The actions of one party toward another are often misunderstood and misconstrued by the other party. We need only look to the press to feel overwhelmed with the difficulties that confront people as they deal across national and cultural boundaries. Our need to understand one another extends into the global perspective on business as well. This need is reflected in many ways, including how people work in cultures different from their own and how to run effective multinational teams by negotiating across national boundaries or forming joint ventures for companies' mutual benefit. Increasingly, people work in international teams and divisions, thanks to the global nature of work. However, business is populated with numerous tales of ineffective global managers who failed to grasp important nuances of their host culture. The result of such inability to adapt and understand local culture is significant and costly to organizations.

Cultural diversity affects individuals in the workplace and affects both the internal and external environments faced by people at work. According to Nancy Adler, a well-known scholar on international management, "Whether organizations produce in multiple countries or only export to them, whether employees work as expatriates or only travel abroad, whether legal ownership involves joint ventures, wholly owned subsidiaries, or strategic alliances, global firms must manage despite the added complexity of working in many countries simultaneously" (Adler, 2002: 15).

Thus, it is important to know how to manage culturally diverse, cross-cultural, and geographically dispersed organizations. Globalization has reshaped human and social interactions in the workplace. You need cultural intelligence even if you never leave home. Cultural intelligence is needed to manage the stress of culture shock and the consequent frustration and confusion that typically result from clashes of cultural differences. Cultural intelligence is essential in facilitating effective cross-cultural adjustment.

In positioning cultural intelligence as a key concept in the global economy, several questions that concern both individuals and organizations can be raised:

- How do individuals develop their ability to adapt effectively across different cultures?
- Why do some individuals possess superior capacity to deal with the challenges of working in different cultures?
- How do individuals reach full productive potential working in culturally diverse work environments in their home countries and overseas?
- How do organizations build the capacity for effective global work assignments in different locations around the world?
- How do organizations optimize individual and collective performance by harnessing the cultural diversity of their people across the world?

In this book, we tackle these questions by explaining what cultural intelligence is and showing how it is applied in the workplace.

A SHIFT IN THINKING ABOUT INTELLIGENCE
IN THE WORKPLACE

Some people argue that if we can just understand why other people act as they do, we might improve how people relate to one another. That is, the secret to helping people get along with one another is a type of human problem-solving. This idea stems largely from the field of psychology and it emphasizes a crucial part of human thought: intelligence. Simply stated, intelligence refers to a person's capacity to solve problems and adapt to diverse circumstances. This ability to adapt to varying circumstances shows an important new flavor to the study of intelligence — it isn't just a reflection of a person's problem-solving, mathematical, or reading skills. Certain individuals seem actually to have an enhanced ability for people-to-people discourse. Just as some people are very capable of solving complex mathematical problems, others are highly adept at figuring out the real power broker at any party or social event. Some have an uncanny ability to judge the mood of another person or to calm down the most agitated person. Some have a knack for picking up languages or musical instruments. And some can pick up a complicated literary treatise spouting the most recent iteration of logic or philosophy and read and internalize it with ease.

Despite abundant interest and timely relevance in global affairs, there remains a large gap in our understanding of personal adjustment to new countries and foreign peoples. Our approach provides a new understanding for the age-old problem of the sojourner (a traveler whose stay in another country, while purposeful and voluntary, is temporary): why is it that some people adjust relatively easily, quickly, and thoroughly to new cultures, whereas others can't? There are many anecdotes about managers who show great empathy within their own culture — who display high emotional and social intelligence — yet don't adjust well to new cultures. In contrast, some of the most effective global managers seem somewhat out of place in their own countries.

Why shouldn't a manager who has high emotional and social intelligence be able to move among cultures with great ease? Take, as an example, an American manager who ran a *maquiladora* in Mexico, on the Arizona border, for a large consumer electronics company. This manager was viewed by his American employees in Arizona as understanding and sympathetic, with good insight into his employees' interests and needs. After being assigned to the plant in Mexico, he decided that he'd get to know his key managers (subordinates) better by inviting his two top managers (who were Mexican) to his home in Arizona for a weekend visit to meet his wife and family. He thought that this would give his managers the opportunity to get to know him more personally and would show them how much he valued their contributions to the factory. However, the managers politely turned down his initial invitation. He waited a few weeks and then extended an invitation again. Again his managers turned him down. After refusing the invitation numerous times, the two managers finally (after a period of several months) acquiesced and visited his home. The next week he returned to the factory only to find that both managers had resigned. How could such a thing happen? Had he offended them during the visit? Were they insulted by the relative opulence of his household? Had the lowered status difference reflected in the visit offended them? These were the various possibilities that he mulled over in his mind as he attempted to contact them and ask them to return to the company.

After a number of calls one of the two managers agreed to return to his job. When the American asked this manager what he had done (or left undone) to offend his guests, his manager replied that he had not done anything to them. They had, in fact, enjoyed the visit, but it made it hard for them to maintain control of their employees at the factory floor. The American asked why; he had assumed that "mingling" with the "boss" would raise their social capital and enhance their prestige and face. The Mexican manager said that the opposite was true. By lowering the power differential between himself and his Mexican managers, the American sent a signal to the employees that there was no significant power differential within the company. As a result, the power base of the Mexican managers (who relied on cultural values of strong power and authority) was undermined. (We wish to thank Mary Teagarden for this example.) Under this circumstance, they felt that they had no recourse except to leave. Although this American manager has great empathy and social intelligence within his own culture, he was unable to discern and interpret the cues provided by individuals from outside it. Obviously, the managers' rejection of the invitation on several occasions was a strong signal, but he hadn't paid attention to it. What the manager was lacking was an awareness and understanding of different cultural practices. More important, he wasn't able to figure these things out himself, which is an important part of CQ. CQ is a characteristic unique to each person; that is, each individual can be thought of as having a unique CQ, and this ability is based upon unique experiences.

So how is our idea of cultural intelligence different from related ideas popular in the management press, such as emotional or social intelligence? Emotional intelligence presumes that a person is familiar with his own culture and (often unconsciously) uses a familiar situation as a way of acting and reacting with others. Cultural intelligence picks up where emotional intelligence leaves off: dealing with people and situations in unfamiliar surroundings.

Cultural intelligence captures a person's adjustment to new cultures. Thus, we define cultural intelligence as *a person's capability for successful adaptation to new cultural settings, that is, for unfamiliar settings attributable to cultural context.*

Cultural intelligence consists of three key parts, including what you think and how you solve problems (cultural strategic thinking); whether or not you are energized and persistent in your actions (motivation); and whether you can act in certain ways (behavior). Cultural strategic thinking refers to the general thinking skills that you use to understand how and why people act as they do in a new culture. This understanding captures not just what people in another culture believe or value, but also the procedures and routines that people are supposed to use as they work and act. The ideas that we have about a new culture concerning what people believe or value is called *declarative knowledge*, or knowledge about the state of things. For example, if I know that in Bali children are named according to their birth order, this is declarative knowledge. Think of it as knowledge of facts. However, if I know that in China after a toast (*gan bei*) you empty your glass, this is knowledge of procedures, or *procedural knowledge*. The cultural strategic thinking part of cultural intelligence has two components: *cultural knowledge* and *cultural thinking and learning.* Cultural knowledge captures both the facts that we hold about another culture as well as our knowledge of how things operate. Related to this is how we gain this knowledge in the first place, which we refer to as cultural thinking and learning. This kind of cultural thinking and learning, called metacognition by the psychologists, has also been referred to as "thinking about thinking" or "learning to learn." So these two elements work together; cultural strategic thinking guides the strategies we use to acquire knowledge about country-specific information. Clearly, both types of knowledge are critical to success.

Creating a way to make sense of new and radically different situations is important for cultural intelligence. A culturally intelligent manager isn't just learning the ways in which people act and behave in a new place. Although learning about a new situation is important, he or she must create a new mental framework for understanding what he or she experiences and sees. Psychologists call this higher level of learning *higher-order thinking* or *cultural strategic thinking,* and it refers to how we learn, not just what we learn. In approaches such as emotional or social intelligence, people use their existing knowledge of how things function in their culture to decide how and when to act in any particular situation.

As important as it may be, "learning to learn" about new situations isn't enough if you consider the challenge of managing people in a foreign country. It requires motivation as well. A manager might understand what is happening and why in a cross-cultural encounter but choose to ignore the situation or not feel confident to act. A German manager working on a multinational team with both German and Brazilian members commented:

> When I first joined the team I was very frustrated by my Brazilian colleagues. We would schedule a meeting for 9 a.m., and they would show up at anywhere from 9:30 to 11 a.m.! It just didn't seem that they cared about the meeting and our team. I mentioned this to them several times, but it just didn't seem to have an effect upon them. Later, I just gave up and focused on my own work outside of the team.

This manager certainly knew what was going on in his team, but he had become so frustrated with his experiences that he became unmotivated and stopped trying. The second element of a culturally intelligent manager is confidence and motivation.

Personal motivation isn't enough either, if you think about it. Certain actions not within a person's current repertoire (inventory of actions that you already know how to do) may be needed for an appropriate response in a new culture, as we will discuss later in this chapter. Simple examples abound from the anecdotes of international managers — e.g., the proper way to shake someone's hand in Ghana (involving a finger click at the end of the handshake) and how to eat a local exotic delicacy without showing hesitation or disgust.

The difficulty is that many of these actions are easily overlooked, yet they have a cumulative impact on the quality of our interactions with others. One manager from Canada relayed the story of meeting a group of managers from a Mexican joint venture. He noticed that after several minutes of talking with his Mexican counterpart that they had moved around the meeting room as if they had been engaged in a dance! He later realized that as they spoke, the Mexican manager would draw closer to the Canadian manager. As he did so, the Canadian manager would unconsciously draw back. As one manager approached, the other manager backed away as if they were two magnets with a common charge. After moving around their conference room in this cultural waltz, the Canadian manager realized what he was doing and purposely stopped moving back. A person's aversion to particular foods or facility for languages (e.g., some people just cannot hear the tones in Chinese or Thai very well) reflects this third component of a culturally intelligent manager; such a person is able to adopt new actions when they are needed.

This means that it isn't enough to understand why young male college students hold one another's hands during class lecture in China or why German MBA students look repeatedly to their watches in anticipation of the onset of class; one must be motivated to adapt and adjust to a new culture. Without proper motivation and a willingness to engage the world, you won't adjust. We will look at several aspects of motivation, including self-confidence (efficacy), setting goals and targets, and self-assessments of personal identity and values. Self-confidence provides you with energy to push ahead, goals provide direction and guidance, and personal identity and values are your anchor in the storm of life. Think about a Korean manager, who said about his experiences on a multinational team: "They were trying not to listen to me, sometimes they changed the subject after I spoke, they were not paying attention; I think it went on for at least one or two months while I was trying to improve my speaking and listening, and this was a bad experience. Later, I just gave up trying to speak." In this example, our manager was able to understand what was going on and why, but he was unmotivated to try and deal with the cultural situation. His attitude reflected his own low motivation; furthermore, he lacked the confidence to work effectively, so he disengaged from his team. CQ means knowing *and* trying.

The final piece of CQ is a person's ability to "do the right thing," or engage in action that is adaptive. The action component is often neglected in most of the current work on intelligence — an unfortunate oversight. We suppose that this is because psychologists often pigeonhole their work, and so-called cognitive and behavioral psychologies have their own independent supporters. From a management perspective, it seems to us that separating what a person thinks from what he or she does is woefully short-sighted. Ultimately, business requires action, not simply intention. But we are not talking about CQ as something stagnant when it comes to behavior. A person's actions are dynamic, and he or she must adjust to the changing nature of the work environment. It's not enough to have a "potential" for action; potential realized through one's actions partly determines CQ.

To summarize, cultural intelligence reflects an intersection of three paths — what I think about a new culture (direction), whether am I motivated and feel confident to act (energization), and whether I create the actions needed for the situation (adaptation). To us, cultural intelligence isn't meaningful unless it means that actions are completed. As in the adage of "deeds versus intentions," CQ reflects a person's ability to enact actions needed in a particular culture. A person may know what to do and feel motivated to act, but without appropriate action, it will all be for naught. For example, suppose you have are visiting your friends in Germany and they take you to a nice restaurant. They kindly order the food for you, and you are served what appears to be a healthy portion of meat. Not wanting to risk acquiring BSE from tainted beef, you politely ask your hosts the origins of the beef, explaining your concerns. Your hosts laugh heartily at this, pointing out that you have no worries whatsoever because you haven't been served beef — you've gotten a nice cut of horsemeat (a delicacy gaining popularity in Europe as a result of BSE scares, foot-and-mouth disease, and other plagues of the twenty-first century). Despite your understanding of why you've gotten horsemeat and your desire (motivation) not to offend your hosts, you find yourself unable to eat dinner. This example reflects one type of difficulty arising from cultural encounters owing to the behavior or action facet of CQ. That is, many of our reactions in cultural settings are sufficiently ingrained that we may find it very difficult to overcome them. There may be other instances in which we're unable to do the expected action, such as trying to master the nuances of a new language. The first author (a nonnative Chinese speaker who has attempted to acquire bits of Mandarin) recalls an incident concerning a well-intentioned colleague who had prepared a careful speech (all in Chinese) to show his Chinese colleagues his appreciation for their hosting him and his family in China. At the end of the fifteen-minute speech the American shook hands with his hosts. Later that evening (well out of earshot of the American, so as to avoid offending him), one of the Chinese professors commented, "I really appreciated his trying to give his speech, but I had absolutely no idea what he was saying." As it turns out, the American seemed completely incapable of producing the appropriate tones during his speech even though he had the correct syllables. Without effective execution, the best of intentions won't translate into effective action, and a person's CQ will not be realized. CQ requires effective adaptation to cultural circumstance, not merely intentions or wishes.

Cultural Intelligence as Competitive Advantage and Strategic Capability

More and more organizations and individuals are seeing cultural intelligence as a competitive advantage and strategic capability. In the following sections, we present evidence that different corporations are already oriented toward cultural intelligence and are enjoying the benefits realized by hiring individuals who are culturally intelligent and by including cultural intelligence as a core part of the organization's corporate strategy.

IBM firmly believes that cross-cultural competence is the glue that enables cohesiveness and collective performance. In the high-performance environment of the global marketplace, cultural intelligence is a strategic capability of leaders and managers. Organizations and individuals who see the strategic value of cultural intelligence are able to effectively leverage cultural differences for competitive advantage and achieve competitive superiority in the global marketplace.

In the global scramble for talent, organizations aspire to be the employer of choice. They hope to attract, develop, and retain the best talents in their organizations. Organizations such as Novartis and Nike see the competitive advantage of hiring individuals who are culturally intelligent. These organizations also adopt cultural diversity as an integral part of their human resource (HR) agenda. They identify focus areas for cultural diversity and link cultural diversity and the HR business case.

Culturally intelligent individuals who can respond effectively to customers from different cultures would also be welcomed at Lloyds TSB. In fact, Lloyds TSB takes the challenge of improving customer relationship so seriously that they have a diversity strategy to deal with it. The strategy has contributed to increased income streams and better cost management.

Culturally intelligent individuals who are able to leverage cultural diversity to align marketing and product development with consumers can provide a competitive edge in product development and marketing strategies for consumer groups in different countries. Levi Strauss capitalizes on this strategy to grow their business globally. Lufthansa, the German airline, believes that culturally intelligent individuals constitute a precious organizational asset during times of crisis. At Barclays, culturally intelligent individuals will be able to help the organization gain local ownership and commitment in the United Kingdom and beyond.

It is evident that organizations leverage on culturally intelligent individuals to achieve organizational goals and strategies. Individuals who are culturally intelligent provide a source of competitive advantage for global multinational companies.

For instance, culturally intelligent leaders can improve cooperation between employees from different countries and cultures. As the management professor Lynn Offermann suggests, a person's ability to work and adapt in an environment where one's assumptions, values, and traditions differ from those in the local setting reflects cultural intelligence. This adjustment requires skills and abilities very different from those that you might use in your own familiar surroundings.

OUR APPROACH

In this book, we develop and describe cultural intelligence in a global and cultural setting, focusing on the modern work organization. Our approach to cultural intelligence can be illustrated using a simple example from the first author's experiences in London. I noticed an unusual event while riding the underground rail system. A middle-aged British woman lost all composure and yelled at another patron (a man in his early twenties) because he refused to give up his seat to her very young child after she politely asked him several times to move. I relayed this story to a British friend, and he suggested that the English seem to operate at very different levels of restraint at times. He said that many British are so used to acting in a restrained manner that "when the top blows off, the mountain comes down." (Perhaps it's no coincidence that *Dr. Jekyll and Mr. Hyde*, which portrays a character struggling with the dual nature of his emotions, was written by Robert Louis Stevenson, a prominent British author.) We might speculate why something such as this train situation might have happened, and we might surmise that it is a carryover from the restraints placed on people during Victorian times.

What went wrong in this transportation encounter? If we recall the three questions posed earlier (What is happening and why? Am I motivated to act? Can I do the right thing here?), we can understand where things went awry. First, the train rider failed to understand the intensity and direction of the mother's feelings. He wrongly assumed that he understood her. Second, he wasn't really motivated to deal with the mother and didn't really persevere in the encounter. Third, his inaction was poorly received by the mother.

To predict his cultural intelligence, we have to see whether or not he learned his lesson. He might notice and confirm with his friends that a number of British operate in at least two rather different modes (restraint versus self-abandon) depending upon the situation. Is he motivated to deal more effectively with other commuters the next time he travels by rail? Would he take the right actions the next time (use appropriate etiquette on the train)? Time will tell. Will his next encounter prove more productive? We certainly hope so!

How do these skills in adapting relate to the skills that a manager might use while working with people from his own culture or country? When you are operating in your own familiar social surroundings, it's much easier to know whether you are getting an expected reaction. The real challenge facing a manager who works internationally is that it's virtually impossible to learn everything that you might need to know about a country you are going to work in. Certainly, general knowledge about the country, its people and customs, food, religion, politics, and so on is valuable. However, it's just not practical or possible to learn all, or even most, of the important nuances of a new culture.

Many companies rely on existing training programs that emphasize critical dos and don'ts in dealing with new cultures or lists of values, practices, and facts. You see them at Heathrow and other international airports: posters advertising the global bank HSBC that show a grasshopper and read, "In the USA, it's a pest. In China, it's a pet. In Thailand, it's an appetizer." Culture is so powerful it can even compound the meaning of even an insect. So it should come as no surprise that the actions, gestures, and speech patterns of human beings in an unfamiliar business setting are subject to an even wider range of interpretations, including some that can make misunderstandings likely and cooperation impossible. As you might expect, these methods have proven to be of limited usefulness, time consuming and tedious to use, and very expensive and difficult to assemble. Given that they are culture specific and country bound, we believe that an entirely new approach is needed, one that recognizes that a different type of understanding and learning determines who can adjust quickly to the challenges of a new country.

What does it take, then, to adapt to a new country and culture? In a new cultural situation many familiar cues and tips may be largely or entirely absent (or present but misleading), and so your natural talents lead you astray. Take a person who gauges another person's feelings and motivation by facial expressions. A smile shows an openness and willingness to move ahead as well as a generally positive mental attitude, doesn't it? Not in Thailand, where a smile may reflect over twenty different thoughts and feelings! Scientists at one time thought that facial expressions universally reflected a person's emotions (a smile is a smile, and it means the person doing the smiling is happy), but we now know that the feelings and thoughts that underlie facial expressions may differ a great deal from person to person.

What can an international traveler do to understand what another person may be thinking or feeling? *He or she must develop a common frame of understanding from available information, even though there may not be an adequate understanding of local practices and norms.* An ability to understand not only the big picture, but a new picture, is one sign of a culturally intelligent manager.

What seems to be lacking in management practice is an integration of the broader cultural and national contexts in which people live and work with this emerging emphasis on cross-border work. To make things even more complex, people from different cultures and/or nations, who do not necessarily share a common way of interpreting and evaluating situations, are more likely to respond dissimilarly to the same context. A work unit consisting of several Malaysian, Thai, and Australian managers will exhibit markedly different reactions to the same organizational intervention compared to a group consisting of Brazilian, American, and German managers.

Thus, our primary focus in this book is the development and presentation of a new approach to global management that can be brought to bear for managers seeking new work opportunities that concern international functioning for people. After completing our book, you will have a personal assessment of your CQ strengths and weaknesses as well as a developmental model showing you how to enhance your CQ. Further, you will have the skills needed to use CQ in developing your subordinates, creating effective multinational teams, and preparing managers for expatriate work.

ORGANIZATION OF THE BOOK

This book is organized into two major sections: Part I (chapters 1–4) is a general introduction to understanding our approach to cultural intelligence; Part II (chapters 5–9) demonstrates ways to put CQ into practice. The appendix gives you an opportunity to assess your own CQ.

Part I: Understanding Cultural Intelligence

In the first section of this book we discuss the value of cultural intelligence and the various bases for it — strategic, motivational, and behavioral. It gives ideas for and examples of critically assessing the areas of strength and weakness in one's own cultural intelligence and provides strategies for playing to the former while at the same time working to improve the latter.

Chapter 1: What Is Cultural Intelligence and Why Does It Matter? We begin chapter 1 by providing an overview of the three aspects of cultural intelligence: namely, cultural strategic thinking, motivation, and engaging in effective action. Next, we describe a system we call PRISM to apply cultural-intelligence practices to your work situation. In addition, you will have an opportunity to turn to the appendix to determine your own level of CQ for each of the general facets.

Chapter 2: Preparing Your Mind: The Cultural Strategic Thinking Basis of CQ. We begin chapter 2 with several sample situations for the reader to think about and solve. We illustrate how cultural strategic thinking can help to resolve cultural problems and dilemmas through thinking and reasoning. We explain how the strategies that people use for gaining cultural knowledge are critical for successfully adapting to a new culture.

Chapter 3: Directing Your Energy: The Motivational Basis of CQ. Although it is critical for managers to think rationally and accurately, they must be willing to persevere during difficulties that arise from cross-cultural misunderstandings. That is, personal effort and integrity are the next critical elements of CQ. In our discussion of CQ from a motivational perspective, we discuss one's core values, preferences, and goals as being central to his or her identity. These values and preferences give rise to personal motivation and, in turn, create a sense of personal purpose and direction.

Chapter 4: Presenting Yourself: The Behavioral Basis of CQ. The action part of our approach looks at a person's ability to draw from an existing repertoire (or to create new actions) to translate motives into successful action. That is, if someone has analyzed the situation accurately (cultural strategic thinking) and is motivated to respond (motivation), how might he or she actually respond in a culturally appropriate fashion?

Part II: Applying CQ to Your Workplace

In the second section of this book we take the ideas of cultural intelligence and show how they apply to key aspects of managing people in organizations. These topics include leadership, multinational teams, global work assignments, and workplace diversity. There is a thematic flow in this section. We begin by examining how people work with other people from different cultures within and outside the organization (chapters 5 and 6). Then we proceed to look at how cultural intelligence is applied in multinational team and global leadership contexts.

Chapter 5: Working Effectively in the Culturally Diverse Workplace. We begin chapter 5 by highlighting how organizations are dealing with diversity issues in the workplace. Then we show how CQ can be used to improve understanding and enhance work relationships for people working in a culturally diverse workplace.

Chapter 6: Succeeding in Global Work Assignments. In chapter 6 we discuss the potential use of CQ to identify key managers for expatriate work assignments as part of a larger selection and training program. In addition, we describe how a company might raise the CQ of selected personnel through various training techniques.

Chapter 7: Building High-Performing Global Teams. In chapter 7 we focus on using the concept of CQ to aid an expatriate manager with a new work assignment on a global team. We describe the role of CQ as an assessment device for a manager to understand where he or she might have difficulties in dealing with people in an international context, with special emphasis on internationally diverse work teams.

Chapter 8: Leading Globally. In chapter 8 we look at how CQ can help a manager become a more effective leader in an international context. How does CQ help a manager understand what it takes to lead in various cultures, and does this person tap into universal leadership qualities? Or do cultural strategic thinking and other capabilities mean that leadership is uniquely tailored to each new situation?

Chapter 9: Summary and Concluding Thoughts. In this final chapter we recap the nature and importance of CQ for a global company as well as for a domestic company operating in a culturally diverse environment. We return to the PRISM framework for applying a CQ-based program in a global organization, with some concluding comments about the future of global management.

Appendix: A Self-Assessment of Your CQ

In this section you can assess your CQ and obtain a profile of your strengths and weaknesses. This instrument is based on our fieldwork with managers in various international assignments.

SUMMARY

There is a story that one day a powerful and wealthy Chinese businessman went to the market with his servant. This businessman was known to all the market vendors, and everyone knew how important and powerful he was in the province. After browsing in various shops, he happened onto an open market where pottery was sold. He looked at the various pots and plates and noticed one that he found very appealing and purchased it. He motioned for his elderly servant to collect the large, heavy pot and to follow along to the next shop. Unfortunately, as the servant tried to lift the pot, it slipped from his hands and fell to the ground, breaking into many pieces. Upon seeing this, his master came over to the servant, shouting at him and berating him for his feebleness. In addition, the businessman took his cane and began to beat the old servant in front of everyone in the market, calling him a senile old fool and humiliating him. However, it was clear to all the bystanders that the true fool was the businessman who expected his elderly servant to carry such a burden. The real shame was the disgrace of the businessman reprimanding and punishing his servant in public. The businessman had difficulty doing business after this, and within months he had lost his fortune. Why? Simply because the businessman lost "face" (personal status and prestige) by abusing his servant as he had. If he had forgiven rather than condemned his servant, he would have gained face rather than losing it. Had he shown benevolence rather than malevolence, he would have gained face; although the Chinese don't readily admit errors if a mistake is obvious, to hide behind one's error using someone powerless is seen as demeaning and unbecoming. Showing one's magnificence in such a situation enhances reputation and face for the wrongdoer.

How can we comprehend such complex thinking across such a wide range of cultural settings throughout the world? Are some people more able to do so than others? More important, can we teach managers skills so that they are able to do so? These are the questions that lie at the heart of our book. We attempt to bridge a gap in the management literature concerning why some people fail to adjust to new cultures even if they seem very empathetic and sensitive in their own cultures. We identify the reasons and explain why these reasons matter. Further, we seek to understand the very nature of intelligence and how cultural situations help to shape it. It is through this approach that we believe it is possible to expand and clarify the most fundamental of human characteristics: intelligence.

I

UNDERSTANDING CULTURAL INTELLIGENCE

1 WHAT IS CULTURAL INTELLIGENCE AND WHY DOES IT MATTER?

It's clear that cultural intelligence is a source of competitive advantage and a strategic capability for individuals and organizations. Effective and efficient adjustment to new countries and cultures brings dividends to individuals and organizations. What isn't clear is, what exactly constitutes cultural intelligence? If cultural intelligence has core elements, why do these elements matter in the context of developing a manager's cultural intelligence? Understanding why the different elements of CQ matter will help us understand why managers differ from one another in their success at international placements.

Take an example described by the anthropologist Edward Hall concerning his early visits to Japan. After returning to his hotel (a small, family-run place), he found that his belongings had been moved from the room where he had been staying for the past week to a new one. Not wanting to create a fuss, he went to his new room. About a week later, he was again moved to a new room (and again without his consent or knowledge). He again made no mention of it to his hosts, simply assuming that he was being treated as *gaijin*, or a foreigner, and after a while went back home to the United States. The following year he returned to Japan to another family-run hotel and found that not only did he get moved from room to room, switched, but, one week, even from one hotel to another. After complaining to a Japanese colleague, his friend told him that this was a compliment — only someone considered family would be moved in such a fashion. Strangers are not bothered, but family (or those belonging to the in-group) can be imposed upon. Why do some managers understand that the hotel was treating them as part of the local family, while others assume wrongly that they are being moved around unexpectedly because they are unimportant and have low status? Why is it that some managers who seem to understand what is going on in a new culture nevertheless fail to work effectively? Is this a motivation dilemma or a manager's inability to adjust properly?

SOME BASICS: CULTURE, COUNTRY, AND UNIVERSALS

Before we describe the details of our approach, it's important that we share with managers our definitions of several key ideas in this book.

- *What do we mean by culture?* The most important starting point for our discussion focuses on the distinction between culture and country. Culture can be thought of as patterned ways of thinking, feeling, and reacting to various situations and actions. Culture is gained and shared among people through symbols, including their embodiment in artifacts. For example, in American culture the eagle symbolizes freedom and independence, as every schoolchild learns at an early age. The eagle appears on our currency, on national emblems, on the presidential seal, and the like. The sociologist and business consultant Geert Hofstede likes to think about culture as a sort of mental programming for people within a nation; it's the "software" of the mind, and it reflects a set of imperfectly shared rules for behavior and meanings attached to such behavior.
- *What do we mean by country?* Simply put, country (or nation) refers to a territorially bounded, multigenerational region with a population organized around a common culture and social system.

Culture and country are slippery concepts at times. For example, one country might consist of many subcultures. Many people would use the United States as an example of such a melting pot of views and peoples. Switzerland, with its four official languages represented in the Swiss parliament and regions dominated by various language and ethnic traditions, represents a different type of eclectic country. However, in both the United States and Switzerland, there is an overarching common view of the world inside and outside the country. This is the national culture. Differences among groups of people within the country represent a different type of cultural diversity, which we will return to later in the book.

Culture and country are not synonymous. Although every country has an overarching culture, many subcultures may exist within a single country. To make matters even more complicated, people within the same subculture do not necessarily see the world in the same way. Over time, people acquire variations on cultural meanings because the ideas that they gain from their parents, friends, popular media, and so on are imperfectly shared. Any two individuals from a common culture may hold different views of the same event, and they may share such views with other people in their country but not with one another.

Another important idea of our approach is that some things are understood and held in common by all people, whereas others are idiosyncratic to certain countries and cultures. An idea or object is culture specific if it has a unique meaning for one group of people but represents something very different to another group. For example, the idea of machismo in Latin culture does not really have a counterpart in Anglo culture. A person from the United States might interpret machismo as "manliness" or "masculinity," but this is only partially correct. Machismo carries other meanings, including honor and obligation, that are often overlooked by non-Latinos.

In fact, some ideas are so rich and subtle that they can only be understood by someone who is from a certain culture or who has spent extensive time learning about it. This is why anthropologists seeking to learn about new groups of people will often live for several years with the people much as they do themselves (eating, sleeping, and working with them). The Chinese concept of *guanxi* has received a lot of attention in the business press and by business professors. Some people mistakenly think of *guanxi* as corruption — bribes and gift giving. Although this certainly may happen with *guanxi*, it's not a basic part of it. *Guanxi* refers to social relationships; gift giving is involved only as a gesture that helps establish and build relationships, not as a bribe. Without these symbolic gestures, the bond among people is weakened.

How does this discussion of universals relate to CQ? At certain levels there are parts of CQ that are universal across all people. For example, people everywhere share an ability to think about new situations and use problem solving to analyze them. Likewise, people are energized when motivated to challenge themselves. This does not mean that everyone is equally motivated or able to solve problems, but it does mean that everyone has some degree of motivation and problem-solving ability.

Nonetheless, some aspects of cultural intelligence are idiosyncratic. CQ is thought of as a unique characteristic of each person, but situation-specific features do appear. For example, the way to address an elderly and educated person in Thailand is properly done with a *wai*: clasping the hands in a prayer position, with the fingers extended facing upward in front of one's face, and bowing slightly forward. This particular sign of respect is unique to Thai culture (although variations are observed in other countries). The practice of showing respect to the elderly and educated people in Thai society reflects idiosyncratic interests and values within Thailand. It turns out that this is true of many things that we think of as universal. Within most universal parts of CQ rest unique aspects of culture.

Thus, it's useful to think about culture and its resulting practices as cascading downward. At the top are fundamental ideas or practices that are shared among all people. These give rise to various specific practices across countries and regions. Local practices give rise, in turn, to specific practices and interpretations by each individual. Thus, we begin with universal aspects of human behavior and end up with a look at each person as a unique individual.

The top of this pyramid consists of aspects of intelligence that capture high-level capabilities such as memory and recall, logic and deduction, and categorization. However, the specific type of logic and deduction used, categories formed, and so on may be unique to a given group of people. For example, some researchers have found that the aboriginal people of Western Australia display a highly developed sense of spatial memory and can use this for problem solving and memory exercises involving spatial locations. However, their memory using other forms of rote memory exercise is not well developed in comparison with Anglo-Australians. Memory and recall at a high level of abstraction exists for both indigenous and Anglo-Australians, yet the type of memory skill differs. To this kind of difference we note that people vary individually as well, based on their innate capabilities and their unique experiences. This suggests that CQ paradoxically reflects a universal quality that is unique to each individual — an idea advanced by the psychologists Robert Sternberg and John Berry in their pioneering work on this topic.

A GENERAL VIEW OF CULTURAL INTELLIGENCE

Cultural intelligence has both process and content features. We illustrate both in figure 1.1. In the next sections of this chapter we describe each feature and return to them in more detail in subsequent chapters of our book. Recall that the three facets of CQ are addressed by three questions:

- Why does cultural strategic thinking matter?
- Why does motivation matter?
- Why does behavior matter?

Why Does Cultural Strategic Thinking Matter?

The first facet of CQ is what we call cultural strategic thinking, or what psychologists and others often refer to as metacognition.

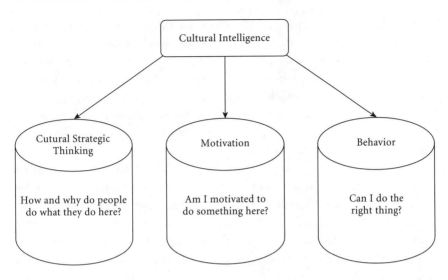

Figure 1.1   Elements of cultural intelligence

We begin our discussion by looking at how people store, process, and retrieve information critical to understanding new cultures. We aren't concerned about other types of intelligence such as arithmetic-problem-solving ability or spatial reasoning.

Each person has a unique psychological "fingerprint," the complex set of memories, thoughts, ways of thinking, and feelings that we have about the world around us. Psychologists call this our self-concept (the sum of our experiences, thoughts, and views of ourselves and others). Our fingerprint refers to the complex way that we define ourselves, and it consists of many roles that we may occupy (such as manager, parent, or golf partner) as well as the specific characteristics that mark our uniqueness (such as a liking for spicy Thai food or a good sense of humor). People differ in these characteristics and in the relative importance of these characteristics. While all people seem to like some spice in their food, they differ on how spicy they like it and in what type of spice is used. If you think about the seasoning on food as a dimension of a psychological fingerprint, you can see how everyone has a desire for some spices but that people differ — some like lots of salt, some like jalapeño peppers, some like sweet sauces, and so on.

The pieces that make up our view of ourselves are organized hierarchically. This helps us understand new experiences. For example, a manager who places a strong emphasis on central control and authority may easily set aside a secondary characteristic of friendliness to his employees if someone has made a mistake or violated company policy. Keep in mind that the amount of information included in a person's fingerprint (self-concept) is enormous, including his or her past and present experiences and anticipated future ones. However, not all this information confronts us all of the time. What we think about at any given time is largely influenced by the situation we are experiencing. The part of our thoughts active at any moment is called the "working self," and it helps us deal with the world around us. The working self is accessible, active, malleable, and tied to current events. So, for instance, if you show up to work and everyone is in a festive mood because of an upcoming holiday, your thoughts may be drawn to your past holiday experiences and make you feel festive too.

Not only do we have these various layers of self-knowledge, but we also have a complex combination of personal role identities. Every person has many hats that he or she wears at any given time. As a manager, you might go to a meeting representing your personal, business unit, or professional identity. Put more directly, each person has separate identities, such as being a student, a family member, and an employee, and depending on the situation, certain roles will dominate over others.

Take an executive MBA student enrolled in a part-time MBA program. In the classroom, with her professor, she is a student. In the boardroom, she is a senior executive and leader in her company. At home, she is both a parent with two young children and a member of the local soccer club. These various separate identities are ordered in a salience hierarchy, in which the most important ones are more likely to be evoked in response to a given situation. But the salience of an identity is also related to your commitment to the various social groups related to these identities.

Returning to our executive MBA, imagine that a family situation arises as she is attending a board meeting: she receives a call from her son, who needs help on a school social problem (perhaps advice on asking out a girl for the school dance). Does she take this call and interrupt her meeting? Does she postpone advising her son until the meeting is over? In this situation, you might expect her corporate-executive identity to be dominant because she is in a company setting, but if her commitment to her family identity is stronger than her work identity, it will dominate her actions even in the boardroom.

Our example illustrates that our identities interact with one another as well as with the situation we are placed in. However, it's not simply that each identity operates as a perfect match to the situation. These identities are in a quasi-battle for our attention, and the winner or winners are the ones to which we are personally most committed. What do we mean by commitment? It's "the costs to the person in the form of relationships foregone were she/he no longer to have a given identity and play a role based on that identity in a social network," according to the sociologist Sheldon Stryker. We measure commitment based on what we stand to lose if it's taken away from us. The more we stand to lose, the more dominant that identity will be in guiding our actions and reactions.

One factor that influences the importance of particular identities is a person's cultural background and experiences. For example, an employee from a team-oriented culture is expected to have a high commitment to a team identity across various situations. That is, a team mentality will arise in the classroom, board-room, and home. As another example, imagine a manager in a culture that emphasizes authority and hierarchy, such as India. In such a situation, power-based relationships can support an employee's commitment to subordinate roles, which aids the use of authoritative management methods such as leadership by directive.

The importance of these identities for CQ cannot be overstated. Role identities help us understand why people do the things they do. In class, our executive-MBA's professor notices that when another student is present she doesn't speak up much. After inquiring about this, he finds out that at her company, she is the subordinate of the other student, and she does not want to say anything in front of him lest she make a mistake and embarrass herself. This example not only tells us that her corporate identity is very powerful, but also suggests that her general values reflect respect for authority and power, characteristic of a highly power-oriented culture.

In thinking about these identities in a more specific way, the analogy of a molecule is useful. That is, a person's self-knowledge and self-concept are made up of various interconnected molecules, each of which represents a different identity. Each individual identity, in turn, is made up of interconnected atoms that represent specific information about people, places, events, and so on. Each of these "identity molecules" is a generalization containing information about your general traits, beliefs about the identity, and actions that you associate with the identity, as well as procedures and rules for dealing with various situations. These identity molecules are a collection of ideas and images concerning what you see as both the ideal and the typical state of things in the world.

What is crucial from our perspective is how these identity molecules lead a person to act one way or another. We do not passively react to the world around us — we actively interpret and seek to understand the situations around us. Our way of interpreting and understanding, however, is guided by our identities and what they imply. Put another way, these identity molecules make up a filter through which our experiences and current situation are channeled. If you can understand a person's identity filters and what atoms make up their molecules, you can predict how he or she will interpret and react to various situations. More important, you may use this information to formulate the most effective course of action for yourself in any given situation.

The element missing from our analogy is how tightly bound these atoms are to their molecules, and the molecules to one another in some larger structure. What is the molecular glue holding together these elements and how strong is it? The stronger the bonds, the more likely it is that people will try and satisfy the demands of all of their identities at the same time. Even if one or two identities are stronger than the others, a person will try and satisfy the others because they are tightly intertwined.

If her identity as a businesswoman and her identity as a mother are strongly connected, our executive-MBA will struggle with her desire to speak with her son and interrupt her meeting. Even more, she will think about her various opportunities as both a mother as well as an executive. If her identity molecules are loosely connected, she can separate her identities, which means that the most dominant one will guide her actions most directly (e.g., having dominant corporate identity means that she asks her assistant to inform her son that she'll speak with him after work is finished). This isn't to say that she doesn't understand herself or her identities. The point is how strongly she clings to them and whether she can adapt them to new circumstances.

The strength of connections is important for understanding which manager is most likely to have the mental flexibility to adjust to new cultures. People who have a strongly intertwined set of identities to which they are strongly committed may experience problems adjusting to new cultures. Their intertwined identities fight for prominence and complicate how a person will react to new situations. This means confusion for others trying to work with him or her. They will see such a manager as sending mixed signals — or, worse, confused and conflicted. To make matters even more troublesome, these strongly connected identities act like a large, strong brick wall that prevents him or her from assimilating new ways of doing things. That is, these intertwined identities mean that it's difficult for such a person to change his or her existing views and opinions — not a good trait for the international manager!

Ideally, a manager knows his or her own identities and how they are interrelated but has the flexibility to adjust, reprioritize them, and so on, as the situation demands. Knowing yourself is not enough for high CQ; awareness does not guarantee flexibility. Flexibility is critical to CQ, since new cultural experiences require you to constantly reshape and adapt to the new situation. Flexibility and the ease with which you integrate new features into your existing identity are related to high CQ, since understanding new cultures may require abandoning preexisting ideas of how and why people act the way that they do. But flexibility is only part of the issue; high CQ requires a person to reform and reconfigure his or her view of the self into complex new configurations. Both flexibility *and* the ability to adapt your self-view to complement a new situation are necessary.

Certain reasoning skills are important for CQ as well. Managers who are high in CQ are good at inductive and analogical reasoning. These two forms of reasoning are important because they are a detective's tools. How can a manager approach and understand a completely new situation without being constrained by past experiences and preconceived ideas? Recall our story of the anthropologist who stayed in Japanese family-run hotels. His existing ideas and identity as a foreigner suggested to him that he was moved because of (his self-perceived) low status. The truth, however, was very different, as he later learned.

> It was my lack of understanding of the full impact of what it means to belong to a high-context culture that caused me to misread hotel behavior at the Hakone. I should have known that I was in the grip of a pattern difference. . . . The answer to my puzzle was revealed when a Japanese friend explained what it means to be a guest in a hotel. As soon as you register at the desk, you are no longer an outsider; instead, for the duration of your stay you are a member of a large, mobile family. *You belong.* The fact that I was moved was tangible evidence that I was being treated as a family member — a relationship in which one can afford to be "relaxed and informal and not stand on ceremony." This is a very highly prized state in Japan, which offsets the official properness that is so common in public. (Hall 65)

Hall interpreted room and hotel shuffling as a sign of low status, consistent with an American perspective. However, inductive reasoning might have suggested to him that only a close friend would be imposed upon by a Japanese host.

A person with high CQ has good inductive skills. He or she can read what seems to be an ambiguous situation and make sense of it by creating a story that fits the facts of the case. If you think about it, figuring out how things operate and what is appropriate in a new culture is largely detective work using the facts of the case — assemble them, order and organize them, interpret them, act on them.

Analogical reasoning is important as well; it helps a person transfer knowledge and experience from one situation to another one. The experiences Hall gained from his hotel stays might be combined with other types of experiences to form a sense of his actual status within the Japanese community.

Thus, CQ reflects several different thinking capabilities. First, CQ captures a person's personal identities and their flexibility. A manager who has high CQ may have several prominent personal identities but is flexible and can deal with each identity separately without conflict or confusion. This means that he or she can incorporate new experiences into her worldview. Second, inductive and analogical reasoning are important for an international traveler since many new cultural situations require that a manager step beyond his or her existing ideas to fully appreciate what is going on. This is not just empathizing with others, because the signals received may conflict with what a manager normally relies on. A high-CQ manager deduces a proper mapping of the situation to his or her actions.

However, a full understanding of the social situation is only the beginning. In the next section, we look at the importance of a manager's motivation and self-confidence.

Why Does Motivation Matter?

Although it's important for a manager to know what should be done, it's also every bit as critical that he or she feel confident and committed to action. Cultural intelligence means that a person is energetic and willing to persevere in the face of difficulty and possible failure. Take our example of the Korean manager who gave up trying to speak with his teammates: it illustrates that knowing what to do is only part of the picture, since a person lacking proper motivation may give up quickly when confronted with challenges or setbacks.

To understand what we mean by motivation, it's useful to draw on some recent thinking by the business professors Miriam Erez and Chris Earley and their approach to expatriate managers. According to their approach, everyone's actions are guided by three central self-motives — enhancement (wanting to feel good about yourself), growth (wanting to challenge and improve yourself), and consistency (wanting continuity and predictability in your life). These three motives vary for each person and are related to his or her cultural background and current work environment.

Self-Enhancement, or Feeling Good about Yourself. The experience of self-enhancement is affected by opportunities in the environment and by how we interpret such opportunities. For example, some people are more sensitive to personally relevant information than to information that is not personally relevant or that conflicts with their personal views. This is sometimes referred to as a self-serving bias, and it means that these people seek out information that reinforces their existing viewpoints rather than examining all information equally. This is not just egotism on a person's part. In fact, a number of research studies have shown that this self-relevant information is easier to remember than other information. Most important for our discussion is that the centrality of this self-relevant information to our thinking shows that our personal view of the world biases our interpretation of events around us.

What this implies is that we tend to focus on information that is consistent with our views of the world, discount conflicting or irrelevant information, and remember things that make us feel better about ourselves. Of course, this is just common sense — we wouldn't expect people to dwell on negative feedback of things that make us think we are wrong! However, we find that a person with high CQ is a bit different here. This type of person has a relatively low motive for self-enhancement. Rather than focusing on the positive and discounting the negative, a person with high CQ weighs all information equally and tries to incorporate both the bitter with the better. Rather than judging others exclusively on dimensions that are personally relevant, high-CQ people seek both positive and negative information about themselves — they don't selectively sample, interpret, and remember just the positive events.

Put another way, some people use negative feedback as a source of inspiration for change. This is a mark of high CQ. Why? When encountering a new culture, a manager will inevitably experience some failure and setbacks; what is critical is how he or she learns from these negative experiences. High-CQ people who accurately use feedback (good or bad) likely have learned over their experiences that both bitter and better lessons are beneficial, so they pay attention to both.

Self-Growth, or Seeking Personal Challenges. Self-growth, or what the psychologist Albert Bandura calls "efficacy," is another facet of the self. According to Bandura, self-growth is "a judgment of one's capability to accomplish a certain level of performance," and work on self-growth tells us that people seek to challenge themselves while avoiding situations they believe exceed their capabilities. Where do these judgments come from? They are based on four sources: our actual accomplishments, vicarious experiences based on watching other people's actions and their outcomes, verbal persuasion or boosterism (e.g., positive persuasion helps people believe that they can achieve very challenging goals, so they become more committed to their course of action), and general physical arousal (e.g., fatigue, stress, and anxiety indicate that a person is not at his or her best and so avoids challenges).

Self-growth has focused primarily on individuals, but it applies to teams as well. In fact, a sense of collective or team growth is absolutely critical for a team's success. Collective growth is crucial for what people choose to do as part of a group, how much effort the team puts into its work, and how persistent it is when facing setbacks. The strength of groups, organizations, and nations lies partly in people's sense of collective growth. It's not clear how the environment shapes collective growth and whether it's more likely to develop in certain cultures than others. Several researchers suggest that cultural background shapes both personal- and collective-growth motives. For example, the first author of this book has worked with managers from a variety of countries and looked at how they make team decisions based on the status of team members.

In working with French and Thai managers who come from a culture of what we call high-power distance (respect for authority and a belief that it's expected for people to have power and to exercise it), we found that these managers were much more influenced by the opinions of team members having high status than were managers coming from the United States or England (low- to moderate-power-distance countries). The French managers who had graduated from one of the *grandes écoles* (very elite private universities) dominated the decisions made by their teams. More important, the team's collective growth and confidence were guided by this high-status manager!

Similarly, Thai managers who had been educated in an elite Western university such as Oxford, Harvard, or Stanford, as well as managers who were older than their fellow teammates, led the team's decision making. This was not true for the American or English managers. These managers seemed to take a more egalitarian approach in which team members tended to average out their differences. The follow-the-leader effect in France and Thailand illustrates the potential influence of cultural values and norms on something as subjective as personal and collective growth.

Self-growth plays an important role in CQ because successful encounters across cultures and countries require that a person who has to jump into a new situation have a fairly high level of personal confidence. Take, for example, a person who has been learning a new language. Even if this person has a very good memory for sounds and words, he or she may still be very hesitant to speak the language in public for fear of embarrassment. Although the person knows the words and phrases of the language, he or she avoids speaking because he or she lacks confidence to do so. A person with high CQ has a strong self-growth motive and will tackle these challenges with great voracity and confidence.

Self-Consistency, or Keeping Things on a Steady Keel. A sense of continuity and consistency helps people attach current experiences to past ones and maintain a coherent view of the world. Self-consistency has two parts — first, it means that we construct our memories in line with previous ones; and, second, it means that people direct their actions so that they are consistent with those people's values, beliefs, and norms.

What does this mean about people and their actions? First, people tend to think about themselves similarly across time. How many of us look in the mirror in our forties, only to think about ourselves as we were in our twenties. A television commercial in the United States illustrates this point nicely: the fifty-plus-year-old actor Dustin Hoffman looks at himself in the mirror and recites a line from his famous role in *The Graduate*, after which he comments, "You don't need any work, you look fine." His self-image as the young star from the movie still lingers. Second, people construct views consistent with their self-image, and these colored lenses filter things so that the self-image is maintained.

As a manager, if I think of myself as a "people person" and I experience a situation suggesting that I was uncaring about a subordinate (perhaps firing him during a tough time in the economy), I am likely to interpret the event as the subordinate's own fault (if he really wanted to keep his job he would have worked harder) or as its only seeming that I was uncaring (this is really for his own good and he'll grow from the experience). I convince myself that what I did was really for the employee's own good.

The implications of these motives for cultural intelligence are numerous. First, a manager's proactivity in new cultural situations is strongly influenced by a sense of self-growth. People with strong self-growth are more likely than others to mix and learn more about people from unfamiliar cultures. Further, high growth means that when they confront obstacles, setbacks, or failures, they will reengage with greater vigor rather than give up. This is critical for sojourners and expatriates, because much of the work of discovering and adapting to new cultures involves overcoming obstacles and setbacks. High-growth managers don't require constant reassurance to persist, whereas low-growth managers are unable under such pressure to maintain their commitment to a course of action.

Second, high-growth managers are likely engaged in setting specific challenges, or goal setting, for themselves, which is very beneficial. For example, the psychologists Robert Wood and Albert Bandura have found that growth expectations are positively related to the goals that people set for themselves, and that this, in turn, shapes the strategies they use and their performance. People who have high growth motives not only work harder, they work smarter as well.

A manager's self-motives are important for cultural intelligence in other ways. For example, self-enhancement implies that we seek out those situations for which we expect the most pleasure and that we avoid discomfort. But what might this imply for the culturally intelligent person? As we said earlier, overly high self-enhancement is a problem for a culturally challenged manager. Adjusting to a new culture often involves delayed positive feedback and immediate negative feedback (we make mistakes quickly, and only over time do we understand the right thing to do). As we discuss further in the next section, delayed gratification is an important facet of cultural intelligence, since people make mistakes early in their cultural encounters and are likely to receive failure feedback before they receive success feedback. Although a person's ability to delay personal gratification is shaped by early learning in childhood, psychologists suggest that adult learners may create short- and long-term goals to help them adapt to delayed gratification as well.

Finally, a manager's consistency motive is negatively related to CQ. A person with a high consistency motive will have a lower CQ. A strong motive for consistency means that a person will have difficulty adjusting to new and different situations, since he or she will try to keep things as similar as possible to the familiar. Adjusting to a new culture requires a manager to think differently about things and to openly incorporate these new perspectives. At an extreme, a very high consistency motive means that a person will ignore or reject information inconsistent with existing biases even if this information may be critical for figuring out the situation. A person whose consistency is overly high is rigid when he or she encounters new ideas and perspectives, as happens when one encounters a new culture.

Imagine a British expatriate manager in Hong Kong who insulates himself from the local flavor of a culture — perhaps by living in an expatriate neighborhood, sending his children to the "English preparatory school," buying from British specialty stores (e.g., Marks & Spencer), and so on. In one area of Hong Kong island (just off the downtown area of Central), it's possible to walk from pub to pub and hear nothing but Australian and English accents. You'd think you were in downtown Sydney or London. Most major cities in Asia have "expat alleys," consisting of pubs, restaurants, shops, and so forth for Western expatriates. This is not intended as criticism — this type of "bringing it with you" is common and functional in many ways. When the first author of this book counsels managers about international assignments, he emphasizes that even people with low self-consistency motives require some attachments to home to maintaining their general sense of welfare. Simple routines as getting a newspaper or buying a cappuccino reconnect an expatriate with his or her home culture. However, an overly active consistency motive may result in isolation and an overreliance on one's own culture. A high-CQ manager balances the need for continuity with the home environment against understanding the unique aspects of his new host culture.

Combining these self-motives with CQ, it becomes clear that CQ requires many complex and subtle aspects of motivation. We have addressed what people know about a new culture and whether they are motivated to push themselves to deal with it. However, we haven't dealt with effective action. This is the last piece of our CQ puzzle.

Why Does Behavior Matter?

As the old saying goes, "Actions speak louder than words." The action part of CQ is based on how people develop skills as well as on their personal abilities. As we have said, CQ not only requires that you know how and what to do and have the energy to persevere and keep trying; it also requires that you have in your toolbox of actions the specific ones needed for a given encounter. A person with high CQ must be able to understand and execute needed actions with great finesse.

CQ refers to a person's aptitude for learning new actions that are needed in a new culture. We used the simple example earlier in the book of shaking hands in Ghanaian culture. The reader should notice that action isn't just thinking about something. There are many actions that each of us can think of but not actually do — for example, you may think about dunking a basketball or running the hundred-meter dash in ten seconds but not be able to perform either action. Some actions require subtlety and sophistication. The ability to learn a new language can be important to one's cultural adjustment, but accurate pronunciation of tones and phonemes in languages such as Mandarin or Thai may elude many Westerners. (We suggest that people who lack an aptitude for learning languages, *at least at some reasonable level of proficiency,* will have a low CQ. This doesn't mean that learning a language causes CQ to increase, or vice versa, but the two are related.) Learning a language is a complex behavior, since linguists tell us that language use and acquisition may be tied both to genetics and to early learning experiences. For example, a Japanese child not exposed to the sound of the letter "r" in English before the age of eight to twelve months may never fully acquire the sound. Although such a child may as a teenager be taught to pronounce the "r" sound, the teenager doesn't report hearing it as a unique sound. Fortunately, much of the behavior we are talking about with CQ is highly malleable and learnable.

A person's behavior is tied to CQ in more indirect ways, too. There are times when someone may know what to do and be motivated to do the right thing but cannot because of some deeply held reservations. Imagine an expatriate manager provided with a plate filled with a local delicacy of grubs, fried earthworms, and grasshoppers: she may not be able to overcome her revulsion and eat her meal. This type of action response (or lack of it) can be thought of in psychological terms. That is, a person's past successes and failures influence what actions he or she is likely to use and how successfully they will be used. Actions done properly require that a person persist, as we mentioned earlier. Persistence is necessary for learning new skills, and so is a person's aptitude. It isn't enough to be willing to try; a high-CQ person determines what actions are needed and executes them.

This means that the action or behavior part of CQ is both what you understand and what you're motivated to achieve. The development and subsequent execution of a new action requires recognition that it's new and different (e.g., a Thai smile for nervousness is different than one for anger or contentment).

This is not the limit to a person's actions. Returning to our example of eating bugs, your personal experiences (past experiences both good and bad) influence your future actions; effective action requires flexibility. Even if you are inclined to skip the interesting bug delicacy, it's possible for you to overcome your revulsion and scoop up the grubs greedily. Whether you really have high CQ is reflected in your ability to control your reactions to the meal (not conveying hesitation, revulsion, etc.). Your file of possible actions (what the psychologists call your "behavioral repertoire") is flexible, broad, and easily adapted.

CQ doesn't just mean that you can force yourself to do things you might find repugnant, as we discuss in chapter 4. Simply forcing yourself to act may convey subtle and negative cues to your host through body language and the like. (We call this nonverbal leakage, and it happens when your nonverbal actions, such as body orientation or facial expression, conflict with what you are saying. For example, if a husband admits that he was wrong concerning the choice of, say, a movie, but he rolls his eyes and has a smirk on his face, the message actually conveyed to his wife is likely to be interpreted by her as not taking her complaints seriously.) A person with high CQ controls his or her physical display so well that nonverbal leakage and other subtle confusions are not conveyed. That is, a high-CQ person has a strong mastery and sense of emotional display and physical presence.

People with high CQ are very good at observing others and mimicking their actions. We know that mimicry has many positive effects as people work with one another. For example, when a person mimics another person's gestures and actions, even if unconsciously, the result is an increased satisfaction with the encounter on the part of the person who was imitated. This does not mean duplicating each and every action — that might seem to be mockery and not mimicry. Instead, it means adopting some of the gestures, postures, social distances, and so on of your cross-cultural compatriot as a way of putting him or her at ease in the encounter. Mimicry has even been found to result in spouses eventually coming to looking alike. Mimicry is subtle and even unconscious, but it has generally positive effects in a social encounter. A high-CQ person is a talented mimic. By talented, we emphasize that this is not savant duplication, but a judicious use of similar actions and gestures to put another person at ease while communicating and working in another culture.

It's not enough that a person be an effective actor who is able to control his or her own actions; he or she must be able to use the actions of others to infer their underlying motives and thoughts. What is particularly tricky about these inferences is that these actions are happening in a strange and unfamiliar culture perhaps involving odd and unfamiliar rituals.

Imagine a Canadian expatriate manager who has been newly hired to run a Thai factory. He goes to the shop floor and begins to wander around the factory. As he encounters various employees, he notices that they stop work and smile at him very consistently, with some of them giving him a Thai *wai*. Later that day he sees an employee who is dealing with a factory problem of a very significant nature and is smiling as well. Finally, on the way home he crosses a very busy road in Bangkok and is nearly hit by a taxi; the driver is smiling at him. The expatriate wonders to himself, why are these Thais smiling all the time? Oh, it must be that the Thais deal with all types of situations by smiling and feeling happy about their situation. The next day, there is a bit of trouble, and the manager has to intervene and strongly reprimand two employees. As he does this, he forces himself to keep a bit of a smile on his lips, since he figures that this will help reduce the general tension of the reprimand. Afterward, he notices that the two employees are very confused and frustrated with the whole incident (based on what he has heard from a second-in-command). The following day, both employees have quit their jobs. What has happened?

The problem confronting our expatriate manager is multifaceted. First, he failed to observe the type of smiling he witnessed in the various incidents, since distinctive smiles were used (Thais have well over twenty different smiles that they use in different situations). Second, he failed to realize that in a high-power-distance culture such as Thailand (that is, one in which there is a large difference between powerful leaders and their followers), there is no compelling reason for a superior to use smiling as a means of reducing tension when reprimanding an inferior. Third, not only was the smile the manager used the wrong type, but also his nonverbal leakage conveyed his own high degree of personal discomfort, and the two employees sensed it. High CQ means having sufficient control and observational skills to know what smile to use and when to use it, what a smile means in the first place, and how to use smiling the right way.

This action component of CQ is strongly tied to the other two features we have discussed earlier in this chapter. Doing the right thing means knowing what the right thing is and having the energy to do it. It means identifying the correct problem and filing it away in order to try and understand and use it in the future. It also means having sufficient control and composure to convey exactly what is intended in a response.

Our description of the action and behavioral feature doesn't require such a deep level of self-analysis, nor does it require an incredible command of one's emotional psyche. For example, consider a method actor (who actually experiences and lives his or her role, including the character's concomitant emotions and views) versus a role-based actor (who mimics the necessary emotions in his or her portrayal); the high-CQ manager is more like the role-based actor. We do not think that it's necessary to "become" your role to be effective in new cultures. However, a high-CQ manager can play a role very convincingly and consistently.

PUTTING THE PIECES TOGETHER: CQ IN AN INTERNATIONAL ORGANIZATION

Armed with an overview of cultural intelligence, the next step to using CQ to your advantage is to assess your own CQ strengths and weaknesses. In the appendix, you will find a short questionnaire that you can use to measure your own CQ. It includes such queries as: How and why do people do what they do here? Am I motivated to do something here? Can I do the right thing? The instructions that come with the appendix show how to calculate your scores for the three aspects of CQ: cultural strategic thinking (the thinking part of CQ), motivation (the energizing part of CQ), and behavior (the action part of CQ). Armed with your CQ strengths and weaknesses, you are ready to investigate and determine the best way for you to manage others. Without question, your next step is to understand how your individual CQ profile influences your aptitude and ability to manage across cultures. This profile helps you understand your particular strengths and, as we will illustrate, whether or not a particular managerial style (e.g., strong and authoritarian versus friendly and participative) will be consistent with the employees' orientation. If it's not, then you must take steps to change the profile of your subordinates (perhaps through special job training) or choose a different management style.

In this section, we begin by discussing how you can use your cultural intelligence features and preferred management practices to complement one another. Next, we describe our framework for developing and enhancing your CQ in your current work situation.

Using the PRISM Model for Developing Your CQ

To take advantage of your natural strengths for cultural adjustment, begin by assessing your relative strengths and weaknesses. It's important that your CQ scores not be viewed as some unchangeable mark that you carry around with you. Just as with other forms of intelligence, CQ can be improved upon with the right type of training, as we will discuss later in this book. However, before you can understand what direction such training for you should take, it's critical that you have a firm foundation of your attributes for CQ. It's important as well that you decide how you might wish to use this information. For example, are you preparing for an expatriate work assignment? Will you lead a team of internationally diverse employees? Do you need to enhance your current assignment by effectively motivating your employees? Your answers to these questions will guide how you follow and implement our model for developing CQ, which we call PRISM. (see figure 1.2)

- *Preparing your mind* (how you acquire knowledge and how you think). Goal: acquiring the rules or cultural knowledge for effective adaptation to different cultures.
- *Reviewing and learning* (how you think about your thinking; how you plan, monitor, and review; and how you learn). Goal: knowing how and when to reconfigure the rules for effective adaptation to different cultures.
- *Identifying your strengths and weaknesses* (knowing your strengths and weaknesses by having your CQ profiled — e.g., are you weak or strong in cultural strategic thinking, motivation, and/or behavior?). Goal: increasing self-awareness of your CQ and developing a road map for training and development to enhance effective adaptation to different cultures.
- *Setting goals and targets* (knowing what you want to achieve and exerting energy and drive to achieve your goals and targets). Goal: establishing the *Focus* for effective adaptation to different cultures.
- *Mobilizing your resources* (displaying appropriate behaviors and actions for adapting to different cultures). Goal: ability to use appropriate behaviors and actions, or repertoires, for effective adaptation to different cultures.

This five-component developmental model for CQ is underpinned by three Rs: rules, reasons, and repertoires. Depending on the specific work and professional needs of the managers and based on the CQ profile ("Identifying Your Strengths and Weaknesses" is placed at the center of our developmental model, as this is the very first step that must be performed), the focus on training and development can be on rules, reasons, and/or repertoires.

An example might help clarify these relationships. A French manager, Jean Pierre, is going to work in Indonesia for the first time. He is working for an electronics company that has a large manufacturing facility just outside of Jakarta in a newly emerging high-technology corridor. His primary responsibilities are to supervise the completion of a new manufacturing plant and to help local staff keep it running smoothly. He will have five direct reports of Indonesian managers who

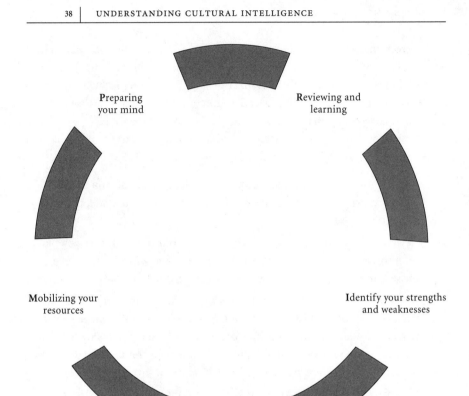

Figure 1.2   PRISM framework

have worked for the local subsidiary for an average of two years. This trip will be our French manager's first visit to Indonesia, but he has worked in a number of countries throughout the European Community. In preparing for his new assignment, he will need to know his present strengths and weaknesses and what his CQ profile is. As it turns out, he has a very good strength for the first feature, cultural strategic thinking (answering the question of why things happen), and the third feature, behavior/action (engaging in the right actions needed).

However, he lacks confidence in his ability to engage his Indonesian managers or to manage in Indonesia. This means that his second feature, motivation, is lacking. What Jean Pierre lacks is efficacy, or perceived confidence. Although he has had several international experiences in nearby countries, he has not had any assignments outside Europe, and he lacks the confidence that he will need for the Indonesian assignment.

Knowing his strengths and weaknesses, there are several options that he can consider. In preparing his developmental plan, not only must he focus on choosing management methods that are appropriate for Indonesian culture, but it's important that he provide himself with simple and immediate opportunities for success before he tackles larger challenges. Why do we say this? People who lack sufficient confidence but also have strong thinking skills will often take on significant challenges — perhaps too challenging. It's likely that such challenges will be met with setbacks, and a person lacking confidence will interpret these setbacks as inevitable defeat. Rather than redoubling his or her efforts and trying again, a person who is low on CQ motivation will interpret these cultural mistakes as a sure sign of defeat. To overcome this tendency, a smart manager will provide himself with small, modest challenges early on whose mastery will create a positive momentum and build confidence. As the psychologist Albert Bandura says, the way to build strong, long-term efficacy is through a careful mastering of immediate achievable goals. Just as a journey of a thousand miles must begin with a single step, so does an expatriate assignment begin with simple challenges such as figuring out how to buy a newspaper or order coffee at the local café!

Once our French manager has had a chance to master some of the basics of Indonesian culture and society, it's important for him to leverage his natural strengths in cultural strategic thinking to look beyond cultural stereotypes. Jean Pierre is very good at moving beyond these stereotypes to understand why people act as they do. This is not to suggest mistakes will not be made — they will. But what is critical is that Jean Pierre is able to use them productively. How can he avoid these stereotypes? One thing he should do is engage in what we referred to earlier as "thinking about thinking." What strategies has he used in the past to understand cultural differences between the French and the Germans or Spanish? He needs to figure out what strategies work and to use them in the new assignment. Or perhaps he could reconfigure his knowledge of these strategies, that is, adapt some of the strategies that have worked well for him to help him in this new situation. Maybe he thinks that the way friends relate to one another is important for determining the proper style of leadership to use, or that the place where people gather after work will show how hierarchical people are in the company. These strategies are ways to understand what he really wants to know: what Indonesian culture is like in and out of the workplace and what that means about management style.

Jean Pierre can also mobilize his resources to put his plan of action into place. His resources include his personal talents, support employees, business resources, and so on. The critical feature here is that he utilizes his personal talents to leverage the most he can from support personnel. If Jean Pierre has done a good job of developing an effective plan to work locally, emphasized small gains to build his confidence, and moved beyond simple stereotypes, then he is ready to choose a managerial style and approach that will capitalize on his subordinates' talents. In Indonesian culture, which is known to be hierarchical but group oriented, he needs to think about the best way to lead. Although French culture is hierarchical, it's more individually focused than group oriented. This will represent a significant change for Jean Pierre, who must be careful to leverage the various strengths of a group-based management style (e.g., using group discussion but with strong leadership). He must avoid another CQ trap — incorrectly assuming that all Indonesians see their culture the same way. It's critical that he organize his subordinates to leverage their individual talents and preferences, since some may differ from general Indonesian culture and prefer an egalitarian management style and lots of individual responsibilities.

Mobilizing your resources means adapting your behavior and actions effectively in the general cultural setting you are operating in as well as recognizing the preferences of individual employees. This might require new actions that Jean Pierre is not used to doing; acting in keeping with local custom is a good way of helping people feel at ease with you.

Our French manager needs to develop a means of reviewing and learning from all his experiences, which will include evaluating his effectiveness. This benchmarking and review process is important because it provides Jean Pierre with important feedback about all three of his CQ features. His review will guide him in the future in how to figure things out, maintain his motivation, and take the correct actions. It's not enough to keep this evaluation informal or unspecified: without proper goals and targets it's difficult to know if one's journey is proceeding successfully.

SUMMARY

In this chapter, we have explored the various features of our approach to cultural intelligence. Given the globalization of business and the ease of international travel, it is very surprising to us that people have not paid more attention to this idea. Why is it that some people adjust to new cultures, understand local practices, and can behave appropriately and effectively, while others flounder? Our anecdotal and preliminary empirical evidence suggests that this is not merely an issue of emotional intelligence, empathy, social intelligence, practical intelligence, tacit knowledge, and the like. A cultural encounter is unique in that a manager cannot easily rely on previous experiences because they may be misleading. Many times the actions and apparent intentions of others are so unexpected as to appear bizarre and random. A person with high CQ has the ability to face such a situation, understand and master it, persevere, and do the right thing when needed.

Our approach addresses three general questions: How and why do people do what they do here? Am I motivated to do something here? And, can I do the right thing? Our first question focuses on thinking, or cultural strategic thinking; our second on motivation; and our third on effective action. A person high in CQ has capabilities in all three areas. Lacking these features means that a person is lower in cultural intelligence. CQ means that a manager is able to observe and comprehend and will feel compelled to react, interact, and implement action.

In addition, we described a general developmental model for a manager to use in assessing CQ for an international work assignment. Our five-component model, called PRISM, involves the critical steps of examining your own CQ, identifying your strengths and weaknesses, focusing on specific areas of developmental needs, and reviewing your effectiveness to learn from your successes and reassess new challenges.

In the next chapter, we explore these basic features of CQ. We begin by looking at how thinking, problem solving, and thinking about thinking are related to a person's ability to understand a new culture. We talk about several types of reasoning related to CQ and how people use these skills to expand their CQ. Afterward, we turn to a discussion of the motivational and action aspects of CQ.

2 | PREPARING YOUR MIND:
THE CULTURAL STRATEGIC
THINKING BASIS OF CQ

You are here like a mystery
I'm from a world that's so different
From all that you are
How in the light of one night
Did we come so far?

Miss Saigon

In the long-running musical *Miss Saigon,* Chris, the American protagonist, calls Vietnam "a place full of mystery that I never once understood." It is evident from the musical, and in the light of the opening quotation of this chapter, that Chris exhibited a low level of cultural strategic thinking — that is, he failed to develop an understanding of the Vietnamese culture. *Miss Saigon,* to a large extent, leveraged on the lack of cultural understanding to develop some of the tensions between Eastern and Western cultures as portrayed in the musical.

Take the example of an airline that had problems when it began operations in Hong Kong. The company had decided to hand out white carnations to passengers without realizing that for many Asians, they represented death and bad luck. Even something as seemingly obvious as language and translation is often ignored; think of Chevrolet's introduction in Mexico of the Nova car. The translation of *no va* in Spanish is "no go" — in other words, a car that doesn't run. These cultural blunders could have been avoided if the companies had done their homework by studying Asian culture and the Spanish language, and by knowing the different taboos and language issues. Failure to understand can have dire consequences not just for individuals (as in the case of Chris in *Miss Saigon,* whose love affair with Kim ended in Kim's tragic death) but also for organizations.

Never assume that you understand what is going on in a different culture, or what a person from another culture thinks or feels. Culture consists of many nuances. Individuals with high cultural thinking would be able to detect and decode these cultural nuances and therefore to adapt more effectively in different cultures. In the airline story, the company might have avoided unnecessary embarrassment by making itself aware of the belief represented by the white carnation and acknowledging the importance of local knowledge. They had not thought through the implications of their choices.

But the type of thinking that we are referring to is not simply local knowledge or awareness of customs. Yes, it is useful to know that the color red represents a stop or alarm in the United States but good luck in China, or that opening a present in front of your hosts is rude in Japan. Our point, however, is that knowing these cultural facts and trivia is insufficient. As a global manager, a person is unlikely to be able to learn the practices and taboos of each and every country he or she works in. Imagine having to learn about eleven new countries in a few short weeks when you've just been assigned as the leader of a new regional product-development team for your company! So what we are referring to in this chapter captures two different aspects of building cultural knowledge for you:

- *Cultural knowledge*, or what you know about a specific country or culture concerning practices, beliefs, and values; and

- *Strategic thinking*, or a more general skill you have about "thinking about thinking," or developing ways to gain new cultural knowledge.

These two areas, cultural knowledge and strategic thinking, are what we mean by *cultural strategic thinking* (CST). If we lack cultural strategic thinking, we tend to interpret other people's behaviors and intentions from our own limited perspective, which is likely inappropriate in many circumstances. As it's not possible to master and speak every foreign language, we need to possess cultural strategic thinking to help us pay attention to what's going on in different cultures, and to understand and process in our minds what's really happening.

In the following sections of this chapter, we will explain what cultural strategic thinking is, why it is important, and how you can develop your cultural strategic thinking.

WHAT IS CULTURAL STRATEGIC THINKING?

Cultural strategic thinking matters in any cross-cultural encounter. Before your company sends you on an overseas assignment, you would normally find out more about the particular country where you will be sent. What you know about the political, economic, and social systems of that country is important. But filling your mind with lots of information about the country to which you will be assigned should not be an end; rather, it should be a means to an end.

We can illustrate the two elements of cultural strategic thinking with an incident described to us by a manager we interviewed for our research. This manager, a young black professional from the United States, was assigned by her company to work in Cairo, Egypt. One day, as she was walking down the street, a small group of Egyptian teenagers greeted her using a word she found very offensive:

> I turned on my heel, went right up to the group of guys, and began to upbraid them as vituperatively as my Arabic would allow. These young men were obviously shocked at my reaction, as I am sure they thought they were greeting me in a friendly way. And once I'd had my say, I stormed off to meet my friend.
>
> After I'd walked about half a block, I decided not to leave them with a cloud of disdain hanging in the air, as I would normally have done. So I went back to talk to the group in a calmer, more diplomatic manner. They asked me why I was so angry, I gave them my reasons, they apologized profusely, and we all sat down and had tea and an interesting talk about words and how the wrong ones can easily cause trouble. This was especially helpful to all of us, as these guys were in school, and most of them were studying English, with varying levels of success. During our conversation, I brought up a number of examples of Arabic expressions that, uttered in the wrong tone or by the wrong person, would spark an equal reaction from them. After about an hour together, I had a group of new friends.

This example illustrates cultural strategic thinking in several ways. First, notice that this manager did not simply get angry and storm away from the situation. Instead, she returned and engaged the group of young men in a conversation. Her knowledge of Arabic greatly aided her in communicating with them. Language ability was one element of her cultural knowledge, as was her awareness of Egyptian culture, food, customs, and so on. Clearly, her knowledge of the culture and language helped her engage the young men and, ultimately, create a new bond.

But this example illustrates also a very important aspect of cultural strategic thinking: she had noticed that their reaction to her anger was one of confusion and hesitation. She had picked up a signal that they did not communicate what they had intended to. Also, notice that she came up with a new way of dealing with the situation, instead of her usual style of just walking away angry. She decided to return to engage the young men in a "more diplomatic" fashion and not just leave things as they were. She developed and put into action a new way of dealing with people. Her method included discussing the matter openly and drawing from examples using her cultural knowledge strategically — using examples from Arabic that conveyed an analogous effect as what they had used. She captured her knowledge of Egyptian culture and language, created a new way of approaching an existing problem, and leveraged the common links between her own culture and theirs to create a positive situation from a negative one.

Learning about a new culture with openness to novelty, active noticing of cultural differences and similarities, heightened sensitivity to different cultural contexts, and awareness of different perspectives on cross-cultural engagements enable you to diagnose and respond more accurately to the demands of new cultural encounters and episodes. Individuals who are high in cultural strategic thinking are fully engaged in each new cultural experience. They are able to use active strategic thinking during new encounters and adapt their actions accordingly by making sense of various dimensions of the situation. These dimensions include verbal as well as nonverbal feedback. More important, managers who are high in cultural strategic thinking are able to detect unstated and subtle nuances that guide them in their cultural adaptation and adjustment.

To use a computer metaphor, individuals with a low capacity for cultural strategic thinking operate like a computer program when they engage with other people from different cultures. It's as if they had been preprogrammed and behave like they are on "autopilot"— they are unable to attend to the cultural interaction and the changes that may take place during it. However, individuals with high cultural thinking have a built-in "artificial intelligence"; they can reconfigure their mental circuitry to enact appropriate behaviors and actions in different cultures and contexts.

Cultural Knowledge

The cultural knowledge aspect of cultural strategic thinking is what most of us consider when we discuss cross-cultural encounters and training. Local knowledge of white carnations or the meaning of *no va* in Spanish are simple examples of cultural knowledge, Hong Kong and Shanghai Banking Corporation's worldwide advertising campaign introduces HSBC as the "world's local bank," and focuses on an appreciation for local cultural knowledge, including such examples as showing the bottom of one's feet in Thailand, the meaning of the color red in Chinese culture, and the family's role in paying for a wedding in various countries. In one television advertisement entitled "Hole in One," it tells of an American businessman coming unstuck because of his lack of local cultural knowledge while playing a round of golf with Japanese businessmen. Unlike in the United States, where it is customary to celebrate by buying a round of drinks in the clubhouse, the American businessman finds that in Japan, the custom is to buy fellow players expensive gifts!

Traditionally, expatriate and cross-cultural training programs have focused on conveying relatively specific knowledge and information to people prior to their leaving for overseas. The emphasis in such training is on teaching a manager what he or she needs to know in a new country in order to operate effectively and avoid cultural misconduct. We can think of this as an elaborate list of cultural dos and don'ts or extended cultural synopses, although most of the sophisticated methods go beyond such a simplistic approach.

By far the most common (and traditional) approach to breaching cultural and national differences is to teach country-specific knowledge and expose trainees to different cultural values. An emphasis on values orientation and understanding others through their beliefs and practices, which are related to values, underlies much of the current work on intercultural training and management education. Intercultural training has become nearly synonymous with models for understanding cultural values by such authors as Geert Hofstede or Charles Hampden-Turner and Fons Trompenaars. For example, a great deal of attention has been focused on the "group orientation" of a country, or what the academics call individualism-collectivism. In a group-oriented culture people think of themselves as part of a group, team, or family, and they prefer activities and rewards that acknowledge this group membership. In an individual-oriented culture people think of themselves as independent of others, and they prefer solo work assignments and individual recognition and reward. However, there is a fundamental problem with a cultural-values-awareness approach: an awareness of cultural values isn't a substitute for more direct knowledge of person-to-person encounters, just as values alone aren't strong predictors of people's actions. A person who is very group oriented might, under the right conditions, prefer an individual assignment with the opportunity for personal recognition, just as a person who is individual oriented might want and enjoy working on a team assignment. Cultural knowledge of values is a useful starting point for cultural thinking, but it is *only* a starting point.

One very influential training method that has received widespread attention from professional trainers and academics is called the cultural assimilator. Developed by a number of cultural psychologists, including Charles Osgood and Harry Triandis, this is a method of training employees by giving them a series of critical incidents for a country. Culture assimilators show people cultural scenarios and ask them to interpret the situation. They often employ a critical-incident approach to present examples of culture clashes between individuals from different backgrounds. A typical cultural-assimilator exercise would have participants read a number of stories about culture clashes. For each incident, a trainee is asked to attribute and interpret the behavior of the actors in the conflict situations. The trainee is then presented with a number of alternative explanations and asked to select one that best accounts for the conflict in the critical incidents. For example: A Greek manager working in Japan goes to a colleague's home for dinner during a holiday. When he arrives, they present him with a wrapped gift. He immediately tears the package open and looks at the gift, much to the dismay of his Japanese colleague. What has gone wrong?

- The present was a disappointment because the Greek manager already had this present.
- The present was very expensive, and now the Greek manager feels obligated to buy his Japanese colleague a very expensive present in return.
- The present should not have been opened in front of the colleague, because it might have caused the colleague to lose face if the present wasn't desirable or appropriate for some reason.

In this example, you read the scenario and decide which of the three responses is best. Next, you turn to a page detailing your answer and why (or why not) it was the right choice. In this example, the third alternative is correct: opening the present right away may cause someone to lose face if the present isn't appreciated.

A variation on a country-specific cultural assimilator was developed by Deepak Bhawuk and Richard Brislin. Rather than focusing on a particular target country, the emphasis is on a target cultural value that can be shared across countries. For example, you might focus on group orientation or power and hierarchy to create critical incidents that apply across countries.

Cultural assimilators are generally useful because they provide basic cultural scripts about specific countries that cover a wide variety of social situations and culturally appropriate actions. If a manager knows which culture he or she will be visiting, country-specific assimilators can be very effective at helping him or her gain cultural knowledge. However, culture assimilators are limited because they are country specific. It isn't clear how the knowledge gained in country-based training programs of any sort might be leveraged in new countries. At least one problem is that people just aren't very good at learning by analogy or case method comparisons: psychologists have shown us that people shown one case example have great difficulty in taking the general principles learned and applying them to other situations unless they are very, very similar. The real challenge seems to be taking some specific piece of cultural knowledge and leveraging it across new situations and circumstances. It is this capability that we refer to as strategic thinking, and it constitutes the second aspect of cultural thinking.

Strategic Thinking

It remains unclear whether cultural assimilators and other country-specific training methods provide benefits for strategic thinking. The focus on a particular cultural value or country may inadvertently lead global managers to overempha-size one aspect of culture over more significant ones for a particular country. For example, although Thailand may be characterized by a certain level of group ver-sus individual orientation, power and hierarchy are more important motivators of people's actions.

The way people view themselves and others varies widely across countries. A number of years ago, a colleague from the United States decided to immigrate to Israel after having lived there for about a year. When she was interviewed by the immigration officer, he asked her about her religion. She replied that she had writ-ten "atheist" on her application form. He looked at the form and then asked her again, "What is your religion?" She replied again, "Atheist." He finally lost patience with her and bellowed, "Fine! Are you a Jewish atheist, a Muslim atheist, or a Christian atheist?" In a country such as Israel, religion is not just a particular philo-sophical belief in God — it represents an ethnic background for personal identity.

Strategic thinking in this example is not learning that the Thais and the French have respect for educational background or that Americans and British managers average their team decisions. In a sense, strategic thinking is "forward" thinking — *what* does this cultural knowledge tell me in general about team decisions in var-ious countries and *how* can I learn about team decisions in new countries that I have yet to visit?

If we explore this team decision-making work in a bit more detail, we can see what is meant by strategic thinking. Recall the study of follower and leader actions of U.S., English, French, and Thai managers we described in chapter 1. Although the Thai and French managers both placed importance on the educational back-grounds of their teammates, the way they actually decided as a team differed rather dramatically. In the Thai teams, the "junior" members (those who were younger or who lacked a high-status educational background) waited for the more senior manager to state his views. They then discussed it with him in a quiet and respect-ful fashion before finally deferring to his view. The experience of the French teams was a very different process. The junior members immediately stated their opin-ions at the beginning of the meeting, and when their "leader" expressed a different view, they confronted him and disagreed wholeheartedly! After discussing the de-cision in a very frank and relatively confrontational fashion, their team decision ended up dominated by the leader, just as with the Thais.

Now if you encountered the American team first, you might conclude that teams make decisions by using an averaging scheme and that every person had an equal say in a decision. Applying this idea to the Thai situation would be wrong, and you might conclude that the strong show of respect and deference seen there reflects a different valuation of authority or decision making. You would say to yourself that something is different here (in the Thai case) and you need to figure out how to understand the new situation. You might conclude that the cultures of Thailand and the United States differ — that people are seen as equal in the latter but not the former. Strategic thinking reflects your inference that values underlie team decision making. You might even test this idea when you next encounter the French team. You will realize that, even though the French seem to make their team decisions very differently than the Thais, both processes still reflect a decision hierarchy.

What you have just done is to "think about thinking" — to ask yourself how to understand new situations. We referred to this type of higher-level thinking in chapter 1. Cultural knowledge might be not showing the bottoms of your feet to people while in a Thai café; strategic thinking might be developing a general strategy for identifying restaurant-related taboos in a new country. For example, if you are asked to read a very complicated chapter, one method might be to read the material slowly to understand it. However, the strategic thinking approach would be to skim the material briefly to decide its difficulty and what specific method might be used to master the material most effectively. This type of strategic thinking might well be thought of as a strategy of learning how to learn, or meta-learning.

These higher-level thinking strategies are part of a person's cultural strategic thinking. This kind of strategic thinking has two complementary elements: meta-level knowledge (general techniques for using cultural knowledge, which has been gained under a variety of circumstances, in new ways) and meta-level experience (the intuition or subtle insights that people have about their cultural world and how to incorporate relevant experiences as a general guide for future interactions). Strategic thinking is a critical aspect of CQ, since much of what is required in a new culture is putting together new ideas and experiences into a coherent picture, even if you don't know what this picture might look like. To do so requires a higher level of strategic thinking about people, places, and events.

When you organize your thinking about people, places, and events, you put them into what we call cultural scripts, or schema. A cultural script is best thought of as a routine that describes how events and people are expected to interact over time. For example, an American has a cultural script for visiting the supermarket that includes taking items in a shopping cart to a checkout clerk and then having these items scanned for price and placed in sacks by the clerk, after which the customer leaves the store with the groceries. This script says that the items should be scanned for price before going in the bag and that you must bring them to the clerk before leaving the store.

What about in England, where you are expected to bag your own items? Or Germany, where you bring your own sacks unless you wish to be charged for new ones? Or China's Friendship Stores, where you tell a clerk what you wish to purchase and he or she collects them for you? All of these examples violate the cultural script for an American. Cultural knowledge is organized into these scripts, and you get them by observing and buying groceries. Meta-level knowledge is organized into more general scripts about grocery shopping in general as well as how to understand new scripts for new countries. In our example, meta-level knowledge reflects a general knowledge that people obtain their groceries from stores (suppliers) in exchange for some valued resource (money, tradable goods) and that this is done differently in different countries. By knowing these things, you are able to make up new scripts as they are needed in new situations. As you walk around a shopping area in Hanover, Germany, you notice that a number of people are carrying a sack of sacks. Further, you watch in the supermarket and see that people take out their own sacks and bag their own groceries. You incorporate this knowledge into a more general way of thinking about the grocery-shopping experience in other countries.

What's important to remember at this point is that strategic thinking isn't limited to the mental strategies that you "think" about. Part of strategic thinking may be unconscious or very subtle. Recall our example of the American manager who encountered the young men in the streets of Cairo. One thing she observed was that when she reacted strongly to the greeting they used, they seemed puzzled or confused. Meta-level experience reflects her sense or intuition about the situation. Some people can just tell if something is amiss in a cultural situation. If you ask them why they think something is wrong, they can't really say, but they tell you they have a feeling or a sense of things. One manager commented, "I don't really know how it is I can tell if something is going on in a new situation, but I kind of get a feeling about it." Some people are just more tuned in to general situations and can sense if difficulties arise. This is not the same as emotional intelligence, since the cues for discomfort or confusion may be very different across countries. No, what we are talking about is a subtle aspect of experience that a person gains through many cross-cultural encounters. It is best thought of as a cultural intuition. In the next section, we talk about how strategic thinking and cultural knowledge can be used and leveraged to your advantage.

THE IMPORTANCE OF CULTURAL STRATEGIC THINKING

Why does cultural strategic thinking matter in cross-cultural adaptation and adjustment? In living and working in a new culture, you need to be open and alert to new cultural experiences. Just being culturally aware — that is, being aware of cultural differences — doesn't mean you're exhibiting cultural strategic thinking. The concept of cultural strategic thinking goes much deeper. Managers who display high cultural strategic thinking have a sensitivity to different cultural contexts that facilitates an active and dynamic strategy for dealing with the world around them.

Individuals who are high in cultural strategic thinking exhibit the following characteristics:

- Open, alert, and sensitive to new cultures
- Able to draw distinctions and to identify similarities between different cultures
- Able to develop different strategies for acquiring knowledge relevant to adapting to different cultures
- Able to engage in active and dynamic thinking in interacting with people from different cultures; able to plan, check, and learn from each encounter; and able to resolve cultural dilemmas or problems in the encounter

Take the example of the third author of this book, who discovered that politeness takes on a varied complexion across cultures. In a small pastoral community in New Zealand, if you get extremely polite reactions when you engage locals, it might be because you've offended the local in an earlier encounter. But if you're not aware that this form of extreme politeness signals social disapproval, you might not think of examining your actions to see whether you indeed had caused offense, intended or otherwise. And such cultural information is not obtainable through reading guidebooks or searching on the internet.

Even though the third author didn't spend a long time in the community, he had to exert a lot of effort to make sense and monitor every encounter with locals, and to think strategically to understand the hidden meaning behind the politeness. To develop your cultural thinking, you should strive to be open, alert, and sensitive to cultural differences; to develop your ability to draw distinctions and activate the appropriate set of reasoning skills; and of course, ultimately, to be able to engage (or, in the third author's case in the above story, to reengage) people from a different culture.

THINKING AND THE NEED FOR CLOSURE

Some people have a high need for what psychologists call closure. The need for closure is a desire for definite knowledge on some issue. It represents a dimension of stable individual differences as well as a situationally evocable state. The need for closure has consequences for how you view yourself as well as your encounters with others, and these consequences are exacerbated when people interact with people from other cultures.

The consequences of how you view yourself and your encounters with others are derived from two general tendencies: urgency and permanence. The urgency tendency means that some people are inclined to attain closure as soon as possible; the permanence tendency means that some people want to maintain closure for as long as possible. People who have a high need for closure have several characteristics that limit cultural strategic thinking. For example, they tend to:

- Generate fewer explanations for things they observe
- Use less information in making their decisions
- Selectively use the information they obtain
- Use stereotypes and decision rules that bias their thinking
- Rely heavily on overly simple cultural scripts

In cross-cultural engagements, quick or premature closure may not be a good thing. Engaging in active and fluid thinking and staying open to different possibilities are traits of people with high cultural strategic thinking.

A high need for closure is negatively related to cultural strategic thinking for several reasons. First, a high need for closure increases the tendency to rely too heavily on previous knowledge and experience to assess the cultural situation, without taking new information into consideration. This results in cultural myopia that leads you to focus on past experience at the expense of new happenings. This overreliance on experience typically leads to the activation of negative stereotypes, inaccurate impressions, and faulty assessments that could impair effective cultural adaptation.

Second, a high need for closure may hinder the creation of new knowledge that is vital for effective cross-cultural adjustment. People who have high cultural strategic thinking are able to create new knowledge, which enables them to resist being stuck with old and rigid knowledge, mindsets, and ways of seeing the world. It's as if such individuals are able to live between the borders and boundaries of different cultures and therefore are more capable of adapting effectively to different ones.

Juxtaposed against the person with higher cultural strategic thinking is the person who is culturally myopic, who fails to pay attention to the perspectives and worldviews of others or even to permit them to permeate his or her way of being. This limited individual is a kind of cultural tourist, moving in and out of cultural boundaries, and is never conscious of how those boundaries might have affected behaviors, never conscious of how the locals live in an unfamiliar location. Glen Fisher, a cross-cultural researcher, calls this type of person (self-absorbed and unaware of the world around him) an intransigent person. In moving across different cultures, these culturally intransigent individuals will likely face severe challenges.

Culturally limited thinkers are also categorized as inactive or passive thinkers. They are unaware of how they think (remember Chris from *Miss Saigon*), and hence they are unable to use appropriate strategies and skills to resolve problems they experience in a different culture. They also rarely monitor or regulate their thinking. They may also exhibit low capacities for self-monitoring and self-awareness.

Lest you get the mistaken impression that it's always necessary to be an active strategic thinker in all cultural situations, we hasten to add that culturally intelligent individuals know when to engage in more extensive thinking and strategizing and when not to across different cultural situations. They have an adaptive capacity to deal with the information demands and complexities of new cultural experiences. The effort and attention you exert depends on the particular cultural problem or dilemma that confronts you. For example, a strong cultural thinker realizes that figuring out supermarket etiquette not only takes less time than understanding how to manage subordinates in a product design team, but also isn't as important. Less time and attention can be devoted to supermarket etiquette because indiscretions are less consequential.

The level of effort you spend on cognitive processing will also depend on your motivation. Individuals can process information in a quick, effortless, and heuristic way or in a more effortful, deliberate, and systematic manner. According to Carsten K. W. De Dreu and his associates, whether individuals will engage in such systematic and thorough thinking depends on how motivated they are to "search for, attend to, encode and retrieve information upon which to base subsequent judgment."

USING THE MAPS MODEL FOR DEVELOPING YOUR CULTURAL STRATEGIC THINKING

In this chapter we propose the MAPS model for developing and enhancing your cultural strategic thinking. MAPS illustrates the steps that can be used to develop a more systematic and effective approach to understanding new cultural situations:

Step 1: Making sense and monitoring

Step 2: Activating thinking and reasoning skills

Step 3: Prioritizing options

Step 4: Solving problems

Individuals high in cultural strategic thinking engage in intelligent sense making (to distinguish what is significant from what is not significant), intelligent search and retrieval (to seek, acquire, or retrieve relevant cultural information to deal with the demands of the situation), and intelligent monitoring (to adopt a deliberate, strategic, intentional, goal-directed, and future-oriented style of thinking) that can be used to accomplish the objectives of the cultural encounter. The idea of deliberate, strategic, and goal-directed thinking is deeply embedded in many scientists' views of how people think about the world around them. Individuals with high cultural strategic thinking possess sophisticated intellectual armory and weaponry that can be applied to diverse cultural situations.

Let's look at a young Chinese business executive and see how she exhibits cultural strategic thinking:

> A young business executive from China sits attentively in the meeting room at the firm's headquarters in Seattle, trying to follow her colleague from the United States, who is explaining how an existing business process needs to be transformed. As she sits there listening to the explanation, she recalls another business meeting on a major organizational change she attended in her previous firm in Shanghai, and she begins to make the connection between the current meeting and the previous one. She thinks she knows what to expect from a meeting like this. However, as the meeting progresses, she has a sense or feeling that she doesn't understand what the change is all about or exactly what her American colleague is trying to say in his presentation. As a result, she tries to concentrate harder on her colleague's explanation. As her U.S. colleague continues speaking, he uses a chart to show how the business process needs to be changed. The chart the U.S. colleague uses is Kaplan and Norton's Balanced Scorecard. The Balanced Scorecard can be considered a strategic management tool that in essence balances financial and nonfinancial perspectives. The chart triggers a chain of memories in the Chinese colleague's mind. She is reminded of her culture's concept of yin and yang, which ancient Chinese philosophy posits as two opposing yet complementary elements of the universe. She then realizes that her understanding of yin and yang can be used to help her understand her colleague's explanation of Balanced Scorecard, which highlights the importance of balancing apparently contradictory yet interdependent perspectives in strategic management of organizations. She redoubles her concentration and is able to follow what her U.S. colleague is saying.

A look at this vignette will illustrate how the MAPS model was used to resolve a challenge in a cross-cultural encounter.

Step 1: Making Sense and Monitoring

You might have noticed that two things stand out in the events described in the vignette. The first thing is that the executive was thoroughly attentive and focused during the entire episode (this is what we mean by being "oriented in the present"). During one phase of the colleague's presentation, she had a sense or feeling that a connection wasn't being made that needed to be completed. It was as if something was missing or inconsistent, though she wasn't sure what. This type of monitoring reflects the meta-level experience we described as part of strategic thinking. That is, she had a sense or intuition that more was being presented than the actual presentation appeared to convey.

The second thing is that she engaged in effortful, deliberate, and goal-directed thinking throughout the episode. She was engaged in constant sense making and monitoring throughout the entire meeting.

Her use of sense making and monitoring helped her realize quickly that her knowledge of another business meeting on organizational change wasn't terribly helpful for her understanding of the current situation. She was aware of what she didn't know and what she didn't understand. Because she was fully attentive, she was able to assess the situation accurately and concluded rightly that she needed to forestall closure and continue with active searching.

The vignette illustrates that cultural thinking involves active monitoring and consequent regulation and orchestration of thinking processes to accomplish tasks and goals. Monitoring, regulation, and orchestration can take the form of checking, planning, selecting, inferring, self-interrogation, introspection, interpretation of ongoing experience, or simply making judgments about what one knows or does not know about accomplishing a task.

However, the vignette also shows that along with the idea of "active" and "conscious" monitoring, regulation, and orchestration of the meeting is the possibility that strategic thinking (thinking about thinking), through repeated use or with learning, may become automatic and consequently unconscious. The challenge for individuals with high cultural thinking is to avoid complacency.

Step 2: Activating Thinking and Reasoning Skills

In the vignette, the young executive activated her analogical reasoning skills. Analogical reasoning is the ability to transfer knowledge from one situation to another to achieve greater insight. The ability to form and understand analogies is used by educational psychologists as a marker of high thinking processes. Your capacity to reason analogically is related to your ability to draw inferences from what you know or have learned. Analogical reasoning can greatly facilitate problem-solving in cross-cultural situations, but, as we pointed out earlier in this chapter, it can be a very difficult thing to do. According to cognitive psychologists, most people just don't reason well using analogies and will often overlook even fairly obvious connections. One mark of the high cultural thinker is a penchant for effective analogical thinking — drawing from one example to a potentially different one.

Consequently, the executive was able to retrieve intelligently the cultural concept of yin and yang in her mind and integrate them with the two concepts of Kaplan and Norton's Balanced Scorecard, helping her to solve the problem she had experienced in the earlier part of the meeting. Her knowledge about yin and yang helped her understand the new concept of the Balanced Scorecard.

The vignette illustrates more than just analogical reasoning. The executive also applied divergent or creative thinking. She was able to form rich associations between a cultural concept she already knew and a new concept she had just learned. Divergent or creative thinking reflects your capacity to elaborate or discover unusual similarities or analogies, and to link ideas in novel and unexpected ways. Educational psychologists sometimes refer to divergent or creative thinking as a component of giftedness. We assert that individuals with high cultural strategic thinking can be considered gifted in this context. However, we also assert that individuals can be trained to develop their analogical reasoning and divergent and creative thinking abilities. These abilities are critical in developing high cultural strategic thinking.

Step 3: Prioritizing Options

Though it's not explicitly presented in the vignette, we can infer that the executive had to make certain decisions such as defining what situation she found herself in and how best to resolve the problem of understanding what was going on at the meeting.

According to a group of management professors at Northwestern University, people apply the "logic of appropriateness" in decision making. The logic of appropriateness suggests that in making decisions and prioritizing options, individuals ask themselves, either explicitly or implicitly, "What does a person like me (*your identity*) do (*rules*) in a situation like this (*situational recognition*)?" This question identifies three significant issues: recognition of the kind of situation encountered, the identity of the person making the decision, and the application of decision rules to guide choice.

In the vignette, the executive had to define the situation she was in. That she ascertained that she was attending a meeting on organizational change then helped her to match features of the situation encountered to features of similar situations she had encountered in the past. Recognition is therefore an act of categorization. However, she had to abandon her categorization of the situation as the meeting progressed, because she experienced serious impediments to her initial and rapid categorization — for example, a new actor, new behavior, uncertainty, attributional ambiguity, and novel contextual information (e.g., the Balanced Scorecard).

Identity is a complex, multifaceted factor in the appropriateness framework. People often differ in many systematic ways. Here, we take a much broader approach than the typical one, which links identity with personality factors. As we discuss in more detail in the next chapter, our assessment of identity includes professional and personal histories, because these can influence the ease with which you'll face a new situation and the way in which you will find analogies that can direct your initial behavioral choices.

We don't know enough about the executive in the vignette to make any detailed inferences about her identity. But we might infer that since she is attending a meeting in the United States, she is likely a high performer with potential in her organization. The fact that she's Chinese might provide some general insights about her based on her cultural background. Her identity affects how she prioritizes her options for solving the problem. In developing your cultural strategic thinking, you need to be aware of your own identity. Also, you need to be aware of the possible psychological filters you may have (e.g., your biases, prejudices, etc.) that could affect the way you make decisions.

Rules and cultural scripts offer people a way to cope with the potentially overwhelming flow of information to which they are constantly exposed. Rules simplify behavioral choices by narrowing options. One important type of rule is called by psychologists a heuristic. Heuristics are best thought of as mental shortcuts, rules of thumb for making decisions. Unfortunately, heuristics may not lead to better decisions, and they often lead to poorer ones. The management expert Max Bazerman describes a number of these heuristics and how they might hinder effective decision making. For example, people have a tendency to use information in memory that is easily recalled, or what is called the availability heuristic. When our executive first remembered other meetings about organizational change that she had been in, this reflected the availability heuristic. Unfortunately, information that is very salient or obvious is often most easily recalled. Her recollections about yin and yang reflect ease of recall, even though they might not have been the most helpful thing to think about. She might have had other experiences in organizational change (e.g., her training during an MBA program) earlier, but she focused on the most available (easily recalled or salient) information. Cultural thinkers are as susceptible to heuristics as everyone else; however, they are able to look beyond these decision traps. Rather than succumbing to the salience of information, a high cultural thinker pushes his or her thinking to go beyond obvious comparisons.

Rule-based processing of decisions is defined as deliberate and demanding of a higher level of cognitive effort. Whether people use heuristics or rule-based processing will depend largely on the situation. In cross-cultural contexts, situations can be vague, ambiguous, or unpleasant, which tend to activate rule-based processing. This was clearly evident in the vignette: the executive had to engage in deliberate rule selection and consciously and constantly to prioritize the options and make the appropriate decisions to deal with the situation.

Step 4: Solving Problems

Just what is a problem? First, a problem is a mismatch between the current situation and a desired future one. The mismatch may occur because a situation is ambiguous or unknown or because resources are mismatched. Second, finding or solving for the unknown must have some social, cultural, or intellectual significance for a person. An ambiguous situation that has no value to a person isn't a problem. You might not understand how to put money in a parking meter in a new country, but this isn't a problem if you don't have a car. Problems can vary in several ways, but in this book we focus our attention on two dimensions that are critical in developing cultural thinking: structure and dynamism.

Problems within and between circumstances may vary in terms of their structure. Well-structured problems can often be solved using a limited and known knowledge base. Poorly structured problems are often encountered in person-to-person contacts in everyday life. They cannot be solved by applying rules, concepts, or principles from a single domain. Poorly structured problems are often ambiguous and may present many alternative possible solutions. In other words, they are complicated and ambiguous, and they do not suggest a clear single answer. Most problems in cross-cultural interactions can be categorized as poorly structured, because one often lacks full information and prior cultural knowledge may not be relevant. Individuals with high cultural strategic thinking are able to distinguish between well-structured and poorly structured problems and to use appropriate strategies and solutions to solve them.

Problems vary in terms of their dynamism. Poorly structured problems tend to be dynamic — that is, the task environment and its factors change over time.

When the conditions of a problem change, the individual who needs to solve the problem must continuously adapt his or her understanding of the problem while searching for new solutions because the old solutions may no longer be viable. For example, investing in the stock market is often difficult because market conditions (e.g., demand, interest rates, investor confidence, etc.) change, often dramatically, over short periods of time. Poorly structured problems tend to be more dynamic than well-structured problems. In the vignette, it was only after the executive redefined the situation as a poorly structured problem that she could discover a useful solution. How did she do it?

First, she constructed a mental representation of the problem. This is also known as the problem space. Think of this representation as an overarching view she has about the problem (understanding the organizational change project presented to her). Her internal mental model of the problem is a multifaceted representation consisting of knowledge about the structure of the problem, a general view of the problem, and procedural knowledge of when and how to use which strategy or option to solve it. She then actively challenged and tested her mental model. Successful adaptation and adjustment to different cultures require individuals to generate and try out solutions in their minds (problem spaces or mental models) before trying them out in the actual encounter.

This two-stage approach in problem-solving — building a mental model, then challenging and testing it — is an important part of the development of strategic thinking.

DEVELOPING YOUR CULTURAL STRATEGIC THINKING

It's clear that cultural strategic thinking is a core component of your cultural intelligence. Most cross-cultural training programs and pre-departure briefings for global work assignments focus on just the acquisition and accumulation of cultural knowledge. We agree that having cultural knowledge is important, but it's not possible to know everything about a country or a culture (remember the example of the extreme-politeness behavior). What's even more critical is to develop and enhance your cultural thinking.

The MAPS model can help you develop your ability to attend to and critique your underlying assumptions and resolve cross-cultural dilemmas or problems. To achieve higher cultural strategic thinking, you need to focus on developing new hypotheses, options, cues, or goals in cross-cultural encounters. Also, you need to assess and analyze what is happening in each cross-cultural situation by continuously and dynamically modifying your interpretation of cues and intentions in each cross-cultural situation. Using the MAPS model, a problem-solving approach, a manager can be trained to exploit personal experience–based intuition in cross-cultural interactions and to handle the uncertainty and novelty that arise when individuals move from one culture to another.

SUMMARY

In this chapter we have defined cultural strategic thinking and why it is such a critical component of your cultural intelligence. Cultural strategic thinking consists of two general elements: cultural knowledge and strategic thinking. Cultural knowledge reflects the information a person has about a given country or culture, such as the language spoken, cultural values, economic environment, social etiquette, and so on. The Thai respect for age, Russian adherence to agendas during meetings, and Japanese subordinates' willingness to criticize their superiors at the local karaoke bar after work are just a few examples of cultural knowledge.

Strategic thinking reflects a higher, or more general, level of thought. We referred to this as thinking about thinking. This is not just thinking about how to run a meeting in Indonesia; it reflects your ability to discover how to run a meeting in any new culture. That is, it concerns how to learn, not just what is learned. Strategic thinking has two elements: meta-level knowledge and meta-level experience. Meta-level knowledge is the general information that you might have about cultures and the way things operate globally, as well as the general strategies you might use to figure these things out. Meta-level experience is a manager's intuition and feelings — a general sense of happenings — about a new cultural situation.

Think of your own experiences when you have to use cultural strategic thinking while interacting with people from different cultures. Are you able to develop strategies for effective engagement with people from different cultures? Would you say, on the whole, that your cultural strategic thinking is high or low?

We introduced the MAPS model for developing cultural strategic thinking. The MAPS model is a systematic four-step approach: (1) making sense and monitoring, (2) activating thinking and reasoning skills, (3) prioritizing options, and (4) solving problems. Through this model, we described specific strategies and skills that you could consider in developing different aspects of your cultural thinking.

In the next chapter, we explain what motivational CQ is and how you can develop this aspect of your CQ in order to live and work effectively in different cultures.

3 | DIRECTING YOUR ENERGY:

THE MOTIVATIONAL BASIS OF CQ

Although it's critical for managers to think rationally and accurately, they must be willing to persevere during difficulties arising from cross-cultural misunderstandings. That is, personal effort and integrity are the next critical elements of CQ. In our discussion of CQ from a motivational perspective, we emphasize the centrality of a person's core values, preferences, and goals. These values and preferences give rise to personal motivation and, in turn, create a sense of personal purpose and direction.

An international sojourner must overcome innumerable challenges. This requires a great deal of perseverance, motivation, and dedication, as well as natural confidence and commitment to the endeavor. It's our experience that many of the difficulties that ultimately deter a manager are based on drive and persistence rather than on thinking through the issues. That is, it's not merely working smarter that predicts success; rather, for a global manager success comes from working harder and longer. Even if you believe that actively engaging others will help you master your new cultural surroundings, if you lack the requisite confidence and courage to do so, you won't. As we suggested earlier, cultural intelligence requires not only knowledge of a new culture, but also requires a personal motivation. In this chapter, we talk about the personal motives and values that are essential for a manager to be successful in international encounters. We discuss cultural intelligence from a motivational perspective, emphasizing a person's values, confidence, and goals as key features. A person's values and preferences help determine what motivates you, and these motives influence the goals that you set for yourself and others.

Adjusting to a new cultural situation is not accomplished merely by understanding the practices and habits of people. A manager has to engage others proactively and to redouble his or her efforts when confronted with failure. If you think about it for a moment, it's clear why perseverance and personal confidence are so critical for a manager. What is the most likely result of a manager's early encounters with others in a new culture? More often than not, early attempts to dive into a new culture are met with mixed results and preliminary setbacks. The problem is that a manager who is already somewhat apprehensive about working in a new cultural situation is very sensitive to these setbacks and will likely weigh them too heavily. That is, early setbacks will be perceived as reflecting a lack of personal capability, so a manager may disengage very early on after a few minor setbacks.

What are the motivational characteristics that help us predict someone who will adjust successfully to another culture? Thomas Vulpe describes his ideal candidate for the Canadian Foreign Service as possessing a number of critical characteristics, including personal and professional commitment. It's this element, personal and professional commitment, that is highly relevant to a manager's personal motivation for coping with new cultural experiences. Those who exhibit this commitment competence "give evidence of wanting to contribute to the local community . . . [and] have a clear and realistic awareness of their own motivation and expectations regarding the assignment and personal life abroad."

The importance of personal motivation for global success is nicely documented in work by the management professor Rosalie Tung, who pioneered work in this field. She studied a wide variety of global managers and found four general areas of competencies needed for a global manager's successful adjustment: technical job competence, personality traits or relational abilities, environmental variables, and family situation. The relational ability of a global manager refers to his or her motivation and desire to adjust to a new work environment. Despite the seemingly obvious importance of such a capability, Tung's work with multinational companies reveals that very few companies (5 percent at the time of her study) assessed or trained for these skills.

The management researcher Simcha Ronen found something very similar in his work with the adjustment of global managers. He identified a number of key factors predicting a manager's effectiveness overseas: job factors (technical competence), relational (empathy, tolerance), motivational state (interest, openness), family situation (the spouse's willingness), and language skills (verbal and nonverbal). Of these various skills, a person's motivation, as well as the motivation of his or her spouse, is a critical key for a global manager's success. (In fact, the most common reason for global managers to fail in completing their work assignment is that their spouses do not adjust! This failure is largely based on the spouse's motivation and satisfaction with a new culture. Thinking about it for a moment suggests that this is a very difficult aspect of an overseas assignment, since the job is for the manager rather than the spouse. In many cases, one's spouse may have to leave a desirable job and take a less suitable one to accommodate the partner or perhaps give up on work completely for a time. On top of this, a manager's spouse is more likely than the global manager himself or herself to feel isolated because of the job changes, because the global manager has a work setting to go into, with built-in social networks and the like.)

Finally, the importance of personal motivation is demonstrated in work by the management researchers Hal Gregerson, Mark Mendenhall, Gary Oddou, and Stewart Black. They have suggested that there are four critical factors for successful adjustment: self-orientation, other-person orientation, perspective taking, and cultural toughness. Self-orientation refers to actions that strengthen your self-esteem and self-confidence, such as on-the-job successes. Other-person orientation refers to activities and attributes that help a global manager interact successfully with host-culture nationals, such as learning local customs or a bit of the local language. Perspective taking refers to a global manager's ability to see things from other perspectives in order to understand why things unfold as they do. This is more than just empathy — it means you really come to understand why it's so important to show respect for age and experience in Thailand, or why Singaporeans like to keep their options open and keep others from getting ahead (*kiasu*) by constantly working and pressuring themselves to produce. Cultural toughness refers to a global manager's ability to endure radically different environments. Cultural adjustment for a French manager working in Montreal, Canada, clearly requires less effort than working in Brazzaville, Republic of Congo. The larger the difference between your home and host nations, the more cultural toughness is required.

What is common to all of these approaches to global manager motivation falls into three general categories:

- personal and cultural values and norms
- self-confidence and personal goals
- roles and personal identity

What we mean by this is that a person's motivation, from a CQ perspective, is best thought of as influenced by values, goals and confidence, and the roles that people take on for themselves (see figure 3.1). If we understand how these values, goals,

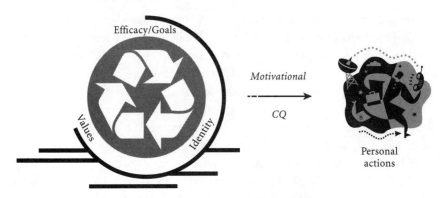

Efficacy/Goals

Values

Identity

Motivational

CQ

Personal
actions

Figure 3.1 How cultural and personal values, efficacy, goals, and personal identity shape motivational CQ

and roles fit together we will use CQ more effectively. A way to think of these three features of a person fitting together is to use the analogy of driving a car to your favorite restaurant for a meal. The choice of restaurant reflects your preferences (values), and your choice to drive reflects your goal and confidence. If you don't have a great deal of confidence in your likelihood of getting to the restaurant (perhaps because of bad weather or car troubles), you won't bother going even if you really enjoy eating at the restaurant. Assuming you get to the restaurant, you will enter it, be seated, order food, and enjoy a nice meal. No one has to tell you how to go to this restaurant and how to get food. You don't try to cook the food yourself, nor do you clean up the tables, because your role as a patron is clear. Getting a meal successfully requires personal preferences (general guidance), goals and the confidence to pursue them (specific direction), and clear roles that prescribe action (rules for what to do). It's with these three facets that we can understand a manager's motivation and CQ.

ANCHORING ON PERSONAL AND CULTURAL VALUES

An important starting point for understanding the motivational part of CQ is a person's personal and cultural values. In this section we explore various values that we have found to be critical for global managers dealing with multicultural environments. We begin by exploring the core values across nations and people.

A useful way of thinking about values is to consider how people interact with each other under various circumstances. According to the researchers Talcott Parsons and Edward Shils, there are general value orientations that guide us as we deal with one another personally (according to my personal wants and needs), socially (according to our mutual wants and needs), and culturally (according to larger wants and needs from society). These value-orientations, or pattern variables, are what some people call cultural values, and they include:

- *Affective versus affective neutrality*, or emotionality and delayed gratification. Affective versus affective neutrality captures two ideas. It looks at how desirable it is for people to experience immediate gratification and display emotionality. In an affective culture, people indulge in immediate gratification, whereas in an affectively neutral culture they show restraint from such excesses.

- *Self-orientation versus collectivity orientation*, or group focus. Self-orientation versus collectivity orientation is a topic of many management aficionados. It refers to a person's relationship to others. In a self-focused culture, people pursue their own interests and "do their own thing," but in a group-focused culture, people think about their actions in terms of others in their in-group.

- *Universalism versus particularism*, or how general are rules applied. In a universalistic culture, a broad set of rules and policies will guide all individuals' actions, and conformity to these standards is expected. In a particularistic culture, however, individuals are guided by the unique aspects of the situation and its relevance to specific people involved.

- *Ascription versus achievement*, or whether position is based on accomplishments. In an ascriptive culture, people are judged by attributes that they possess (e.g., group memberships and possessions), whereas, in an achievement culture, people are judged by their actions and performance (e.g., skills and work habits).

- *Specificity versus diffuseness*, or the degree of interconnection between things. In a diffuse culture, the relationship of a person to the world around him or her can be quite indirect, whereas in a specific culture this relationship is quite narrow and limited.

Each of these pairs is a specific value that implies certain patterned behavior. For example, Italians are high on the affectiveness dimension (as are most people from southern Europe and the Mediterranean), which is illustrated by their strong emotionality and animated conversation. Contrast this style with the reserve of a German manager, who is high on affective neutrality. Universalistic cultures such as that of Singapore believe that rules apply to everyone regardless of who a person is, whereas neighboring Indonesia endorses a view that rules must be adapted to the person and circumstance uniquely.

Of course, we find that people in most cultures are not at one extreme or the other. The management professor Charles Hampden-Turner suggests that many cultures endorse both ends of these continuums but differ in their emphasis. For example, he finds that although Japanese managers often put their relationships with others ahead of formal rules and laws, they will use their relationships to try and obey the rules. In one example, he uses a story of a person who is traveling in a car with a friend who is speeding. The friend hits a pedestrian and ends up in court. As it turns out, only the person traveling with his friend is a witness. What will the person do in court? Protect his friend and lie? Tell the truth and harm his friend? Or something that combines these two extremes? He finds that many Japanese managers say that they would lie to protect the friend but encourage the friend to tell the truth in court and admit the mistake for the sake and honor of their friendship. Indeed, Hampden-Turner has found that the most successful global managers and leaders are those who are able to integrate these cultural extremes. It appears that they are able to integrate various perspectives; after all, this is the essence of effective management.

The importance of these traditional approaches to cultural values is evident in much of the popular writing, by various authors, on cross-cultural management. In fact, there has been an explosion of management books focusing on cultural differences by documenting differences in people's values. While these various frameworks are an important starting point for understanding how cultural values and diversity influence employees' actions, they don't provide us with a coherent framework for understanding the relationship of value orientations to personal motivation (and hence, CQ). Instead, most of the work along these lines focuses on describing people from various cultures using these values but ignoring the complex interplay of the values. More important, they don't describe with much precision how these values actually influence a person's actions and thoughts.

Values play a central role in our self-concept as well, which influences the motivational component of a person's cultural intelligence. An approach the first author developed with our colleague, Miriam Erez of the Technion in Haifa, Israel, provides a way to understand how cultural values influence personal motivation. We mentioned earlier that people use three primary motives to regulate their personal motivation — enhancement (wanting to feel good about yourself), growth (wanting to grow and challenge yourself), and consistency (wanting to keep continuity in your life). Cultural values play the most direct role in a person's self-enhancement motive, because they provide the benchmark for judging what happens around you and how you feel about yourself. Put simply, our values enable us to evaluate which one of several social cliques will help us feel better about ourselves if we join it. A person who has a strong motive for self-enhancement is more likely than others to seek out people in a new culture as a source of self-affirmation.

This influence of cultural values also reflects the nature and structure of our self-image. For example, a person from a group-focused culture likely views himself as a member of a number of overlapping groups, including family, work, hobby, religion, and so on. A person from a self-focused culture perceives these various personal identities as separable and malleable. You might think that someone from a group-focused culture should have higher CQ than someone from a self-focused culture, because getting along in groups requires strong social skills. However, this may not be the case. Although group-focused people have more overlapping identities (I view myself as a husband *and* an automotive engineer *and* a pitcher for the local softball team), the boundaries around these identities are rigid and well defined. That is, I may see myself in an overlapping fashion as a company man, a family man, and a member of my sports team in an overlapping fashion — but not just *any* company, *any* family, or *any* sports team. Rather, I am a General Motors man, the husband of Susan, and a member of my Pontiac, Michigan, neighborhood's intramural softball team. These identities are overlapping and integrated but very clearly defined. The self-focused person may have a less-integrated self-concept (at work I am a Unilever man, but at home I am husband to Susan, but at the workout field I am a bowler on the cricket team), but the particular role memberships are more flexible (having quit the cricket team, I am now a member of the local golf team, and tomorrow I may switch to the local tennis team).

What might this flexibility mean with regard to motivation and CQ? A self-focused manager is constantly moving from one social group to the next as excessive demands are placed on the person. In order to fit into a new social group, a person must be motivated to learn about it. Thus, a self-focused person is likely to have a higher motivation to learn about new groups, and hence greater openness to new experiences, than a group-focused person who perceives group memberships as long term and quasi-permanent. A group-focused person is very good within his or her own group but not necessarily across other groups. This is just one example of how cultural values may impact a person's actions at work.

Our suggestion is that although a self-focused person's view of himself or herself may be less well integrated than a group-focused person's, it may require greater motivational CQ to satisfy their tendency to move across social cliques.

A company can buffer these differences, as we describe later in the book. For example, if your employees are group focused, then it's useful to send them in existing groups or teams. Global managers who arrive in a large group have a fully functioning reference group, support group, and the like, so they are not as motivated to integrate themselves into the local setting. This, of course, is characteristic of how Japanese companies place their overseas managers. Japanese managers are often placed in teams overseas with an emphasis on moving the managers and their families together. Contrast this with the typical American approach to placement. A single global manager lacking such support and referents is sent who must then integrate himself or herself into the local culture in order to function. This places significant adaptation demands on the global manager if he or she is to integrate him- or herself into the local culture.

In the next section, we explore the importance of two additional forces behind motivation and CQ — self-efficacy (confidence) and goals. Knowing a manager's cultural and personal values gives rise to energy for behavior (and choice of direction), but we need more to understand what actually guides action.

DEVELOPING SELF-EFFICACY AND SETTING GOALS

In the previous section we described a number of different personal and cultural values and showed how they influence a person's motivation to engage and understand a new culture. But values address only one part of the formula we use to predict choice and action. Values don't address the important question concerning a person's perceived confidence to act successfully in dynamic environments. This confidence is called "self-efficacy" by the concept's creator, Albert Bandura. In addition, managers are motivated by other factors, such as wanting to look good in front of others and seeking continuity in his or her life. All three motives are important for understanding how CQ works.

As we described earlier, a person's actions in a cross-cultural situation are guided by three motives — enhancement, efficacy, and consistency. Enhancement, or wanting to feel good about ourselves, is largely tied to our values and groups of people we respect. Our values tell us what is good and desirable or bad and to be avoided; they also lead us to join certain groups rather than others. Our choice of health club XYZ instead of club ABC is based, in part, on what we think that club will reflect about us to other people. That is, our membership choice is guided by our judgments concerning what we appraise as positive and desirable; these judgments guide us to develop attachments to various social groups over others. Likewise, some people have strong values for seeking out new and foreign groups of people and getting to know them. Their sense of self-worth is tied to their learning about new people and places; they are modern-day explorers. People with high motivation CQ go out of their way to learn about new cultures through personal exploration of food and restaurants, shopping, travel, cultural events, and so on. More important, they feel better about themselves when they explore.

However, our choices are not based only on values. We not only need to value the endeavor of exploration, we need to feel capable of doing so and to be guided appropriately. This personal efficacy is the key behind a person's motive to seek challenge and grow. A person lacking a self-growth (or *efficacy*) motive avoids engaging people from a new culture even if he or she positively values such actions. Without a strong sense of self-efficacy, a person will avoid challenges and give up easily when confronted with setbacks. The motivational aspect of CQ requires a personal sense of efficacy and desire for enactive mastery.

Thus, self-efficacy is a central aspect of a person's way of engaging the world. Self-efficacy is the level of confidence you have in your ability to accomplish some specific action. For example, your self-efficacy for running a marathon on a hot and muggy New York afternoon will guide your choice as to whether to participate, or, if you do participate, your choice as to whether and then when to give up during the race. Self-efficacy guides decisions ranging from trying to make the green over a 200-yard carry over water at the golf course to accepting a new job heading up the Asia-Pacific region for your company. Efficacy promotes the choice of situations and tasks with a high likelihood of success and eliminates the choice of tasks that exceed one's capabilities. However, efficacy is not just what you think about some situation, as Albert Bandura (1997: 37) describes.

> Effective personal functioning is not simply a matter of knowing what to do and being motivated to do it. Nor is efficacy a fixed ability that one does or does not have in one's behavioral repertoire, any more than one would regard linguistic efficacy as a collection of words or a colony of preformed sentences in a verbal repertoire. Rather, efficacy is a generative capability in which cognitive, social, emotional, and behavioral subskills must be organized and effectively orchestrated to serve innumerable purposes. This is a marked difference between possessing subskills and being able to integrate them into appropriate courses of action and to execute them well under difficult circumstances.

Put simply, your efficacy helps you organize your skills, emotions, frame of mind, and so on into a coherent package as you tackle some new challenge. For example, a mountain climber doesn't just think about his confidence in his ability to scale a summit. His or her musings about efficacy lead him or her to strategize about how to achieve the summit, what must be done, the actions that need to be taken, and the amount of effort and persistence required. In trying to discover "can I do it?" a person mentally works through "how to do it"—high self-efficacy means you work smarter as well as harder. Further, a person with high self-efficacy will be a self-starter when it comes to the need to learn new things. This may include learning new actions (how to give the proper *wai* when going to Thailand or handing a business card to your Japanese colleague with the correct etiquette) or information (what the core values are of the Chinese employees in Shenzhen).

There are, however, important limits to personal efficacy, because it's highly situation specific. That is to say, a person's efficacy expectations are best tied to the specific context at hand. Although my prior mastery experiences with cultural encounters might enhance my general efficacy, it does not guarantee a high sense of efficacy for any particular *newly encountered* culture. For example, a global manager who has had three successful assignments in central Europe is now sent to Indonesia. Will these prior experiences provide a strong sense of enactive mastery and hence high self-efficacy? Bandura cautions that such generalizations across domains and tasks may on occasion be a problem. For example, one obvious change for the global manager is that he or she is now going to Asia, though the three previous assignments were all in Europe. Likewise, he or she may be asked to perform activities in Asia (e.g., start-up a new plant) very different from those he or she had done in central Europe (e.g., new brand development and management). In fact, if this global manager fails to recognize the potential differences among these operating contexts, he or she may have an unrealistic (and therefore inappropriate) level of efficacy, which will be a significant problem for the assignment.

The role of efficacy in motivating adaptation is both direct and indirect. High self-efficacy enables a person to persevere in the face of difficulties. However, persistence is only one benefit of strong efficacy. Another important benefit is the influence of efficacy on proactivity.

Yet another important feature of self-efficacy relates to its generative capacity for controlling oneself. People with high self-efficacy regulate their feelings and emotions better than other people. Put another way, emotional intelligence (and related approaches to intelligence) incorporates a strong motivational component. The generative aspect of self-efficacy is very important in cross-cultural encounters since everything is new and requires our careful attention. Self-efficacy helps us regulate this information overload.

However, there is an important limit to self-efficacy: it may not work as well in extremely turbulent and uncertain environments. This effect is very important for CQ, because understanding a new culture is inevitably a complex and uncertain undertaking. The complexity of mastering a new culture is ultimately a challenge for self-efficacy, though not an insurmountable one. As we suggested earlier, highly efficacious people not only persevere, but they will set goals and expectations such that they will proactively search for new and useful strategies with which to approach the goal of cross-cultural interaction. That is, a person's efficacy motive is an important feature in their creation of new ways of doing and thinking about things in an unfamiliar culture.

Another important aspect of self-efficacy is that it leads us to set beneficial goals for our personal actions. What kind of goals are these and how do they operate? To understand the complex interplay of values, efficacy, and goals we must return to figure 3.1. Remember, efficacy alone does not dictate the target or goal of action — self-efficacy and goals are complementary features in an overall frame for motivational CQ. We can't fully describe the importance of self-efficacy without describing the interactive role of personal goals.

Goal setting has a long tradition in management. It can be traced back to the seminal work of Edwin Locke on motivation and goals. In his original formulation, goal setting operated according to:

$$Environment \rightarrow Cognition \rightarrow Evaluation \rightarrow$$
$$Intentions\ or\ Goals \rightarrow Performance$$

Early work on goal setting in companies focused mainly on the relationship between a person's goals and his or her performance.

Goals have several influences on a manager's self-efficacy. For example, goals provide a sense of purpose, direction, and clarity concerning performance expectations. They influence individuals' beliefs of what they think they can and should try to perform, through what psychologists call "anchoring-and-adjustment." According to researchers, anchoring-and-adjustment refers to a person's tendency to make decisions in line with information (anchors) that they receive, even if the information is not terribly relevant. That is, in the absence of concrete information, people will rely on all sorts of available information. This means that clear, specific goals will anchor your self-efficacy and bolster your confidence if the goals are challenging. In turn, high efficacy means that you are more likely to tackle challenges with great vigor and will therefore perform better. Goals and efficacy are integrally tied to one another.

Positive evaluations of goals lead to goal commitment. Goal commitment is a decision made by a person after he or she evaluates a given goal. It is based on one's level of efficacy (what one thinks one can do) as well as on what value one places on achieving the goal. Your decision about committing yourself to a particular goal can be influenced by who is involved in setting it. We see this especially when we look at goal setting across cultures.

Participation is a well-known way of getting buy-in from employees for setting challenging goals. Participation allows a person to have more control over decisions concerning his or her own future, and a goal is more likely to be accepted when an employee participates in its selection. However, cultural values and expectations come into play when we talk about this kind of participation. For example, people in very egalitarian cultures (e.g., Sweden, Denmark) expect to participate in goal-setting, while those in other kinds of cultures don't (e.g., Thailand, Indonesia). In a study on participatory goal setting, Miriam Erez and Chris Earley looked at goal setting in three different cultures — the United States (moderate power distance, meaning that people are used to taking directives from their superiors), Israel's kibbutz sector (founded on strong principles of worker democracy and socialism), and urban Israel (founded on principles of worker democracy, but strongly capitalist). What they found was that participatory goal setting had its strongest benefit in the more collectively oriented Israeli kibbutz sector, but much less benefit in the United States. It seems that many Americans are used to receiving assigned goals from their company, while members of a kibbutz don't view such matters as legitimate.

Returning to our discussion of personal growth, we can see the interdependent nature of goals and efficacy for understanding motivational aspects of CQ. There is a generally clear path from self-efficacy to personal goals, with a significant feedback loop from one's performance and these goals to one's subsequent efficacy. Connecting this idea to motivation and CQ, it's clear that people high in motivational CQ are likewise high in personal efficacy and tend to set challenging goals for themselves.

Managers high in motivational CQ are confident in their cultural interactions. They have a strong sense that they can deal with the divergent perspectives of others and with changing and unfamiliar situations, and that they can handle complexity and uncertainty. However, a strong sense of efficacy alone isn't enough for understanding CQ, because actions are goal directed; the nature and type of goals that people set are critical for understanding and predicting the outcomes of intercultural interactions. For example, take two global managers, Suzanne and Michele, each with comparably high levels of self-efficacy for cultural encounters. Suzanne goes into her first encounter without any specific goals or outcome expectations other than a desire to learn more about the other culture (comparable to a "do your best" or general goal). Michele, in contrast, goes into her first encounter with specific goals for cultural understanding concerning the way people greet one another, how respect for authority is accorded, how exchanges take place between friends and between strangers, and whether or not the culture endorses discrimination based on demographic considerations, among other things. Michele will take away much more useful information as a result of the encounter, and she is more likely than Suzanne to use this information constructively for subsequent interactions. Further, Michele's sense of mastery from understanding these various specific features of the target culture will provide her with a further enhanced sense of efficacy as well as with a strategic frame for acquiring further information. More important, Michele will be more strongly motivated to continue her cultural explorations.

We are now in a position to combine our earlier discussion on values with our use of efficacy and goals. The goals that people set for themselves are determined by their efficacy *and* by cultural and personal values. They're determined not only by whether we think we can achieve them, but also by what they can get for us.

Thus far, we have discussed the contribution of values, self-efficacy, and goal setting to a person's motivation and CQ. What has been left out of the discussion is the relevance of one's social groups and role identities as a key contributor to the formation of goals and efficacy as well as an active shaper of personal values. In the next section, we discuss the importance of social setting and context to the motivational aspects of CQ, using the roles that people adopt for themselves.

ADOPTING ROLES AND ADAPTING TO SOCIAL SITUATIONS

Cultural intelligence can't be considered outside the setting where people interact with each other. By the "social setting," we don't mean the physical surroundings; we mean the people involved and how the social milieu may influence how people deal with each other. For example, a manager might be very aggressive and goal focused while he's at work, but very sociable and fun loving while at home. Here the social setting sets the scene for how he acts and works with others. How we choose to act in various circumstances is based on such things as our past experiences in similar situations (social history), cultural values, and self-enhancement motive.

Your personal experiences in various social groups influence the motivational aspect of CQ because they shape your personal values, self-efficacy, and goals. With regard to personal values, it's nearly axiomatic to say that our past experiences provide the foundation for our values and how we view the world around us. Your past experiences are related to your self-consistency motive as well. A person with a high self-consistency motive tries to keep a connection of the past with the present and future. For such a person, history will play a central role in shaping motivational CQ. Such a person will rely heavily on interpreting new information in terms of preexisting ideas and perspectives. Likewise, new situations encountered are likely to be discounted or adapted if they appear inconsistent with existing ideas.

Other key features of your social setting influence your CQ motivation level. First, the roles that a person plays in his or her everyday life are critical for understanding CQ motivation. Identity is complex, multifaceted, and dynamic, and it adjusts to changes in one's social situation. Think of a person as a compilation of various overlapping roles such as we described at the beginning of this chapter. Each has a variety of traits and characteristics. These roles are organized in a hierarchy, with the most general way you think about yourself (perhaps based on your nationality, profession, gender, or religion) at the top, followed by more specific and secondary ones. This means that your most salient roles (those that are high in the hierarchy) have the greatest effect on how you interpret new situations and how you act.

For example, a Russian manager, Nicholas, working for Citicorp spoke with us about his view of leadership. Raised in the former Soviet Union, he had witnessed the difficult transition to independence and the reorganization of Russia and had himself now made the transition to working in a Western multinational company. Nicholas commented that despite having worked for Citicorp for a number of years in the West, he still saw himself as a Russian first and foremost. Interestingly, his preferences and beliefs about leadership are not those of his current home (London) or his company; his leadership style reflects the hierarchical and authoritarian approach he was accustomed to in Russia. He says that a good leader is someone who is willing to make difficult decisions using a strong and authoritarian style. Nicholas uses a strong and authoritarian leadership style in his job even though it's somewhat at odds with the cultural norms at Citicorp. His core identity of being a Russian influences his role as a manager in his company (a secondary role). Obviously, our cultural values are an important factor that influences the roles we act out.

Understanding a person's composite identity requires us to remember that people (usually) want to feel positive about themselves. Two of the key ways that we feel good come from group memberships. Why? First, we compare our personal groups (social, work, etc.) to others and evaluate outsiders in a negative way to bolster our personal sense of worth (e.g., reminding ourselves how mediocre they are makes us think of how good we are). This idea was shown in work by the psychologist Henri Tajfel, who illustrated this by an "in-group favoritism" effect. (An "in-group" is a group that you belong to; all other groups that you don't belong to are "out-groups.") In-group favoritism means that you will favor your own in-group over all others even if you are only tenuously related to that in-group. As an extreme example, Tajfel showed that people assigned randomly to one of four groups in a room (by picking at random a card from a deck and being assigned to a group corresponding to the suit of the card picked as they walked into the room) still showed in-group favoritism in giving out limited rewards. That is, if I were a member of the diamonds group, I tended to give more resources to other diamonds even though I had never even met the other diamonds before this experiment. Why should a person favor a randomly assigned in-group? Tajfel argues that by giving more to my own group I strengthen the idea that my group is better than the others, and, therefore, I must be more important than others.

Second, if my group is better than the others, then I must be better as well. That is, people join groups they think will give them personal prestige and status. Do you belong to the "right" clubs, live in the best area, drive the best car, wear designer clothes, visit the best restaurants, and so on? Associating yourself with prestigious groups causes some of that prestige to rub off on you, so you gain personal status. In some places, personal status, or face, is very central to a person's identity, and a manager may do lots of things to make sure he or she maintains his status. For example, Japanese companies tend to send middle managers to negotiate important deals at the early stages of a business negotiation. Why? If their negotiating partners get the upper-hand in the deal, it's not the senior Japanese company officials who lose face. (Also, these more junior managers can defer a negotiated settlement by feigning a need to get back to their superiors before a deal is closed.)

What implications do these roles that people hold have for the motivational aspects of CQ? The roles people adopt are critical for understanding several aspects of their cultural adaptability. Take, for example, two countries similar in size and population but very different in character — Switzerland and Singapore. Switzerland is moderately hierarchical and group focused, with a relatively homogenous and small population despite the apparent differences between its subpopulations of German, French, Italian, and Roma groups. Despite its central location in Europe, a Swiss manager's motivation for integration into new cultures may be limited. That is, such a person is not overly interested in understanding outsiders, and he or she won't likely seek them out as a potential reference group for self-image. A traditional and homogeneous culture such as we find in Switzerland means that people are somewhat less interested in seeking out new cultures and are satisfied living within their strong existing community.

If my roles and group memberships are very complex and interdependent, such as may be found for a dynamic country undergoing significant technological transitions, then I will be highly motivated to understand new cultural situations because this is what I need to do in my everyday life to cope with change. Like Switzerland, Singapore consists of a small number of distinctive subpopulations (Chinese, Malay, India, and Westerners consisting predominantly of the British and Australians). Despite this similarity, Singaporeans are more outward looking and focused on regional actions and activities. Further, the country's national policy emphasizes the adoption of high technology and information exchange. In this type of turbulent environment people must constantly deal with cultural pluralism, global issues, and the impact of technological innovation on each individual. To cope with this dynamism, Singaporeans must focus their attention on learning about others within their small community and adapting accordingly. They are strongly motivated to adapt in order to continue moving forward as a nation.

Such motivation interacts with a manager's goals and expectations about adjustment. My motivation to understand another culture is affected by how similar that culture is to my own as well as by how much it has to offer. If I think this other culture is very different from my own and doesn't have much to offer me, then I won't feel motivated to learn and adapt to it.

Living in a hierarchical and group-focused country may mean that a person has high motivational CQ instead of being an isolationist. Despite having a strong collective and hierarchical orientation, Chinese culture consists of many complex and interwoven groups to which people belong. The elaborate stratification of roles in Chinese culture (e.g., member of a family, an extended family, a community, a work unit, an organization, a university) and their interdependence suggests that a great deal of attention must be paid to very complex cues in order to avoid offending related others. A Chinese manager must be very careful to avoid insulting another person in case he belongs to one of these subtle common groups. The need to be highly sensitive to very subtle social signals is likely to be associated with a strong motivational CQ. But it's not merely a matter of recognizing common social groups. A Chinese manager must readily understand a person's relative status, or position, in these various groups. We refer to this social status as "face," or a person's position on some social scale. While hierarchy and homogeneity might lead to low motivational CQ in Switzerland, it may be associated with high motivational CQ in China. The key difference between these two countries has to do with the level of hierarchy: although it's moderate in Switzerland, it's very high in China. Status and position in China are marked by many different factors, while in Switzerland they are based on fewer characteristics, such as professional and educational background.

One of the chief ways that we think about social groups and status uses the idea of "face." We can use this to further understand motivational aspects of CQ. The reader will recall our discussion of self-enhancement, or wanting to feel positive about oneself. This is the essence of face. Individuals who place a great deal of emphasis on status are highly motivated to understand people from other cultures as long as these outsiders are thought of as a potential source of status. Why do most Asians exchange business cards when they meet a new person? Your business card conveys many things about your own status and importance: your company, your position, your education, and so on. To an Asian, this card signifies a person's importance and significance, and respect is given accordingly. Western managers are often surprised at exactly how much time and attention is given to studying a business card in China or Japan; there is even a protocol concerning how to hand the card to a stranger. A European manager who is given a card by his Asian colleague, gives it a quick glance, and casually sticks it in his pocket has insulted the card giver.

In Asian cultures there are two important parts of face: social position and personal character. Social position means that people are motivated, at least initially, to understand strangers because they may become a source of personal status. Global managers may find that some people befriend them quickly, while others remain aloof. Why is this? The first type of person sees a global manager as a source of personal status; the second doesn't.

The second aspect of face has to do with character and ethics. People who have a strong personal sense of morality try to understand new cultures so that they can act appropriately in a new situation and not offend their host. However, strong morality may imply some rigidity, so a person may understand what to do but choose not to do it. A person with a very strong moral anchor may have the thinking skills of CQ but not be motivated to act because he or she disagrees with what is expected of him or her.

People who are concerned with face are likely to be high on motivational CQ. These people have an instrumental need to understand a new culture that they will need to function in. The only way to ensure that a person can maintain or enhance status in a new culture is by a complete understanding of its functioning and rewards.

As we said, an extremely strong concern about face reflects high motivational CQ but not necessarily effective adjustment. Energy and commitment make up only one aspect of CQ, and that aspect represents only a part of what we mean by motivational CQ. For motivation to contribute to cultural adjustment, it's necessary that confidence and personal goals be aligned effectively so that the manager can gather important information and draw accurate assessments of a new situation. The right kind of goals will help a person adjust. For example, if you have challenging goals for adjusting to a new culture, you are likely to be motivated to search for new ways to understand that culture. You might search out key people to tell you about the culture, you might actively participate in it by attending social events such as concerts, you might read up as much as you can, and so on. However, this may not be enough if the culture you are trying to master is very complicated or not well understood by outsiders. Having challenging personal goals for mastering a new culture motivates you to search for ways of understanding — but if that search is misguided, you may never learn about that culture. What's critical is that motivation be guided by effective strategies.

Someone who is "energized" or motivated has high motivational CQ, but, as we said, this does not guarantee effective adjustment. A desire to maintain and improve face and social status may inspire a person to try and discover the social rules for a new culture. At one level, such enthusiasm seems a very good attribute for a global manager. However, cultural understanding is a lot like predicting the stock market — it's a complex task, and there are many possible strategies to pursue. Unless a person has the kind of meta-level ("learn-to-learn") skills that we described in chapters 2 and 3, this motivation will be a problem. A combination of challenging personal goals and high self-confidence may be troublesome if a person lacks proper guidance and direction.

Take, for example, a friendly global manager who tears down the barriers of status with high-power-distance colleagues by soliciting their input, only to find that he is viewed as incompetent or lazy. (For example, an employee from a hierarchical culture wonders why he is being asked for opinions about a new project. Does this suggest that the global manager is unable to make these decisions for himself? Is the global manager incompetent to do so?) One American manager reported that during his first global assignment to Thailand, he used a very participatory style of leadership and decision making. In an effort to bring his team together, he would have meetings to encourage active disagreement and discussion among the members of his management team. He found the team very unwilling to engage in strong debate — particularly among Thais if their ranks differed. One of his senior managers finally confided to him that several team members were concerned that the global manager did not have full control over the situation nor adequate expertise, and that was why he was sloughing his responsibilities off onto his management team.

Our point is that motivation must be aligned with our ways of thinking about a new culture and how we act in it; a person cannot adapt successfully on the strength of motivation and confidence alone. As we have discussed in this chapter, motivation is made up of a number of facets, including energy and confidence, goals and direction, and links to the job situation.

DEVELOPING YOUR MOTIVATIONAL CQ

How do confidence and energy work in CQ? In general, people need both confidence and energy to adjust to new cultures. Except when unusually high confidence develops into overconfidence, the influence of confidence on cultural adjustment (and as a critical feature of CQ) is positive. You might ask whether overconfident managers are at a disadvantage — whether they get themselves into situations they aren't really capable of handling. Generally, overconfidence is better than a lack of confidence. Even if such a mismatch occurs, the general benefits of high confidence for searching, persistence, and so on outweigh other, potentially negative consequences. For example, some researchers found that regardless of whether children were of superior or average mental ability, those with a strong sense of personal confidence did better at solving conceptual problems than those children with lower confidence. The more confident students at each ability level managed their time better, searched more effectively for work strategies, and were more persistent than students lacking confidence *even if their high confidence was not justified by their actual skill level.*

This idea about confidence helps us understand the limit to the thinking part of CQ as well. The thinking part alone doesn't help us predict who will adjust the best. Confidence and personal goals stimulate action as well as guide it and, most important, energize people who have useful adjustment techniques to use them effectively. Even if he or she lacks an appropriate strategy for cultural adjustment, a highly confident manager will be more likely than a less confident one to develop his or her new way of learning and coping. However, as with all things, there are limitations. If a new culture is very unpredictable and in turmoil, confidence alone won't be enough to eliminate the confusion a manager may experience.

An important role that setting personal goals plays with the motivational aspect of CQ is that it complements the influence of personal confidence on searching, selecting, developing, and using techniques and strategies for adjustment. That is to say, confident people generate their own goals to guide and energize their actions. For example, a French manager decides that he'll learn the proper form of greeting his Japanese colleagues within a week of being posted to a Tokyo assignment. The immediate benefit of this goal is that it will guide his personal adjustment strategies in productive directions, solidify his personal commitment to adjusting, enable him to persist in the face of failure or confusion, and so on. Imagine the first time he greets his Japanese counterpart: he takes the offered business card, glances at it, and then pockets it. He notices that his colleague looks at him disapprovingly but says nothing. The French manager realizes that he's done something wrong but is uncertain as to what. He watches how two Japanese businessmen introduce themselves and present their cards to one another. In his next encounter, he mimics the actions he witnessed but again receives a quizzical reaction from his Japanese colleague. Rather than simply giving up, the French manager watches now how the Japanese colleague relates to other *gaijin* (foreigners) and sees that the procedures for Japanese-to-Japanese versus *gaijin*-to-Japanese encounters differ. His goal for mastering the greeting within a week has led him to redouble his efforts to understand social matters in the face of setbacks, rather than simply to give up.

A related but indirect influence of confidence and specific goals is an enhanced interest in getting to know the new culture. Confident managers with challenging adjustment goals actually become more interested and committed to understanding a new culture. Why is this? Confidence gives rise to personal goal setting, and these goals provide one with a sense of challenge and excitement. Trying to achieve a personal goal can be highly motivating. It's not just learning social etiquette for exchanging business cards that is important — the goal of doing so within a week becomes its own challenge!

Finally, motivational CQ reflects a person's general willingness to engage and master a new culture. It's this point that reflects the interdependent benefits of appropriate personal and cultural values, self-confidence and goals, and a personal sense of who one is. People with high motivational CQ not only value cultural experience but see it as a positive and motivating influence on their actions. They are guided by personal challenges that they set for themselves and are rewarded by their achievements in learning.

SUMMARY

In this chapter we have explored various aspects of CQ using a motivational perspective. Unfortunately, most people talking about "intelligence" in its various forms (general, emotional, social, etc.) have ignored personal motivation. We have discussed it as a key part of adjustment. Personal motivation requires both intelligent and motivated action. Neither one is by itself sufficient for cultural adaptation and adjustment.

Think of your personal motivation when you have to interact with different people and adapt to different work environments in different cultures. How would you rate your self-confidence, on the whole, in working with people from different cultures? Would you conclude that you possess high or low motivational CQ?

We described our approach to motivation using the three things that motivate peoples' actions — enhancement, efficacy, and consistency — and we talked about how personal and cultural values, confidence, and goals guide a person's actions in various situations. Values provide a benchmark for assessing various actions and outcomes. Personal confidence provides us with the energy to set and pursue personal goals as well as to redouble our efforts in the face of defeat. Goals provide the guidance and intrinsic challenge we need in order to delve into the cultural soup.

The major challenge facing us in this chapter was to show how important energy and motivation are to CQ. Simply put, thinking without energy won't help anyone adjust. Rigorous knowledge of cultural facts or rituals doesn't guarantee adjustment. These facts and bits of information become useful only if a person is appropriately motivated and guided. It's essential for a manager to incorporate good thinking with high confidence and directed action.

4 | PRESENTING YOURSELF:
THE BEHAVIORAL BASIS OF CQ

Jack is fuming! He had been waiting patiently for well over thirty minutes to verify a duplicate charge on his credit card over the phone. By the time he finally reached a customer representative on the other end, he found himself not understanding a single word the person was saying. The credit card company had outsourced its call center operations overseas, and the customer representative was a non-native English speaker with a very heavy foreign accent. Not understanding Jack's request, the customer representative constantly asked Jack to repeat his question slowly. To make matters worse, when the customer representative tried to reply, it was with squeaky, high-pitched, rapid jerky stutters. After ten minutes, Jack slammed down the phone in frustration.

When Nancy, a British senior executive, was busy, she asked her secretary to reschedule her appointment with her business counterpart in Taiwan. Later on, Nancy found that her Taiwanese counterpart canceled all plans for furthering their business dealings. Nancy, by asking her secretary to change the appointment rather than contacting her Taiwanese counterpart personally, had inadvertently offended her Taiwanese business associate.

It is clear from the two examples that actions and behaviors are critically important in cross-cultural interactions. The cultural anthropologist Edward Hall believes behavior and actions are the most critical elements for effectively dealing with people from other cultures. In his autobiography, Hall described his many years of experimenting with different forms of cultural training at the United States Foreign Service. Hall discovered that although servicemen benefited from basic knowledge about the general social, political, and economic backgrounds of target nations, facts and knowledge alone didn't prepare them with critical skills for success. In fact, foreign servicemen — despite their extensive general country knowledge — were culturally, socially, and behaviorally awkward. They were uncomfortable in these new cultures and at a loss as to how to act them appropriately.

After years of trying various approaches, Hall directed his training toward behaviors in everyday encounters with foreigners. He taught fewer geographical and historical facts and more social, behavioral, and cultural skills. Servicemen learned from Hall the appropriate "hidden dimension" or "silent language" of cultural communication — greetings, farewells, beckoning gestures, and starting and carrying on conversations or small talk in both formal ones, such as business meetings and negotiations, and informal situations, such as meals and parties.

IMPORTANCE AND MEANING OF BEHAVIORAL CQ

The experiences of Jack, Nancy, and Edward Hall remind us that words, speech, actions, and gestures are extremely critical in intercultural interactions. When we meet strangers from other cultures for the first time, their outward appearances and overt behaviors are the most immediately obvious features, not their hidden thoughts and feelings. First impressions count. How someone dresses, stands, talks, jokes, or laughs affects the way we view that person.

Because your actions, speech, and nonverbal behaviors are what others can observe, you must be careful about how you present yourself when dealing with people from other cultures. By presenting yourself, we mean the impressions on others you created by your appearance and actions.

Behavioral cultural intelligence (or behavioral CQ) therefore refers to your ability to observe, recognize, regulate, adapt, and act appropriately in intercultural meetings. A person with high behavioral CQ possesses a wide repertoire of expressions — both verbally and in body language. High behavioral CQ means you are able to pick up subtle cultural signals from others and to adapt to talking with people from other cultures in an easy and relaxed manner.

Of all the facets of cultural intelligence, behavioral CQ is perhaps the most difficult to acquire. Many of our behaviors are habitual. We grow up acting and speaking in a certain way. Unless we are trained as actors, we have not learned to vary the way we speak or act.

In this chapter, we survey the fascinating range of human behaviors across the world. We categorize human behaviors into universal and culture-specific.

Universal behaviors refer to human behaviors that are the same or similar across cultures, so you will not need to feel uncomfortable, suspicious, or awkward when you encounter these behaviors. Culture-specific behaviors, on the other hand, are those that differ in meaning and expressions across cultures.

We explore many behavioral "homonyms"—behaviors that sound and look the same but have very different and often opposite meanings in different parts of the world (for example, nodding in some cultures means agreeing, while in other cultures it means disagreeing). We provide numerous examples of verbal expressions and body language that differ across cultures. We describe strategies at the end of this chapter to help you through difficult real-life cultural situations. We believe that by raising your level of consciousness and awareness of the universal and culture-specific behaviors, this chapter will empower you with information, tips, and stories on increasing your level of behavioral CQ.

DIFFERENTIATING BETWEEN UNIVERSAL AND CULTURE-SPECIFIC BEHAVIORS

What percentage of human behaviors is universal in nature, and what proportion is culture specific? If a large percentage of human behaviors is universal in nature, and only a small portion of human behaviors is culture specific, then we should not be worried about crossing cultures and getting tripped up in our daily self-presentations.

The search for universals in human behaviors has fascinated scientists for centuries. The earliest search for universals in human behavior dates back to the nineteenth century. The renowned Charles Darwin then conducted an extensive study of key administrators, missionaries, and explorers and discovered a wide range of universals in the emotional expressions of human behaviors.

Since the nineteenth century, two specialized fields of research, ethnology (the study of human behavior's biological basis) and cultural anthropology, have accumulated evidence of universals in human behaviors. A social scientist by the name of George Murdock developed an extensive ethnographic thesaurus called the Human Relations Area File (HRAF; see http://www.yale.edu/hraf/). In the thesaurus, Murdock documented a significant number of universal behaviors — actions and human responses that occur in all cultures and societies. These universal behaviors are very wide ranging. People in all cultures share a number of common actions, such as using language to communicate; producing, processing, and consuming food and drink; making clothing; conducting economic exchanges; traveling; manager interpersonal relationships; and so on. However, the specific expressions

---

BOX 4.1
Nobody can speak this language, that's for sure

SAN SEBASTIAN (Canary Islands)

Mr. Juan Cabello does not use a cell phone or the Internet to communicate. Instead, he puckers up and whistles. Cabello's language, Silbo Gomero, is whistled, not spoken, and can be heard more than 3 km away. This language is thought to originate from early African settlers 2,500 years ago. Now, educators are working to save it from extinction by having schoolchildren study the language up to age 14.

Silbo— the word comes from the Spanish verb *silbar*, meaning to whistle. It has four "vowels" and four "consonants" that when strung together form more than 4,000 words. It sounds just like bird conversation.

A strong whistle saved peasants from trekking over to send messages or news to neighbors. Then came the telephone, and it is hard to know how many people use Silbo these days.

Little is known about Silbo's origins. Silbo-like whistling has been found in pockets of Greece, Turkey, China, and Mexico, but none is as developed as Silbo Gomero.

It is good for just about anything except for romance, says Mr. Cabello. "Everyone on the island would hear what you're saying!"

Adapted from a news release by Associated Press, reported in *Straits Times Online*, November 21, 2003

---

of these characteristics vary dramatically. Take as an example, language and how it is expressed, as described in box 4.1.

CULTURE-SPECIFIC BEHAVIORS

Even though people exhibit many fundamental, universal behaviors, such behaviors often differ in how they appear in specific contexts. For example, intimate behavior — behaviors that express our love and liking for each other — may be universal, but the way intimate behaviors are expressed differs across cultures. In some cultures, people hug strangers, while other cultures do not hug at all except with very intimate spouses and family members. Physical contact in one place may be seen as sexual harassment in another. Another example is laughter. Although laughter is deemed a universal behavior in triggering a happy mood between inter-acting parties, depending on how one laughs — how wide we open our mouths, how much our teeth are showing, and so on — the act of laughter can be misinter-preted and misconstrued. Laughter expressed with an open mouth and bared teeth may be misconstrued as clumsy, uncouth, and even aggressive behaviors in some cultures.

Similarly, aggression is regarded as a universal act, but the specific acts that are seen as aggressive vary across cultures. Abortion, for example, is judged a criminal act of violence in one culture but is perfectly legitimate in another. Other acts, such as physical or verbal abuse, are sanctioned in some societies but deemed unlawful or inhumane in others. Michael Bond, a cross-cultural expert, and his associates find that verbal insults delivered by a boss to a subordinate in Hong Kong (where power distance is high) were deemed acceptable and were not considered aggres-sive, whereas the same verbal insults occurring in the United States (where power distance is low) would be regarded as aggressive.

Let's explore more systematically the intriguing culture-specific nature of human behaviors. We will begin with the challenges of cross-cultural verbal com-munication and then proceed to nonverbal communication.

Communicating through Language

Verbal communication across cultures presents many challenges. Here we describe three of the main ones: foreign languages and language barriers; direct versus in-direct speech acts; and conversational styles and paralanguage.

Foreign Languages and Language Barriers. In cross-cultural encounters, one or more parties speak a language that is not their native language. Proficiency in for-eign languages becomes a critical facet of behavioral cultural intelligence. Learn-ing a foreign language as an adult may be one of the most difficult tasks to master. But the ability to speak a foreign language has many advantages. Languages in themselves are culture carriers. Mastering foreign languages not only increases your ability to adapt; it also allows you to access a body of cultural knowledge, be-liefs, and values beyond those expressed in your native language. For example, un-less you know Mandarin, you may not be able to access fully the Chinese heritage of the ancient crafts, drama, poetry, and the arts.

Sometimes not knowing how to speak the language can be interpreted as arro-gance. Some overseas ethnic Chinese businessmen who cannot speak Mandarin fluently keep quiet when interacting with their counterparts from China. Because outwardly they look Chinese, the mainland Chinese expected them to be proficient in Mandarin. The overseas Chinese's silence therefore could be misconstrued as arrogance.

Language is so important that Indonesia is pressing ahead with plans that require foreign businessmen and students to take language tests before they can work or study in the country. Indonesian officials believe that it is critical that foreigners reach a minimum level of proficiency in the Indonesian language before they can effectively work or study in Indonesia.

Even if two individuals speak the same language, such as English, by choosing specific words to communicate, you signal that you are a member of a particular culture or subculture. As the playwright George Bernard Shaw observed, "England and America are two countries separated by a common language." The problem becomes more severe with people who speak English as a second language or do not speak the language at all. When interacting with people from a different culture, it is critical to pay attention to local pronunciations, local accents, tonal emphasis, and vocal variations.

Languages also never translate word for word. So the use of slang, idioms, jokes, and local sayings poses problems when you are speaking to people from other cultures. "Are you crook?" can only be understood by Australians as "Are you ill?" "Stop being so *kiasu*" can only be understood by Singaporeans as "Please lighten up."

The Cantonese (a southern Chinese dialect) spoken in Hong Kong differs from the Cantonese spoken in Singapore. In Hong Kong, you will ask a storekeeper who speaks Cantonese for "black soy" if you want to buy a bottle of dark soy sauce, whereas, when you are in Singapore, you will ask for "black oil" (in Cantonese dialect).

Direct and Indirect Speech Acts in Low-Context versus High-Context Cultures. The greatest cultural difference in intercultural communication is the degree of directness of speech acts. A speech act refers to how a speaker structures his or her speech and how a listener interprets the structure and content of the speech.

Edward Hall discovered that a speech act can vary across cultures depending on whether the culture is a high-context culture or a low-context culture. Cultures are either high or low context depending on the degree to which meaning comes from the settings or from the words exchanged. Table 4.1 shows how high-context and low-context cultures differ.

High-context cultures rely less on verbal communications and more on nonverbal communications, environmental setting, and relationship histories. In communicating, listeners infer the whole meaning of the message from contextual cues such as the setting of the conversation, the status of people taking part in the conversation, and past history of those who are conversing. High-context cultures

TABLE 4.1
Differences between high-context and low-context cultures

High-context cultures	Low-context cultures
1. People are in very dense interpersonal contacts.	1. People have fragmented their interpersonal contacts.
2. Everyone is linked to everyone else directly or indirectly through relatives, friends, relations, or acquaintances. They tend to stay in touch, with ties in the dense networks.	2. Contacts are fragmented because people relocate once every few years and so they tend not to develop strong interpersonal networks.
3. Examples: India, China, particularly the Nanyang or overseas Chinese and the Indian diaspora.	3. Examples: United States, northern European nations.

look for meaning and understanding in what is not said — in nonverbal communication or body language, in silences and pauses, in relationships and empathy. High-context cultures rely strongly on nonverbal communication.

Low-context cultures value sending and receiving accurate messages directly using words. People in low-context cultures need detailed backgrounds of the people they meet, each time they meet. Verbal messages contain most of the information — very little is embedded in the context or in the participants.

In high-context cultures, meanings are implicit. Speech conveys only a small part of the message. Message is also conveyed through status (age, sex, education, family background, title, and affiliations), and through an individual's friends and associates. Communications in high-context cultures are often considered vague, indirect, and implicit. Information is provided through gestures, use of space, and even silence. In low-context cultures, speech is explicit and meanings are direct and taken literally. Everything needs to be stated and stated well — so it is important to speak up and say what is on your mind in low-context cultures.

Members of high-context cultures view people who rely primarily on verbal messages for information as less credible. High-context cultures think silence often sends a better message than words, and anyone who needs words does not have enough information. People in high-context cultures tend to be more aware of their surroundings and their environment and can communicate their feelings without words. Those in low-context cultures admire a person who can express himself or herself well and clearly, possesses a large vocabulary, and articulates ideas well. People in low-context cultures tend to be less aware of or more oblivious to their surroundings and environment.

In conflicts, people in high-context cultures tend to be less open; they hold that conflict is damaging to most communication encounters. In fact, too much directness in the speech is seen as blunt and insensitive. Those in low-context cultures confront conflict openly and explicitly. They avoid vagueness and ambiguity and get directly to the point.

In a high-context culture, the discourse is contextual, with affective emphases and the use of more qualifiers such as "maybe," "perhaps," "probably," and "slightly." In low-context cultures, a high degree of explicit information is required for understanding and communication. As a result, the discourse that is deemed ideal is that which is direct, explicit, and instrumental.

Crisp, precise, and direct messages are heralded as hallmarks of effective communication in low-context cultures. Indirect and allusive messages are seen as effective communication in high-context cultures, where self-effacement, face saving, and harmony are values held in highest esteem.

A "no" in high-context cultures comes out as "maybe," or "yes," or a "yes" comes out as "no." In low-context cultures, a "yes" comes out directly as "yes" and "no" as "no." So, if you are entertaining visitors from a high-context culture such as, say, China or India, it's better that you offer them a drink even if they say expressly that they do not need one. And if you are from a low-context culture — say, an American — and visit a high-context culture, just accept food and drink with grace even when you have indicated explicitly that you are not thirsty or hungry.

Conversational Styles and Paralanguage. Conversational styles refer to features such as rate of speech, rhythm of turn-taking, tolerance for simultaneous speech, and topic shifting. Paralanguage refers not to the words or the message of the speech, but to the sounds made — particularly voice quality, vocalization, and vocal qualifiers.

Voice quality refers to a person's degree of vocal power, resonance, articulation, and agility. In some cultures, vocal power and resonance are revered, while in other cultures, strong vocal force conveys arrogance and rudeness. Vocalization refers to the use of nonword fillers such as "ahem," "uh-huh," "um," "er," "you know," "okay," clicking one's tongue, or sucking in one's breath. In some cultures one hisses or inhales while talking to others as a sign of showing respect and giving the other person time to think. Other cultures use more pauses in between sentences to allow the listener to process the speech.

Vocal qualifiers refer to the pitch and overall intonation of the spoken word, and even to silence. Silence is a particularly intriguing vocal qualifier, one with a huge range of meanings and interpretations in different cultures. Again, silence seems to be misinterpreted most frequently whenever there is a clash between people from low-context cultures and those from high-context cultures.

Muriel Saville-Troike, an expert on communication and linguistics, related a deadly incident that occurred in Greece because of a difference in the interpretation of what silence means. Greeks regard silence as an outright refusal, while Egyptians interpret silence as consent. So, when Greek air traffic controllers responded with silence as Egyptians requested to land their planes; the Egyptians proceeded to land. As they approached, the Greeks fired on the Egyptian planes as they approached the runway. A flurry of diplomatic activities ensued to calm both sides and prevent the incident from escalating into a bilateral conflict.

In low-context cultures, silence is deafening. Silence indicates the absence of communication and is interpreted as communication that has gone wrong. In low-context cultures, people are regarded more positively the more they talk and articulate their ideas expressively. In high-context cultures, silence is preferred to conversation. Silence is seen as a way of showing respect, of not disagreeing openly, or of contemplating a problem at hand; speech is seen as interfering with deep thinking. In many Asian countries such as Japan, silence is observed to maintain harmony. In Middle Eastern cultures, women are expected to remain submissive and silent, and not to speak or to disagree with male counterparts. Depending on the cultural interpretation of silence, silence may serve to create greater interpersonal distance or to punish, avoid embarrassing, or show respect for others.

It is difficult to translate complicated ideas from one culture to another. At work, conflicts may arise because of differences in conversation styles and paralanguage between co-workers from the same cultures. In a culturally diverse workforce such differences may become more stark, because different cultures emphasize different conversational styles and paralanguage. The different rate of use and meaning behind each type of vocalization varies across cultures and can interfere with cross-cultural communication. Unless one is culturally intelligent enough to know that differences in conversational styles and paralanguage do not make one person better or worse than another but instead reflect underlying cultures or places of origin, people with different styles or paralanguages may experience discomfort in communicating without knowing why.

People who talk too slowly may be shut out by people who talk fast, or they may be thought of as less intelligent. One manager from the southeastern part of the United States (where speech is typically slower and more drawn out than in the Northeast) commented that his colleagues from New York think of anyone with a southern accent as slow and backward. Slow and deliberate speaking is often thought of as indicating slow and deliberate thinking. A manager speaking in a foreign language he has not fully mastered may be thought of mistakenly as a bit "simple."

Displaying Nonverbal Behaviors. Although what we say is important, much of the success of communication hinges on our body language and nonverbal gestures, not just what we say. To understand fully how people in any particular culture communicate, we must become familiar with their body language. Body language carries a message of its own and helps us interpret the verbal messages that come with it. And body language, like verbal language, is culture specific.

You may encounter a wide range of body language abroad. Nonverbal signals can be misinterpreted just as easily as verbal messages or words. Learning to identify and interpret body language by geographical region will enhance your behavioral cultural intelligence. Learning to use the appropriate body language to supplement your verbal message will help you to more effectively convey your ideas and views to someone from another culture. Let's explore some of the most important and common types of nonverbal communication that vary in their meaning and use across cultures.

Physical appearance and attractiveness. Whichever culture you are in, first impressions count! Physical appearance and attractiveness influence episodes in cross-cultural communication. Anyone who does not fit a culture's norms of physical appearance will have trouble communicating in that culture. But what is regarded as attractive in one culture may not be attractive in another.

Norms and acceptability in height, weight, skin color, hair color, hairstyles, clothing, and dress vary from culture to culture. Some cultures, such as the United States view tall, slender women as most attractive; others, such as Japan, believe petite females to be most attractive; and in Africa and some parts of China, plumpness is considered a sign of beauty, wealth, and health. If you do not look like you belong to the culture, you will find it challenging to communicate successfully with others. You may even find yourself being ignored and not listened to. You will find it difficult to persuade others and influence others with your ideas, thoughts, and beliefs.

Gestures. The biggest cultural difference in body language is the use of gestures. Sign language for the deaf is a good example of the use of gestures in nonverbal communication. Gestures often involve the hand, although more recent research has shown that different cultures also make use of different body parts. Beginning with the head and face and going down to the legs and feet, people gesture in a variety of ways. You may be familiar with many gestures, but don't make the assumption that the same gestures mean the same thing in different cultures. Some cultures may share the same gesture but give it different meanings. Some cultures use different gestures to communicate the same meaning. And some cultures use gestures unique to them alone — they have no equivalent in other cultures.

TABLE 4.2

A sampling of gestures across cultures

Categories of gestures	Examples
1. Signaling arriving and departing	Blowing a kiss; fist-to-chest pounding; handshaking; hugging.
2. Showing approval	Applause; arms up; high five; nodding "yes"; thumbs up
3. Showing disapproval	Yawn; folded arms; choking; finger wagging; nodding "no"; holding nose; wrinkling nose
4. Attracting mates	Eyebrow wiggling; eyelid fluttering; holding hands; staring; winking
5. Offensive and profane gestures	Chin flicking; nose thumbing
6. Gestures for emphasis	Chin stroking; making a fist; drumming fingers; snapping fingers; shrugging
7. No words needed (or replacing words)	"Call me": finger and thumb mimicking the shape of a telephone receiver; "come here": palm held face up and index finger crooked toward body; "this person is crazy": index finger on one hand traces a circle near temple

Anthropologists have long been fascinated by the range and variation in the meaning of gestures. The social anthropologist Desmond Morris is perhaps the most celebrated researcher on culture and gestures. Morris and his colleagues found that many gestures extend across national and linguistic boundaries, and that few can be truly labeled as belonging exclusively to any single nation or culture. Desmond coined the term "gesture boundary" to describe the point in a certain linguistic or geographical region where certain gestures are observed to stop abruptly or change meaning. For example, the ring gesture — an "O" made with your finger and thumb — switches from "OK" in northern Italy to "zero" or "worthless" in the south. The same gesture is taken to mean "orifice" in Tunisia, Greece, Turkey, the Middle East, and parts of South America. In Japan it means to ask for change for a bill, since the shape of the fingers resembles a coin.

Nancy Armstrong and Melissa Wagner's fascinating book *Field Guide to Gestures* presents the usage, origins, and meaning of a wide repertoire of gestures, along with a step-by-step guide to their appropriate display. According to Armstrong and Wagner, every gesture falls into one of seven categories (see table 4.2).

Not all of these gestures are culturally universal. For example, in Argentina, the "this person is crazy" gesture, with the index finger on one hand tracing a circle near the temple, is used to let someone know he or she has a phone call. In Bulgaria, some parts of the Middle East, Africa, and India, a person nods in disagreement and shakes the head in agreement. In some cultures, nodding may simply mean continued attention, not necessarily agreement.

Nowhere is bowing more important than in Japan. The bow initiates an interaction between two or more Japanese. A study of bowing in Japan showed that the correct forms of bowing (slight, medium, or deep bow) signify respect for hierarchy in relationships. A Japanese subordinate will remain in a bowing posture when greeting a superior. Because bowing is so ingrained in the habits of the Japanese, sometimes they even unconsciously bow to someone with whom they are speaking on the phone, even though they can't be seen.

Facial expressions. A plate of fried scorpions is offered to a Singaporean businessman by his Chinese hosts, who say: "This is our best dish. Try it." What do you think the Singaporean is feeling?

If you want to identify and interpret a person's emotions, scrutinize his or her face and facial expressions carefully. Faces and facial expressions communicate most effectively the underlying emotions a person is feeling at any given point in time. Paul Ekman, a psychologist who is renowned for his work on faces and facial expressions, finds that there are some basic facial expressions that people are almost always able to decode correctly because the emotions associated with these basic facial expressions are transmitted universally across Western Europe, South America, Asia, and even parts of New Guinea.

However, many facial expressions are culture specific. For example, faces in Western cultures are more expressive than in Asian cultures. Asians are raised to hide emotions and maintain a consistent "face" to the outside world. For example, Korean and Japanese managers show stoic facial expressions when they meet strangers. But they relax and become more animated with friends and family members. Sometimes what seems to be one facial expression may represent many moods and feelings. For example, earlier in the book we described the many different types of smiles used in Thai culture. A Thai smile may indicate happiness; but it may also indicate anger, apprehension, or disgust.

Although Asians don't express themselves facially, they are able to discern subtle nuances better than most Westerners. Being in what we referred to earlier as high-context cultures, Asians tend to look for nonverbal cues, including facial expressions and changes in facial expressions, in the course of a conversation.

Culture and space. A U.S. expatriate experiencing the crowds along the Chingay festival in Singapore complained: "People kept pushing me from behind although no one was moving in the front! I finally got mad and turned to the person behind me and blared: 'Stop pushing!! I can't go anywhere!'" A New Zealand professional working in Hong Kong grumbled, "People kept cutting into my lane — don't they ever learn to walk or drive straight?"

Although milling through the crowded streets of India, Hong Kong, and Singapore is taken for granted in the locals' day-to-day lives, foreigners who from countries with more wide-open spaces find crowds stifling and uncomfortable. Preference for space is another nonverbal behavior that differs substantively across culture. Personal space refers to the distance someone wants between himself or herself and other people in an interaction. Although space preference is affected by factors such as density of population and nature of relationship (whether it is formal or intimate), space preferences are most dependent on cultural norms. Some cultures establish much closer proximity when interacting, while others establish wider distances.

Studies on babies have shown that we need to be touched to grow and thrive, and that older people are healthier mentally and physically if they are touched. But some people are more comfortable with touch than others because they grow up in families or cultures that touch a lot, hug as part of a greeting, and hold hands with casual friends.

Edward Hall observes that people who are raised in "contact" cultures prefer social distances that are more proximate. North Americans, Germans, English, and many Asian cultures are generally non-contact-oriented cultures, while southern Europeans such as Greeks or Italians represent contact-oriented cultures. So Asians and North Americans prefer greater distances when talking with each other than do southern Europeans, Middle Easterners, and South Americans.

Westerners, including Americans, Germans, and English, are more offended by the accidental touch of strangers than are people in Asian cultures. Although Asian cultures are typically non-contact cultures, because many Asian nations are densely populated, people have learned to ignore accidental touching and are not unduly bothered by it.

Space thus nonverbally communicates various meanings across cultures. To be culturally intelligent, you must learn to understand the space and touching norms of other cultures. Remember that if you stand too far away from someone who expects you to stand close, you might be perceived as aloof or cold. By contrast, if you stand too close to someone, you might be perceived as pushy or aggressive, even offensive!

A British manager from Deutsche Bank commented that he found one of his Indian colleagues a bit troublesome. It seems that they had desks that adjoined, and her materials (papers, books, files) kept spilling over onto his desk. He said that she didn't seem to respect his space and thought that she was allowing her "clutter" to impose on him because she wanted to irritate him. Of course, it turns out that the idea of a clearly defined and delimited desk space is inconsistent with an Indian perspective — our desks are to be shared and are thought of as communal.

Culture and time. The psychologist Robert Levine provides a fascinating observation of time variations across cultures in his book *A Geography of Time.* Some cultures, such as North America, keep time by the clock. Time is money! North Americans emphasize scheduling and segmentation. The clock is the controller, and efficiency is highly valued. Americans like others to be on time and judge people by how prompt or late they are. North Americans measure time in, at most, five-minute blocks. (With the world of television news sound bites, we now measure time in ten-second blocks!) In North American culture, if you are five minutes late for an appointment or a job interview, you are written off as sloppy, undependable, or unreliable.

By contrast, other cultures, such as Latin America, keep time by the seasons, by "internal body clocks," or a personal feeling of whether "the time is right" or "the time is ripe." Latin Americans are less concerned with being punctual and perceive time quite differently from their North American counterparts. A half-hour segment may be the smallest unit of measurement for time.

Starting something late is seen as a sign of respect in some cultures. In the Chinese culture, it is not unusual for wedding banquets to begin two hours later than scheduled so that due respect is given to every single guest who took the trouble to make it to the feast. However, such displays vary with the circumstances, and punctuality is prized in Chinese business meetings even if it is avoided in wedding ceremonies.

Hall makes the distinction between monochronic and polychronic time cultures. Monochronic time cultures view time linearly and as a scarce resource. Again, "time is money," and time must be managed and controlled using proper scheduling and appointments. By contrast, polychronic time cultures view time as flexible and plentiful.

Monochronic time cultures emphasize efficiency — how to get things done in the quickest time possible. Polychronic time cultures are more concerned with creating and maintaining harmonious relationships. Time must be flexible so that people can pay attention to the needs of the people around them.

As with body language, time nonverbally communicates diverse meanings across cultures. To be culturally intelligent, you must learn to discern the silent concept and measurement of time of other cultures. Remember that if you over-schedule meetings, you may be viewed as too time conscious. If you schedule too few events in a comparable period of time, you may be seen as inefficient or lazy.

DEVELOPING YOUR BEHAVIORAL CQ

Thus far, we have explored the many cultural nuances, explicit as well as subtle, in verbal communication and body language. All of us are motivated to present ourselves to others in the most ideal light. As part of our basic psychological need for wanting to look good in front of others, we take actions that lead others to think of us as competent, well adjusted, and desirable. If we find ourselves in an unfamiliar culture, no matter what else we may be doing at that time, we want people in that culture to view us in desirable ways. Because social norms can differ dramatically with respect to such actions as greetings, physical contact, speech patterns, and so on, it's vital that you know how to act appropriately and avoid offending others.

Some people suggest that we ought to "act naturally and not adjust"—we ought not to bother too much about others' impressions. Disregard for others may not lead to problems if cross-cultural encounters are short lived, such as when visiting a foreign country as a tourist. However, if managers show the same lack of concern for self-presentation during longer stays, they will find themselves ostracized by locals on account of their disrespectful and boorish behavior. At the extreme, people with absolutely no regard for others' impressions may be written off as "culturally autistic."

Cultural Autism

The term "cultural autism" refers to people who are seen as socially inept or even mentally disturbed. Technically, clinical psychologists would classify people with prolonged socially inept behaviors as "abnormal"—as either clinically depressed, schizophrenic, or autistic. Clinical psychologists and psychiatrists diagnose patients based on the unusual, out-of-pattern behaviors common to individuals who display these conditions. Behavioral handicaps therefore become the primary signs of abnormal conditions. For example, autistic people tend to have several of the following characteristics:

- Absence of speech or severely impaired speech with unusual patterns, such as echoing the speech of others;
- Lack of awareness of salient cues, sounds, and objects around them;
- Indifference to being linked to others by relationships; little or no affection;
- Frequent behaviors that seem to provide only self-stimulation without concern for others in social settings: rocking a chair back and forth incessantly, screaming incessantly, or fluttering their hands in front of their eyes.

Autistic individuals show either behavioral deficits (too little behavior of a type deemed appropriate in a certain context), behavioral excesses (too much behavior of a particular type deemed appropriate in a certain context), or both.

Drawing on the characteristics of autism, we introduce the term "cultural autism" to describe people who have a major deficiency in behavioral cultural intelligence. An individual with extremely low behavioral CQ, unable to make sense of the shared norms and corresponding set of appropriate behaviors of a foreign culture, may, in unfamiliar cultural settings, display such extreme forms of behavioral deficits or excesses that he or she is perceived by locals as displaying autistic-like behaviors.

We live in an era in which working effectively with others in an increasingly diverse workforce is the norm. By carefully implementing the following strategies, you can improve your behavioral cultural intelligence and work more effectively with others from cultures different from your own.

Know yourself. Understand your cultural heritage and be aware of the country of origin and culture your communicating partner comes from. Remember that low-context cultures place meaning on exact verbal descriptions or expressions. Individuals rely on the spoken word, and you will want to say what you mean. Make sure your verbal instructions can stand on their own, independent of context or situations.

Learn the foreign language, or at the very least some common foreign phrases. Learning the language will not only enable you to communicate better, but will help you appreciate the cultures with which you are interacting. You will also gain instant rapport with and respect and appreciation from people of the foreign cultures for your openness and willingness to learn more about their society.

If you do not know the language, you may have to improvise and rely on other visible cues. Jan, a Singaporean working as a regional information technology network manager, demonstrates her unusual behavioral cultural intelligence at work. Jan effectively manages hundreds of foreign network servers located all over the Asia-Pacific region. The network servers span from China, Korea, and Japan in the north to Singapore, Malaysia, Indonesia, Australia, and New Zealand in the south, and from the Philippines in the east to the Indian continent — India and Bangladesh — in the West. Jan is proficient only in two languages — English and Tamil (an Indian dialect)— and therefore cannot read the language displayed on the computer screens in China, Taiwan, Japan, Korea, and other countries.

Despite the language handicap, she is able to interact with network servers from these countries by relying on her in-depth knowledge of Microsoft's operating systems. She possesses vivid images of the English-language interface of computer screen shots that she automatically superimposes onto those foreign-language servers she is unfamiliar with. She also relies heavily on Microsoft's system of universal visual icons (e.g., an icon showing "open file" is the same in any country) to troubleshoot foreign servers. As a result, Jan manages to support network servers that span cultural boundaries.

Speak slowly in verbal communications. Emphasize every vocalization. People often speak too fast, and in particular, if the listener is not used to your own regional accent, you may not be able to get the message across. Use visual aids to supplement your communication; remember that a picture is worth a thousand words. Internationally recognized pictures or icons may help you convey your message. Make sure the photos, pictures, and illustrations are free from gender, racial, and age bias. Listen patiently and check frequently for clarification.

Observe body language. Facial expressions and emotions will tell you whether your speaker or listener understands what is communicated. Always actively look for signs of confusion in your listener. Ask him or her to paraphrase what you have just said. Remember that "yes," nods, and smiles do not mean that they understand you. Also, "yes" may not necessarily mean agreeing.

Try to get a sense of your partner and your environment by asking yourself specific questions. What are you seeing? Be as specific as possible. What is your partner wearing? Where are his or her eyes directed? At you or somewhere else? What setting are you in? What are you hearing? What is the level of noise around you? Can you hear your partner? Do you need to read your partner's lips? How is your partner behaving? Is your partner smiling or frowning? Is your partner leaning forward?

Research and try mimicry. Sean Penn, preparing for his portrayal as an autistic man in the movie *I Am Sam*, spent months with a man who was autistic to find out exactly how autistic people spoke, moved, and behaved. Some people pick up cues and mimic quickly; others may need to practice longer before they are able to mimic. Keep experimenting and practicing.

SUMMARY

In this chapter we have explained the importance of the behavioral aspect of CQ. How you present yourself, how you act, and how you behave in the presence of people from other cultures in different cultural encounters will affect how others perceive and relate to you. Ultimately, your self-presentation can help or hinder you when you engage in social interactions in different cultures.

Think of how successful you have been in self-presentation in your interactions with people from different cultures. Are you generally able to adapt your verbal and nonverbal behaviors to social norms of interaction in different cultures? Would you say, on the whole, you have high or low behavioral CQ?

We have offered several strategies and tactics for enhancing your behavioral CQ. Learning to differentiate universal behaviors from culture-specific behaviors is an important first step. We described in detail the three major challenges in cross-cultural verbal communication: foreign languages and language barriers, direct versus indirect speech acts, and conversational styles and paralanguage. We focused your attention on the differences in verbal communication between high-context and low-context cultures. We also described in detail the key challenges in cross-cultural nonverbal communication: physical appearance and attractiveness, body gestures, facial expressions, space, touching, and time. We concluded this chapter by offering some practical strategies and tactics on developing your behavioral CQ.

II APPLYING CQ TO YOUR WORKPLACE

5 WORKING EFFECTIVELY IN THE CULTURALLY DIVERSE WORKPLACE

The *Wall Street Journal* has predicted that in the twenty-first century, managers and organizations will have to handle greater cultural diversity. Cultural intelligence matters! Cultural intelligence is becoming even more important as countries around the world undergo major demographic shifts in their workforce. Organizations are coming to terms with issues of cultural diversity in the workplace. A key question is, "How do companies manage cultural diversity in the workplace?" At a more fundamental level, we can ask, "How do managers manage cultural diversity in the workplace?"

Diversity management is now accepted as part of the organizational landscape in many global organizations. In the United States, diversity management is the latest in a long history of organizational-level initiatives related to employment equity for minorities. A level of consciousness of and body of experience in diversity issues in the U.S. workplace has helped to produce a more diverse workforce over the years. The character of diversity management in the United States is closely intertwined with affirmative action (AA) policies.

Diversity management in the United States is very different from diversity management in Europe and elsewhere. For instance, the industrial relations systems in Europe, or more specifically, trade unions, play a much stronger role in employment relationships and have more organizational influence than trade unions in the United States. In Europe, the responses of trade unions to immigrants and ethnic minorities in their countries are very different. Thus, diversity management can cover a variety of emphases and contain different mixes of components and approaches.

What exactly does the term "diversity management" mean? In essence, diversity management (or DM) has two core characteristics:

- DM is an organization-wide strategy for improving organizational effectiveness and efficiency. This may be motivated by competition. Organizational outcomes such as greater efficiency, greater competitiveness, increased productivity, and increased profitability are cherished.

- DM recognizes the cultural differences between groups of employees and, concomitantly, the importance of making practical allowances for such differences in organizational policies. This forms part of a broader human-resource management approach that is characterized by a focus on relationships both between employer and employees and between employees themselves.

Although it appears that DM can help companies achieve positive organizational outcomes in the marketplace, the jury's still out. In an extensive review of over forty years of research on diversity in organizations, Katherine Williams and Charles O'Reilly concluded that the mantra of "diversity is good for organizations" has been overstated. They caution companies to avoid an excessive rush to diversify their global personnel without thinking through the actions carefully. According to Williams and O'Reilly, "Diversity is a mixed blessing." Careful and sustained attention to diversity management is needed to unleash diversity's positive benefits.

Nonetheless, the inability to manage diversity in the workplace has real business and organizational costs. For example, diversity affects employee turnover, the ability to attract and retain top talent, discrimination suits and litigation expenses, and corporate reputation. If organizations and managers know how to manage cultural diversity, they can at the very least keep the risks to a minimum. Cultural intelligence can help organizations and managers successfully manage cultural diversity in a fashion most appropriate to their own organization.

TRAINING PROGRAMS IN CULTURAL DIVERSITY MANAGEMENT

Different kinds of training programs are offered to deal with cultural diversity in the United States and Europe. Information, cultural-awareness, and cultural-sensitivity training programs, the most common and most popular, are intended to facilitate cross-cultural awareness and understanding and develop cultural sensitivity. The underlying assumption of these training programs is that cultural awareness, understanding, and sensitivity will result in behavioral change. Based on our discussion of the model of cultural intelligence in chapter 2, it is evident that such an assumption is untenable and grossly inaccurate. There's no simple, linear, cause-and-effect relationship between cultural knowledge and behavior that is culturally adaptive and flexible.

Another type of training is known as an equalities training program. Equalities training programs appear to be targeted at changing behavior. They provide participants with clear instructions for dealing and interacting with colleagues from other cultures that constitute the set of appropriate norms and behaviors. In our analysis, such training programs have value, but they fall short of enabling participants to become more effective and adaptive when working with colleagues from different cultures. Prescriptions formulated in lists of dos and don'ts define cultural boundaries, but they don't show people who work in culturally diverse workplaces how to manage or transcend cultural boundaries in that workplace.

More recently, especially since about 1995, "diversity-management" training programs have become increasingly popular in the United States. Diversity-management training programs include earlier types of training programs such as information, cultural-awareness, cultural-sensitivity, and equalities training programs. One of the major objectives of diversity-management training programs is attitudinal and behavioral change. For real behavioral change, diversity management training programs need to build on cultural intelligence, because behavioral CQ is a core component of cultural intelligence.

Let's take a look at how two global organizations have tackled the challenge of managing cultural diversity in the workplace and examine how their approaches could be enriched using a training program that is centered on cultural intelligence: IBM (box 5.1) and Shell (box 5.2).

IBM's training program anchored on cultural intelligence, which can assist IBM in developing a systematic training methodology to help their leaders and managers acquire the cultural strategic thinking, motivational, and behavioral pieces of CQ so that they will be effective in managing "deep sources of [cultural] differences." The typical training program that is framed as cultural awareness or cultural sensitivity will not be able to build IBMers' deep capabilities to deal with the complex, multifaceted, and multidimensional challenges of working in the culturally diverse workplace.

Let's take a look at how Shell differs from IBM in its approach to diversity in the workplace.

At Shell, the focus is on mentoring. This approach works well on a personal level. Shell also provides positive reinforcement through attractive incentives to

BOX 5.1
How IBM deals with cultural diversity in the workplace

IBM employees are required to develop and exhibit a high degree of cultural competence (that is, the skills to appropriately translate and localize intentions and initiatives). IBM understands that diversity is a business imperative for the company, its organizational structure, and its suppliers and customers. As defined by Ted Childs, vice president of workforce diversity at IBM, issues such as cultural awareness and acceptance, ethnic minorities, and multilingualism are key elements in IBM's global workforce diversity challenges. IBM has developed a unique and innovative "Shades of Blue" management development program to foster learning and awareness of cultural diversity and multiculturalism in their workplace. The objectives defined include:

- Broadening the definition of diversity to include the variety of ways in which people differ and develop a framework that supports the notion of global diversity.
- Recognizing that the majority of differences occur "below the surface" of what is observed. Differences involve behaviors, cognition, and emotions, each deeply rooted in the orientations each person brings to the business environment.
- Equipping managers with the necessary global mindset, skills, and competencies for dealing with and managing deep sources of difference and the resulting complexity in the workplace.
- Developing leadership skills that are firmly rooted in effective strategies for global diversity within the organizational culture.

Source: www.ibm.com

BOX 5.2
How Shell deals with cultural diversity in the workplace

As group managing director of the Royal Dutch/Shell Group of companies, Steve Miller was responsible for transforming the company's "downstream" operations — everything from selling gasoline at the company's 47,000 filling stations to selling lubricants to factories. His model for change? Relying on a diverse group of rank-and-file managers and employees organized in cross-functional teams to identify exciting new business opportunities and solve thorny business problems.

Today, as CEO of Shell Oil, Miller has a new and even more important job. And he's got a new strategic priority: diversity itself. By using the same model of grassroots leadership built on frontline involvement across a range of businesses, he is helping make Shell Oil more diverse with regard to age, race, gender, disability, and sexual orientation.

Two years ago, when Miller became CEO and focused on making diversity a strategic initiative, senior leadership spelled out the business case for creating a diverse talent pool. The thinking went like this: If you build a diverse workforce, you've got one more weapon in your arsenal for winning the talent wars. Ultimately, great people want to work with other great people, and great people come from all kinds of backgrounds. "We are competing for talent against Silicon Valley and Wall Street," Miller says. "To have a good shot at talent, we have to recognize that it comes in all shapes and colors."

In 2000 Miller began a pilot program within the chemicals business to mentor candidates for global positions. Meanwhile, employee networks wanted to expand the scope of the mentoring and received funding from the Global Diversity Center to reach more network members.

More recently, at Miller's prompting, each Shell Oil business started to define the scope of a more formal mentoring program — determining, for example, whether a division would focus on developing new recruits or higher-level managers. A division's budget would depend on the audience and the level of training involved. Now divisions are budgeting for their different training audiences and programs. With a budget in place, managers and employees hope that mentoring will become a regular line item in division budgets.

And that leads to the third piece of Miller's strategy. Miller wants managers in the coming year to focus on developing a pipeline of candidates. That means leaders will become talent developers or "sponsors" as well as business managers. They must train candidates and open doors so that nobody is denied a job for lack of preparation.

The incentive for managers? Compensation. If a manager isn't developing, hiring, or promoting enough candidates with diverse backgrounds, it affects his or her performance review. Miller himself presents an annual report on diversity to his board of directors. "Although the wellspring of ideas is always at the grassroots, employees can't do it alone," Miller says. "That's why the link to senior management is important."

Of course, Miller realizes that each business within Shell sits at a different point along the diversity spectrum. Some businesses, such as Shell Legal Services, have won awards for their minority-development programs. Others are just starting to think about training. "I'm not worried," Miller says. "I'm concerned that we build momentum toward a diverse workforce, not that all Shell businesses arrive at the same point at an arbitrary time."

Source: www.shell.com

promote and champion diversity in the workplace. Role modeling is critical to the success of Shell's diversity endeavors. A training program that is built on cultural intelligence would help create a cadre of culturally intelligent mentors throughout the organization that can help Shell "build momentum toward a diverse workforce." Mentors need to be culturally intelligent, and new mentors in the pipeline can develop greater efficacy for handling diversity issues if they can identify their strengths and areas of further development using the cultural intelligence profile.

In the next section, we will examine how cultural intelligence matters in the culturally diverse workplace. We focus our attention on the U.S. workplace and examine how culturally intelligent managers can deal more effectively with professional behavior, or expectations of professional behavior, in the culturally diverse workplace.

CULTURE AND THE WORKPLACE: CQ AND PROFESSIONAL BEHAVIOR

Acting or behaving professionally in a diverse workplace requires high cultural intelligence. Notions of what constitutes professional behavior differ across different cultures. Immigrants, expatriates, and employees from abroad on developmental assignments all usually act in the best way they know how, yet their culturally conditioned behavior may not be regarded as fully professional by their local counterparts. For example, the differences between U.S. and European, Latin, or Asian notions of acceptable professional behavior may not be strikingly different. Rather, they are often nuanced and subtle.

Culturally intelligent managers will be conscious in a general way of appropriate professional behaviors in various cultures. A client had a newly hired employee born and raised in another country, and now in the United States, who was perceived to be representing the firm in a way that did not do it credit. Those who witnessed her behavior described it as "not professional." Why did this happen? What can be done to prevent it?

In the U.S. workplace, there appears to be very little precision and clarity about the meaning of professional behavior. The word "professional" as used in the U.S. workplace has two meanings:

- Types of work that, to be performed well, require a high degree of knowledge, skill, sound judgment, and constant practice. For example, physicians and lawyers do professional work.

- A set of qualities of one's personal behavior in work-related situations. This meaning of professional, particularly in the United States, may be problematic for employees from different cultures.

In order to function effectively in a culturally diverse workplace, managers need cultural strategic thinking to help them discover how to balance and reconcile apparently contrasting cultural values (or cultural dilemmas) and how to strategize their interactions with their colleagues. Of course, before they can do this, they need to be able to recognize and identify the cultural dilemmas in the situation. They need motivational CQ to help them channel their energy to reconcile cultural dilemmas. They need behavioral CQ to help them adapt and act out professional behaviors that are appropriate, striking a delicate balance between apparently opposite cultural values. This strategy of reconciling cultural dilemmas, according to Fons Trompenaars, is central in the culturally diverse workplace.

In this section, we specify five cultural dilemmas that need to be reconciled in the culturally diverse workplace. These dilemmas are among the many cultural dilemmas that have been indentified by Fons Trompenaars and Cornelius Grove and their associates.[1]

1. Independence versus interdependence
2. Egalitarianism versus hierarchy
3. Assertiveness versus sensitivity
4. Accuracy versus diplomacy
5. Punctuality versus patience

[1]The five cultural dilemmas are used with permission from the original authors, Cornelius Grove and Willa Hallowell of LLC. These five cultural dilemmas (of a total of seven) originally appeared in Strategic Account Management Association's (SAMA) "Focus Europe"; used with permission.

By expressing each of these cultural dilemmas in the form of "X versus Y," we are suggesting that culturally intelligent managers will be able to exhibit professional behavior by reconciling two apparently opposing cultural values. Furthermore, we assert that individuals with high CQ will be able to strike just the right note in their professional behavior with colleagues from different cultures.

Reconciling Cultural Dilemma No. 1: Independence versus Interdependence

Many Western countries have an individualistic culture in which independence, individual freedom, and personal objectives are emphasized. But independence is not license to behave in an unrestrained manner. Culturally appropriate professional behavior in the culturally diverse workplace is guided by the social and business-related expectations of others. Culturally intelligent behavior means that managers must demonstrate their independence, on the one hand, but must also observe prevailing social norms and the expectations of colleagues, on the other. Individuals with high CQ will be able to perform this balancing act more effectively than individuals with low CQ.

For example, managers in the United States have an expectation that those who report directly to them will get things done more or less independently, that is, without constant direction from above. Employees who are "initiative takers" and "self-starters" are valued — up to a point. The balancing act for employees is to take initiative that is bounded and guided by the strategies of their superiors and the overall strategy or mission of their organization.

Acting in a businesslike fashion in the United States means two things with respect to the reconciliation of this cultural dilemma. First, it means demonstrating independence in ways that are subtle, that observe locally prevailing norms of behavior, and that do not annoy or unduly distract the others with whom one is interacting. For another, it means not demonstrating independence in ways that strongly call personal attention to oneself. Behaving professionally means taking initiative on behalf of the firm in ways that support the strategies of one's superiors. Initiative is properly directed in support of the superior's objectives, not one's own unique ideas. However, in more group-focused cultures, the opposite seems to hold true. In Japan employees are expected to take care to consult with their superiors on a wide variety of decisions and practices. To run off and make decisions on one's own violates proper conduct. Culturally intelligent managers know how to reconcile the cultural dilemma of independence versus interdependence.

We present two scenarios to highlight the difference between culturally unintelligent and culturally intelligent behaviors in the culturally diverse workplace.

Culturally unintelligent behavior in an individual-focused culture: An individual is an avid fan of a certain baseball team. In work-related settings, he loudly proclaims the superiority of this team and often discusses details of the team's games, players, and operations. His behavior is unprofessional partly because his topic is not business-related, but even more because he is monopolizing office conversations in order to endlessly draw attention to his personal interest.

Culturally intelligent behavior in a group-focused culture: An individual is charged with helping her firm expand operations in a particular line of business. While contacting others during her exploration of opportunities, she realizes that there may be an expansion opportunity in a related line of business. Rather than taking the credit for this alone, she writes a report introducing this possible opportunity and suggesting the next steps, then takes the report to her colleagues and superiors for their input. After seeking their feedback, she incorporates their ideas into the report. Managers admire her for both taking initiative and remaining subject to direction.

Reconciling Cultural Dilemma No. 2: Egalitarianism versus Hierarchy

Countries such as Sweden, Denmark, and Norway are well known for having an egalitarian culture. People in the British workplace can interact with one another in ways that lack, in most instances, the overt recognition of power and status found in many other cultures. But it's a mistake to imagine that people, and especially businesspeople, ignore hierarchy altogether.

People in these egalitarian countries respect and defer to roles and responsibilities at different levels. The people who fill those roles and responsibilities are nevertheless "just people like you and me." Norwegians demonstrate their common humanity with others by being overtly friendly and informal with all others. At the same time, they are alert and ready to comply when someone with power acts "in role."

Culturally appropriate professional behavior in a country such as Norway means being respectful of power — of roles and responsibilities at different hierarchical levels and of the rights and privileges that belong to those levels. But powerful people are human beings, no more and no less, and we therefore are expected to be more or less informal with them.

We present two scenarios to highlight the difference between culturally unintelligent and culturally intelligent behaviors in the culturally diverse workplace.

> *Culturally unintelligent behavior in a hierarchical culture*: An individual is a junior manager at a firm. She is friendly toward others above her in the hierarchy. She tries to engage them in conversation about key issues facing the firm and offers advice about how management should handle certain matters. Her behavior is unprofessional. It's acceptable for her to act informally toward her superiors, but not to freely contribute her recommendations to them.

> *Culturally intelligent behavior in an egalitarian culture*: An individual is a senior manager at a firm. He has great responsibility and authority there, including the power to hire and fire numerous employees. In his daily interactions with employees, he behaves informally, occasionally asks about their individual interests and family members, and listens if anyone wants to share a concern. Though aware of his high status, he behaves in some ways as an equal.

Reconciling Cultural Dilemma No. 3: Assertiveness versus Sensitivity

In some cultures, self-reliance is admired, an attitude that goes back to a tradition that is the bedrock of independent-focused cultures such as Australia, Canada, or the United States. Individuals are able to be self-reliant, in part, by obtaining what they want through acting assertively toward others. Personal assertiveness, or "directness," is expected and admired, but too much assertiveness is quickly felt to be aggressive and abrasive. The difference between enough and too much is determined by the individual's sensitivity to others.

Self-assurance or self-confidence is admired up to a point. When it tips over into arrogance, others react quickly and negatively. Being described by others as opinionated, dogmatic, or arrogant is never complimentary.

Culturally appropriate professional actions in the United States involve putting a boundary on one's assertiveness and self-assurance, a boundary that varies across times, situations, and people. This shifting boundary is governed by one's awareness of the likely effect on others of varying levels of assertiveness. The professional constantly endeavors to be sensitive to others, thereby learning how to temper and modulate his or her behavior. This is where the cultural strategic thinking aspect of CQ is most critical.

We present two scenarios to highlight the difference between culturally unintelligent and culturally intelligent behaviors in the culturally diverse workplace.

Culturally unintelligent behavior in a low-assertiveness culture: An individual is acting as an assistant trainer. The training topic is something with which he has personal experience. He speaks frequently, sometimes interrupting others, and tells extended stories about his experiences. His behavior is unprofessional. Although he does have relevant experience to share, he is being too assertive; he is not being sensitive to others' needs to benefit from other perspectives besides his.

Culturally intelligent behavior in a high-assertiveness culture: Among the members of a team of six consultants is an older woman who is much more highly trained and experienced than any of the others, but who is not their supervisor. In dealing with the others, this woman is careful to avoid the impression of excessive self-assurance. She listens with interest to their ideas about how to proceed with clients and always explains her own point of view fully and patiently.

Reconciling Cultural Dilemma No. 4: Accuracy versus Diplomacy

Explicit truth and accuracy are valued in many cultures. To be accurate means that, in verbal and written communication, one discusses people, events, things, and one's own internal states in a manner congruent with reality. Americans pepper their speech with phrases such as "honestly" and "to tell you the truth" as a way of emphasizing their accuracy. But whenever a discussion touches on the shortcomings of someone present or on an embarrassing situation, accuracy encounters another valued quality: diplomacy.

The desire for harmony in communication and relationships is valued less in Western cultures than in many Asian cultures. But the importance of diplomacy in the West shouldn't be underestimated. The person who publicly says or writes something that, while accurate, is harsh or embarrassing or causes loss of face will be noted and criticized behind his or her back in strongly negative terms.

Culturally appropriate professional behavior in countries that stress accuracy (e.g., the United States) means overtly striving to be accurate in communication, yet striving as well to be sensitive to the feelings and reputations of others. However, accuracy must always be tempered by diplomacy, even to the point of one's occasionally stopping short of being 100 percent accurate. When shortcomings must be fully revealed, the bad news should be restricted to those who are directly involved.

We present two scenarios to highlight the difference between culturally unintelligent and culturally intelligent behaviors in the culturally diverse workplace.

Culturally unintelligent behavior in a high-accuracy culture: A manager becomes aware that the output of one of her project groups is not up to expected quality standards. During a meeting attended by all of her direct reports, she describes in exquisite detail the flaws in the output of the errant group. Her behavior is unprofessional. She may have been accurate, but because she spoke publicly, she was undiplomatic. She should have dealt with group members in private.

Culturally intelligent behavior in a low-accuracy or diplomatic culture: A middle manager strongly suspects that his firm is engaging in unethical accounting practices, and because he deals with the firm's accounts, he's in a position to know. He arranges to speak in complete privacy with the CEO and he brings with him detailed exhibits of the matters that concern him. His action is admirable because it demonstrates concern for the firm's long-term reputation as well as his own.

Reconciling Cultural Dilemma No. 5: Punctuality versus Patience

Western countries such as Germany or England have cultures in which people are highly conscious of time, even minute by minute. People say things such as "Wasting time is bad" or "Only if I could buy a free moment for myself." Time is treated like a commodity and a scarce resource. People schedule activities well in advance and then follow these schedules as much as possible. Activities are expected not only to begin on time, but also to end on time. Being punctual is about being sensitive to the needs of others, who are also following preplanned schedules.

Another characteristic of these Western cultures is that people have many responsibilities and tasks to attend to daily. A particular responsibility or task, therefore, may take more time to accomplish than might seem reasonable because one has many, many other things to do to as well. So along with punctuality, one needs patience. Being patient is about being sensitive to others' workloads and priorities. However, deadlines are taken seriously in these cultures. When a task clearly has high priority and its completion is critical to the work of others, the deadline should be met. It's not good to miss a deadline. Rather, one should agree in advance only to a "realistic" deadline.

Culturally appropriate professional behavior in punctual cultures means being acutely conscious of constraints on other people's time. One respects others' carefully planned schedules by arriving on time and by meeting deadlines that are viewed as critical. But one also respects others' huge load of responsibilities by not constantly prodding them about the completion of tasks other than, of course, the tasks that are most critical.

We present two scenarios to highlight the difference between culturally unintelligent and culturally intelligent behaviors in the culturally diverse workplace.

Culturally unintelligent behavior in a punctual culture: An individual arranges to meet a colleague at 9:00 a.m. He doesn't take into account, however, the possibility that rush-hour traffic could be slowed by an accident. So he arrives twenty-five minutes late. His behavior is unprofessional. He should have planned for possible traffic problems by allowing extra driving time. And he should have phoned as soon as it became clear that he'd be more than five minutes late.

Culturally intelligent behavior in a patient culture: A consultant is asked by a client firm to submit a proposal for a new training program and does so. When she makes her first follow-up call, her contact at the client firm states his interest in the proposal but also says he's overwhelmed with higher-priority matters. Time passes. The consultant calls back about six weeks later, but the situation hasn't changed. She asks when in the future she could call back again.

To be seen as behaving "professionally," individuals need to behave so as to maintain a delicate balance between two contrasting sets of values and to reconcile cultural dilemmas. This is precisely what culturally intelligent individuals are able to do.

We believe that a very important, but often overlooked, fact stands out in our analysis of professional behavior. Although American businesspeople are widely said to be individualistic, assertive, and focused on their own personal advancement, they actually expect of each other behavior that is consistently sensitive to the needs, constraints, and feelings of others. This is what we hope readers will take away.

Expatriates in the United States and their American colleagues face difficult cross-cultural challenges. These are perplexing and frustrating for all concerned and invariably result in sharply lowered productivity. These challenges follow predictable patterns, leading to the possibility of prevention, which always is far more cost effective than remediation.

Following are the stories of two Asian professionals who went to the United States on expatriate assignment and whose presence in the American workplace led to problems that illustrate how cultural intelligence could be applied. The lessons we will draw from the experiences are supplemented by our acquaintance with numerous other Asian-U.S. cross-cultural upheavals in American offices. The authors thank Cornelius Grove and Associates for the following example.

The case of Mr. A

Mr. A was the first individual from his Japanese division sent to the United States. The company designated his assignment as "developmental," and he viewed himself as a trainee. Soon after arriving at his new office, Mr. A was assigned to an internal trainer, an American who was responsible for Mr. A's learning according to a set of objectives jointly developed by the Japanese sending division and the American receiving division.

After only a short time, Mr. A complained of adjustment difficulties and stress, and he reported confusion and dissatisfaction over the content and purpose of his developmental program. It became apparent that, even though there had been direct communication between the sending and receiving divisions regarding this program, there had been almost no mutual understanding. The Japanese sending division had put forward broad objectives such as upgrading Mr. A's ability to communicate in English and enabling him to improve his abilities as a global manager. These objectives were easy for the American receiving division to accept. But the American side interpreted the objectives quite differently from what the Japanese side had in mind.

A closely related problem was that Mr. A's expectations regarding acceptable training methods were sharply at variance with the expectations of his American trainer. These differing expectations touched on several levels of the learning process.

How do individuals best learn? From Mr. A's Japanese perspective, learning is best accomplished through watching, listening, talking with people, and other such experiences. He expected to absorb useful knowledge by immersing himself in a wide variety of culturally and functionally different situations during his sojourn in the United States.

From the American trainer's point of view, learning is best accomplished through active, hands-on completion of carefully chosen tasks and assignments that have specific, measurable learning outcomes. He viewed immersion or absorption as passive and thus a waste of time.

How do trainees best interact with trainers? As a Japanese, Mr. A was accustomed to a supportive senior–junior relationship between trainer and trainee. Although he hoped primarily to absorb information, he also was accustomed to receiving assignments; in this case, he expected specific instructions from the trainer on the nature of the task *and* on the process of completing it. He assumed that he, the trainee, would do precisely as instructed, and that the trainer, a knowledgeable and involved guide, would be responsible for ensuring successful learning outcomes.

The American trainer expected people in his role to set learning tasks for trainees, then to provide comparatively little instruction. He assumed that trainees learn best by using a do-it-yourself, trial-and-error approach. The American viewed trainers and trainees as near-equals; to him, trainees were self-reliant individuals who accepted responsibility for ensuring the successful outcome of their own learning. He also subscribed to the American expectation that trainees may negotiate with trainers about the nature and extent of their assignments.

What are appropriate learning objectives? We return here to the lack of effective communication between the sending and receiving divisions. Experts in cross-cultural management recognize Japan as a high-context culture — one in which people constantly communicate with colleagues and friends about a very wide range of topics, thereby coming to have a comprehensive knowledge and nuanced understanding of people, events, things, procedures, and social and political realities. In short, people know the entire context of their daily lives.

When people who already are highly context oriented work together, their communication about any specific matter, even a relatively new one, tends to be brief but loaded with shared understanding because they already are well aware of all the factors directly and indirectly impinging upon it. Of course, the process of *becoming* highly context sensitive requires much time and effort.

However, the United States is widely viewed as a low-context culture in which people tend to communicate with others not only less thoroughly but also about a less comprehensive range of topics. Thus, low-context people are less well informed about the overall context of their daily lives. When low-context people work together, their communication about any specific matter of importance (e.g., an assignment) requires careful, focused attention in order to "get everyone on the same page," identify and analyze relevant factors, and develop shared meanings.

One can now appreciate that the single set of learning objectives so readily agreed upon by the two divisions was subject to two interpretations. For the Japanese, those objectives meant that Mr. A was to become highly context sensitive in the ways of American business and social life, best realized by his broadly immersing himself in U.S. daily life for an extended period of time. But to the Americans, those objectives meant that Mr. A was to complete a series of assignments, such as mastering computer software programs, that would introduce him to discrete features of how things get done in the United States. This discrepancy is not just theoretical. The situation wasn't merely stressful for Mr. A. It actually caused a serious setback in his developmental program, wasting his highly paid time as well as that of his American trainer.

Source: Used with permission of the original authors, Cornelius Grove and his associates, from Grovewell LLC. This case was first published in *International HR Journal*, a publication of Thomson West.

The case of Ms. B

Ms. B came to the United States from Shanghai, China, where she held an important and relatively senior position. She was assigned to work with an American supervisor, who recognized that she was a very able individual; consequently, he quickly gave her several responsibilities.

A cross-cultural conundrum soon emerged. She viewed herself as a trainee. Her American manager, who suspected that she outranked him in the company hierarchy, knew that her assignment was "developmental" but actually treated her as a full-fledged professional who could get things, and lots of them, done. The outcome was that Ms. B soon became completely overwhelmed.

This conundrum was not merely a simple misunderstanding about the purpose of Ms. B's overseas assignment. Trying to be cross-culturally sensitive about Ms. B's abilities and position, the American manager did a very American thing: He assumed that Ms. B was a self-reliant learner and doer who could keep up with his unit's insane timetable, and he therefore gave her one assignment after another and left her alone. What he meant to do was convey his confidence in her; he assumed that if he gave her a great deal of advice and assistance, he would be implying doubt about her abilities, thus causing her to lose face. He also avoided giving her any direct feedback about the burgeoning shortcomings in her performance, perhaps because of "face" considerations, and perhaps because he thought she outranked him. When her faltering became serious, he assigned American staff members to assist her, presumably to avoid taking assignments away from her as well as to forestall total failure.

From her Chinese perspective as a trainee, Ms. B did *not* view herself as a self-reliant learner and doer. She wanted the manager to give her exactly what he was deliberately not giving her: step-by-step instructions about both content and process, and lots of supportive guidance so that she would master the learning and not fail in any way.

Ms. B also did not view herself as being of higher rank than her manager; she considered herself to be of lower rank because she was the learner and he the teacher (the salient feature of the relationship from her point of view). Therefore, face considerations compelled Ms. B to never question the wisdom of her multiple assignments, never protest her deadlines. A Chinese learner-follower would not cause her master to lose face by questioning his judgment. Actually, as an American, the manager probably would have been open to feedback from a direct-report subordinate as well as a superior.

Source: Used with permission of the original authors, Cornelius Grove and his associates, from Grovewell LLC. This case was first published in *International HR Journal*, a publication of Thomson West.

Americans are often advised to try to take the face of Asians into account when dealing with them. Asians naturally pay attention to issues of face. In this case, however, we see that even when both sides were consciously trying to do the right thing, they got it wrong.

ANALYZING THE FAILURES

As we review these cases, we find several instances where individuals could have dealt more effectively with the challenges of interacting with each other in the culturally diverse workplace. In striving to work more effectively in the culturally diverse workplace, it's vital for employees to develop their capability to enhance their cultural strategic thinking, increase their motivation, and adapt their behaviors to each other. Let's examine what kind of failures occurred in these two cases, and then we will illustrate how CQ could be applied to improve work relationships in the culturally diverse workplace.

Failure No. 1: Failure to Plan & Adjust Mental Frames

In the case of Mr. A, both the Japanese trainee and the American trainer, failed to plan and adjust their mental frames to deal with the cross-cultural differences manifested in their interactions with each other. The same failure also occurred in the case of Ms. B. It's often been said that if we fail to plan, we plan to fail. It's evident from both cases that the parties involved failed to plan on how they would engage with each other as they interacted with each other. Both the Asians and the Americans failed to plan on how they would reconcile stark differences in several cultural dilemmas they face in their work relationships. Differences in preferences for learning, differences in expectations about what constitutes appropriate professional behavior, and differences about how to communicate are just some of the many cultural differences both parties failed to plan on how to reconcile in their relationships. Failing to plan on how we could approach people from different cultures have adverse consequences on work relationships in the culturally diverse workplace.

Both the Asians and the Americans in the cases also failed to adjust their mental frames of what would constitute an appropriate professional relationship between a trainer and his trainee or a new assignee and her manager. The Asians largely viewed the trainer-trainee and manager-new assignee relationships from their cultural standpoint of "master-disciple," whereas the Americans viewed the relationships as one of equals.

Failure No. 2: Failure to Direct Energy and Effort

In the case of Mr. A, both the Japanese trainee and the American trainer failed to direct their energy and effort to actively engage with each other. In the case of Ms. B, the Chinese assignee failed to direct her energy to engage with her American manager. She did not question her multiple assignments. She did not protest the deadlines that were set for her. In the culturally diverse workplace, active engagement is important in navigating and negotiating the interactive and communicative aspects of working together. In both cases, there was insufficient motivation by the involved parties to engage with each other. This has adverse consequences, particularly when assumptions were made and taken for granted in both cases. A high motivational CQ is important for effective relationships to thrive and flourish in the culturally diverse workplace.

In the case of Ms. B, there were some attempts by the American manager to be "cross-culturally sensitive" in dealing with Ms. B. Perhaps, the American manager in the case of Ms. B may have higher motivational CQ compared to the American trainer in the case of Mr. A. The American manager's attempt is commendable but his attempt had the opposite impact or outcome, as can be seen in the case, on the Chinese assignee. As we have discussed earlier in Chapter 3, having a high motivational CQ does not guarantee effective adjustment. The American manager may have high motivational CQ but if he fails to align his behaviors and thinking, he will not be able to work effectively with people from different cultures in the culturally diverse workplace.

Failure No. 3: Failure to Adapt and Enact Appropriate Behaviors

In both cases, the Asians and the Americans failed to adapt and enact appropriate behaviors that would have improved their work relationships with each other. In the culturally diverse workplace, actions and behaviors are critically important. This is the most tangible and most observable part of cross-cultural interactions. Failure to communicate appropriately and adequately prevented both the Asians and the Americans from checking their assumptions about each other. This failure also prevented both parties from directing their efforts and energy to reconcile several of the cultural dilemmas they encountered in their interactions.

As evident in our analysis, interacting and communicating in the culturally diverse workplace can be really daunting and challenging. How then can CQ help in preventing these kinds of failures that can occur in the culturally diverse workplace? We propose three recommendations that can help you develop your ability to work more effectively in the culturally diverse workplace.

1. *Develop your cultural strategic thinking.* Ample research has shown how we think can affect our job performance, particularly in problem-solving and decision-making. In the culturally diverse workplace, individuals face a number of intricate and complex challenges as they interact and communicate with colleagues and customers from different cultures. Some of the problems

that have to be solved and some of the decisions that have to be made in the culturally diverse workplace require cultural strategic thinking. Use your cultural strategic thinking to acquire cultural knowledge and develop strategic thinking. Developing your cultural strategic thinking will enable you to formulate and test hypotheses about your cultural knowledge and check your assumptions about others, and understanding and learn from your interactions with people from different cultures. Cultural strategic thinking will enable you not only to learn *from* cultural differences but also to learn *across* cultural difference. This kind of deep learning will enhance your ability to reconcile cultural dilemmas you encounter in the culturally diverse workplace.

2. *Build bridges of goodwill and understanding by enhancing your motivational CQ.* For people to work effectively in the culturally diverse workplace, it's important for people to reach out to each other, and build what we call "bridges of goodwill and understanding." In the two cases we analyzed, it's clear that these bridges or "an atmosphere of active engagement between people of different cultures" were conspicuously missing. To build these "bridges of goodwill and understanding" that are so vital in the culturally diverse workplace, you'll need to enhance your motivational CQ. Think of ways on how you can actively engage with your colleagues from other cultures. Learn how to reduce or minimize your sense of discomfort, anxiety and uncertainty of working with people from different cultures by increasing your self-efficacy and confidence in dealing with people from different cultures. Learn how to overcome your natural fear of the unfamiliar, step out of your comfort zone, and reach out to people from different cultures.

3. *Broaden your behavioral repertoire by enhancing your behavioral CQ.* Motivational CQ needs to be aligned with behavioral CQ. Enhance your behavioral CQ and broaden your behavioral repertoire by acquiring and practicing new ways to communicate with people from different cultures. Ask for specific behavioral feedback, be conscious of non-verbal messages, and listen actively.

SUMMARY

In this chapter we examined how cultural intelligence can help organizations and individual managers increase their efficacy in managing diversity in the culturally diverse workplace.

We examined how training and development programs that are anchored on cultural intelligence can propel companies to higher levels of effectiveness in diversity management. Cultural intelligence can help individual managers develop effective strategies for working with people from different cultures by identifying, recognizing, and reconciling cultural dilemmas. Managers who are culturally intelligent are generally viewed by their colleagues and customers as demonstrating appropriate professional behaviors.

To develop and enhance your ability to deal with the challenges of working in the culturally diverse workplace, reflect on how you generally reconcile cultural dilemmas you encounter when working with people from different cultures. Would you say that you have been ineffective or highly effective in reconciling cultural dilemmas?

No matter what cultural dilemmas you face, you can improve your ability to deal with cross-cultural challenges by applying the three recommendations we have proposed in this chapter. The culturally intelligent manager is one who never stops learning about other cultures. Acquiring cultural knowledge and sharpening one's cultural strategic thinking are developmental goals that culturally intelligent managers routinely set. The culturally intelligent manager never stops planning — he or she is always thinking about how he or she can plan to succeed in the next encounter with another person from a different culture. Culturally intelligent managers will constantly strive to build bridges of goodwill and understanding that will facilitate effective interaction and build an atmosphere of healthy and active engagement in their teams and organizations. Culturally intelligent managers will think of how they can enact appropriate behaviors that facilitate cross-cultural understanding as well as accomplish organizational goals effectively.

SUCCEEDING IN GLOBAL

WORK ASSIGNMENTS

Tony Lee* looks worried. His boss has just hit him with a bombshell. Tony is to leave for Bangalore in ten days' time to negotiate with a major Indian IT consulting firm for outsourcing its entire IT data center operations. He is expected to live there for a couple of months, and then make frequent trips after that to manage the outsourcing contract. Tony has no experience working with Indians. He wonders how much of his Chinese business background and negotiation styles will translate effectively in his interactions with his Indian counterparts.

The U.S. recession in 2000 has hit home for Carol Jones.* Working in a highly successful and profitable high technology company has not provided her with any job security. Her job has just been axed, and there have been no U.S. job postings within the company. Carol started exploring company job postings in Europe and Asia. A Singapore posting attracted her attention. It involved program design and process reengineering of the human-resources function of the Asian operations. After much deliberation and consultation with her partner, she decided to take up the Singapore challenge.

Today we face economic and societal trends that thrust us on a very different work journey. Globalization and technological advancements have made the world a much smaller place. The reality of a global world beckoning boundaryless careers awaits us. Exactly what are these irreversible trends?

- *The search for new markets for goods and services.* Workers are expected to travel to and work in countries where potential new markets exist.

---

* Not the real name.

- *Advances in transportation technology.* Aircrafts and bullet railways move business executives to different parts of the world within hours rather than days or months.

- *Changing redistribution of the world's working population.* The world's population increases on average by about 80 million each year. Not only is the population growing, it is also on the move. The number of people working in foreign countries continues to rise. With economic growth in their own nations stagnating, more and more individuals want to improve their economic opportunities and long-term quality of life by seeking employment outside of those boundaries. As many as 175 million people live outside their home country — 3 percent of the world population.

FAILURE RATES OF GLOBAL WORK ASSIGNMENTS

Despite the strategic importance of global work assignments, the success rate of GWAs is troublesome. Reports of U.S. expatriates failing to complete their assignments range from 10 to 15 percent; companies from Europe and Japan report the failure rate to be around 8 to 10 percent, according to researchers Randall Schuler and Peter Dowling.

The cost of any failed global work assignment is enormous, both to the organization and to the individual. From the company's standpoint, the costs of a foreign work assignment include financial outlay — paying for the travel of the expatriate and his or her family; shipping their belongings overseas; managing housing and property; insurance; and return and/or home travel and allowances. The estimated average cost per failure ranges between US$250,000 and $1 million, depending on the specifics of the expatriate assignment. Some studies show that the costs of first-year relocation alone can be as high as US$350,000.

The costs also involve downtime arising from disruption to the home unit as a result of displacing the individual from the home unit operations and the initial disruption of the host country unit operations as the expatriate settles into the new work environment. Because expatriates are generally selected on the basis of their high level of competence domestically, transferring these individuals to a foreign location means a significant loss of the person's expertise and networks to the domestic operations. Downtime pre-departure from the home country and downtime at the start of the global work assignment can amount to three to four months of relatively low productivity from the individual.

The reputation of the expatriate as well as the organization can be ruined by failed global work assignments. A failed assignment will probably leave a sour taste among the locals, who will be less trusting of expatriates in the future. A failed assignment will also disrupt the relationships the company has with local customers, government officials, suppliers, and associates.

Given the huge financial, personal, and reputation costs involved in failed global work assignments, how can more effective strategies be crafted to better prepare individuals and organizations alike for global work assignments?

IMPORTANCE OF CULTURAL INTELLIGENCE IN GLOBAL WORK ASSIGNMENTS

The key factor in determining who succeeds in an assignment is the employee's level of cultural intelligence. Cultural intelligence provides a critical lens through which people see and make sense of their world. It determines what things are important in businesses, work, and life, what things are despised, what things are valued most in businesses, and what things are not worth striving for.

Cultural intelligence is particularly important for workers who are about to embark on or already working in global assignments. Balancing work and life is a challenge in a working world that is driven by global competition and by the Internet, where we struggle to keep up with all the emails and information we receive. For example, the people in the United States now have the longest working hours compared to other industrialized economies. More than 78 percent of U.S. workers described their jobs as stressful, and 50 percent say they experience high levels of stress every day. U.S. corporations spend over $1 billion each year on medical bills for their stressed employees. Twenty-five percent of all U.S. employees describe their jobs as the number 1 stressor in their lives.

In global work assignments, the typical stresses we experience daily in both work and life are heightened considerably because we are working and living in a culture that we are not familiar with. Learning how to be culturally intelligent is complicated because there are so many cultures in the world.

In this chapter we discuss real-life challenges faced by workers who embark on global work assignments. We begin by discussing the different types of global work assignments and the different types of global workers. Then we present a guiding framework that describes the cultural challenges global workers face in two domains when working in a foreign country: general adjustment to living in a host country and adjustment to working in a host organization.

We offer several examples of culturally intelligent global workers and discuss strategies you can adopt to increase your cultural intelligence as a global worker.

We end the chapter with questions that serve as catalysts for your own reflections about possible applications to help you develop into a culturally intelligent global worker.

TYPES OF GLOBAL WORK ASSIGNMENTS

People travel overseas for many reasons. In the 1960s global travel fell into three categories: study, volunteer work (such as the Peace Corps), and military assignments. These groups of travelers are collectively identified as "sojourners."

A new breed of sojourners has grown up with the impetus of business globalization. They are the short- and long-term business travelers and executives. Companies send their employees overseas for four main reasons:

1. *To fill a position overseas because of the lack of local talent.* This is the most common reason for sending people for international work assignments. When local expertise or skills are scarce and there is no technically qualified local individual to fill the position, companies will often look to people in the home country to fill the position. These positions may be permanent positions as long as the company has no plans to develop local talent for these positions. Top management positions such as country managers and regional headquarter directors are often filled by home-country nationals.

2. *To transfer knowledge in production and operations to a new local operation.* Organizations move employees from one geographical location to another globally so that technical expertise, technology, standard operating procedures, and organizational routines can be transferred from one location to another, typically from the parent company to a local unit. When a company wishes to set up operations in another country, it will usually send its team of managers, technical supervisors, and even front-line production workers so that production technologies can be transferred from skilled host-nation workers to local workers.

3. *To develop home-country managers with a global mindset.* Workers are moved globally as part of a strategic human-resource management initiative to groom global leaders so that individuals, especially those from the home country, can learn the diverse range of resources and market conditions facing subsidiaries or local units overseas.

4. *To develop host-country managers with parent-country cultural orientation.* Many foreign governments are pressuring companies to "localize" management talent — that is, to hire locals in top management positions.

Multinational companies have begun to send bright, promising local talent to the parent company for management training and development. For example, Exxon-Mobil in Singapore identifies local talented management trainees from all over the world and sends them to the company's U.S. operations to work for a three-to-five-year stint so that they can understand Exxon-Mobil's global strategy, learn the corporation's culture and philosophy, and develop strong social networks with their counterparts in Exxon-Mobil's global workforce.

TYPES OF GLOBAL WORKERS

The typical profile of global workers is people who work in cultures or nations that are different from their home countries. Their work assignments in the foreign nation are temporary and voluntary. Either they are employees of a company, institution, or organization, or they are self-employed traders or entrepreneurs. Global workers who are employed by institutions are either traditional expatriates or localized expatriates.

Traditional expatriates. The stereotype of a global worker is the traditional expatriate. These are global workers sent out to fulfill many of the functions listed above. They are sent abroad to establish an overseas operation, manage for a few years, and then return home. Some expatriates lead a nomadic life. They have never been repatriated or sent back to their home country. They move from one country to another, working in different countries as expatriates.

Expatriates are expensive because they receive many benefits for relocating. In addition to a base salary, the compensation package includes, at a minimum, a housing allowance, an education allowance for the employee's children, a hardship allowance, and cost-of-living and tax-adjustment allowances. These allowances can amount to twice the base salary the individual would have received as an employee in his or her home country.

Localized expatriates. These are global workers who venture overseas for better job opportunities and the opportunity to gain international exposure. Many seek secure entry-level jobs. They voluntarily take on employment in the host nation on local terms; no premium benefits like those received by traditional expatriates are attached to their compensation.

A localized expatriate is therefore any foreign or guest worker who may have applied directly for a job as an employee to a local or parent unit in another country. Such employees are regarded as global workers because they will be working on short, temporary work assignments in a country different from their own.

TABLE 6.1

Guiding framework for successful global work assignments

Strategies for successfully living in a foreign country	Strategies for successfully working in a foreign country
1. Anticipating national culture shock	1. Anticipating organizational culture shock
2. Minimizing cultural toughness and culture distance	2. Developing cross-border technical and managerial competencies
3. Assessing and developing your own cultural intelligence	3. Managing and minimizing cross-national mixed identities and role conflicts
4. Assessing and developing the cultural intelligence of spouse and children	4. Providing local mentoring and formal CQ training and support

FRAMEWORK FOR SUCCESSFUL GLOBAL WORK ASSIGNMENTS

Whether you are a traditional or a localized expatriate, you will have to learn to adapt and adjust effectively in two major domains: life and work. Table 6.1 presents a guiding framework for successful global work assignments. In the left column, we list the challenges you face in adjusting to living in a foreign land, and in the right column, the challenges you face working in a foreign land.

FOUR STRATEGIES FOR LIVING SUCCESSFULLY IN A FOREIGN COUNTRY

Strategy No. 1: Anticipating National Culture Shock

Sojourners experience tremendous stress in the form of culture shock when they first embark on global work assignments. Removed from their familiar daily living habits and routines, sojourners typically suffer general symptoms of somatic complaints and anxiety attacks.

Table 6.2 is a tool to help you anticipate or evaluate the symptoms that may contribute to the degree of culture shock you would experience as a result of living in a foreign country. With this tool, you rate yourself on each of the following sixteen factors, on a scale of 1 (lowest) to 10 (highest). Each of the factors listed contributes to your overall culture shock in some specific way. Keep your self-rating within the context of how you typically respond or would respond when living in a foreign country. Be as honest and accurate with your answers as you can. There are no right or wrong answers. Fill in one circle in each horizontal row.

TABLE 6.2
Personal culture shock profile

Culture shock symptoms	1 Low	2	3	4	5 Average	6	7	8	9	10 High
1. Confusion upon arrival	O	O	O	O	O	O	O	O	O	O
2. Difficulty getting around	O	O	O	O	O	O	O	O	O	O
3. Difficulty adjusting to local food	O	O	O	O	O	O	O	O	O	O
4. Difficulty adjusting to the climate	O	O	O	O	O	O	O	O	O	O
5. Difficulty making friends	O	O	O	O	O	O	O	O	O	O
6. Feeling a general sense of helplessness	O	O	O	O	O	O	O	O	O	O
7. Frequent spells of homesickness	O	O	O	O	O	O	O	O	O	O
8. Level of impatience	O	O	O	O	O	O	O	O	O	O
9. Level of irritability	O	O	O	O	O	O	O	O	O	O
10. Frequent spells of insomnia or poor sleep	O	O	O	O	O	O	O	O	O	O

After you have completed the profile, go back and rank the factors contributing to culture shock that are most problematic for you. This information is invaluable for helping you face the truth about the aspects of your life overseas that need special attention.

Strategy No. 2: Minimizing Culture Toughness and Cultural Distance

How much a sojourner needs to adjust in a new environment depends largely on the degree of similarities or differences in cultural norms, values, and beliefs between the host nation and the sojourner's home nation, as well as differences experienced in the hardships of daily life.

The difficulty or challenge of adjusting to a new culture varies according to several different dimensions in the living environment. The critical factors to consider in deciding how difficult it might be to adjust to a new culture include a harsh climate, pollution, lack of personal freedom, security, different food, poor health care, lack of conveniences, and cost of living. Americans rank the following continents in descending order of toughness: Africa, the Middle East, the Far East, South America, Eastern Europe, Western Europe, and Australia and New Zealand.

Security concerns have heightened since September 11, 2001. In the past, political conditions were so unstable that expatriates were forcibly evacuated — for example, more than 100,000 expatriates were forced out of Iran and Libya in the 1980s. With threats of terrorism worldwide and the bombings in Indonesia (in Bali and at Jakarta's Marriott Hotel), the insurgence of terrorist activities in the Philippines, and the bombings in Spain, Saudi Arabia and Turkey, more nations find their culture-toughness index rising.

Note that these challenges we have discussed are hardships tied to general living conditions and not to cultural differences in values or norms.

Of course, there are variations in the degree of toughness within these regions and countries. For example, although located in the Far East, which is generally regarded as a culturally tough region, Singapore is often touted as a benign and safe environment. With a citizenry made up of four races, Singapore's dominant language of common parlance is English. All signs, notice boards, and instructions are written or displayed in English. Public transportation is efficient — with ample cabs and a well-oiled, user-friendly mass-rapid-transit system. Singapore has a low crime rate, and the streets are clean. The island has preserved much of its tropical character, with huge boulevards flanked with rain trees and well-manicured parks. Cuisines from all corners of the world are available on the island — Chinese, Malay, Indian, German, Greek, Italian, Japanese, American, and others. Other nationalities have equivalent cultural enclaves. For example, the Americans, British, Japanese, and Germans have social clubs they can belong to for a nominal fee. Regular social functions allow foreigners from the same home country to seek out culturally familiar peers or ethnic contacts on foreign soil.

Cultural distance based on values is also a factor for how multinational companies (MNCs) adjust to local conditions. The concept of cultural distance was used by Bruce Kogut and Harbir Singh in their work on MNCs. At the organizational level, for example, MNCs find it easier to transfer their technologies, human resource practices, and operating procedures and to achieve internal consistency through standardization when the cultural values between the host and home countries are more similar than different. For example, Japanese MNCs were found to be better in transferring their HRM practices to the rural areas of the United States, because the values of rural Americans were perceived to be more similar to those of the Japanese. Therefore, we would expect an expatriate to be better in adapting and adjusting to living in places where the locals' values are similar to their own because the cultural distance or novelty is not as great as in some other places.

Strategy No. 3: Assessing and Developing Your Cultural Intelligence

The most important step in a global work assignment is confronting the truth about your own level of cultural intelligence. Recall that the three important facets of cultural intelligence, which refers to a person's capability of adapting effectively across cultures, are cultural strategic thinking, motivation, and behavior.

We now return to Carol Jones, whom we introduced earlier as a global worker from the United States who volunteered to take a job posting in Singapore. Her story serves as a typical case example of what you can expect to face in your ever-more-challenging global environment and how to leverage your cultural intelligence to succeed in your global assignment.

Box 6.1
*Ms. Carol Jones**

Place of Birth: United States
Foreign Work Assignment: Singapore

EDUCATION AND WORK BACKGROUND

Carol majored in four disciplines in college — political science, philosophy, sociology, and psychology — which she combined with her desire to be a lawyer. After graduation she worked in a law firm as an attorney specializing in corporate immigration.

Her work has led her to many interactions with global clients and client organizations that operate in many locations around the world. The people she interacted with were primarily engineers and other professionals, such as accountants and researchers, from Europe, Asia, and Eastern Europe. After working in corporate immigration for ten years, she moved to the human resources area of a Fortune 500 high-technology company.

PERSONALITY

Carol describes herself as a fairly easygoing person who thrives on change. "I get tired of doing something after about two years, which seems to be

* Not her real name

---

my attention span from the job perspective, for you can only take so much and so far. . . . I like new challenges — to keep learning and do different things. So, I have been lucky that others have said, 'You've done good work, we want you to come and work with us.' "

Carol says she is an avid traveler. "I have done quite a lot of traveling. I went all around Europe in 2001. I've been there three times. Then South America, Panama, Mexico quite often. Canada. Had a layover in Greenland. For personal reasons. Never traveled internationally for business. I have visited most places in the United States.

"I like to be active, see new things. I just love to go to Italy and be there for four days. The people are wonderful, the wine is fabulous, the history — I am not much into historical references, but I like the architecture and just the historical domains. You know Boston — I like going there because they have the Red Sox. I like baseball. But going somewhere. . . .

"I don't go traveling because I like the food. I don't eat when I travel. I am a very particular eater. Typically when I travel I lose weight regardless of how good the food is, because I just don't eat."

IMPETUS FOR A GLOBAL WORK ASSIGNMENT

Recession hit toward late 2000, and Carol's job was cut. According to Carol, "My preference was to stay in the United States. There were no jobs in the United States, because the U.S. economy was down. Job cuts everywhere. Then I started exploring Europe and Asia. This sounded interesting because it involved program design, process reengineering." Carol described her preparation for her overseas work assignment to Singapore. "Frankly, I did not have time to think about the assignment. The company did not offer cross-cultural relocation training. I talked to my tax consultant to find out what the tax impact of my overseas work assignment would be on my personal income taxes.

"I didn't know what to expect. I had no idea. My uncle had traveled to Singapore some years back, he said that it was like an Asian San Diego. Lots of sun, tall buildings, trees. Even the people, language. . . . I had no idea what to expect. I did not have an apartment lined up. I was booked into a hotel, and that was all.

"The other steps I took were — there was a movie on TV about Malaysia starring Sean Connery and Catherine Zeta-Jones, with great shots of the Twin Towers in Kuala Lumpur. So I watched that to see what KL looked like. That was primarily it. I think I looked at one travel book to look at what the public transportation was like, what was the food like. But really not much. I did a will before I left, as it was after 9/11."

Carol assumed that since Singapore is in Southeast Asia, the country would be culturally similar to other nations in the region. However, she discovered Singapore to be very different from the rest of Southeast Asia.

FIRST IMPRESSIONS UPON ARRIVAL

Upon arrival, Carol realized how long a flight it had been and discovered how tired she was. "When I walked outside to get the cab it was like, 'Oh my goodness! I can't breathe!!! The humidity!!!' Driving from the airport to the hotel was like, 'Wow! This is really pretty!!!' We go through the nice tree-lined roadway. I was struck a little shortly, after not being here for very long — probably somewhat disappointed as well in the lack of Chinese architecture. I was hoping to see more Chinese culture and more architecture. Very standard. I won't say very American — very pretty, but standardized buildings. I was disappointed at not seeing Chinese architecture and Chinese buildings."

INTERCULTURAL ENCOUNTERS WITH
LOCALS OUTSIDE OF WORK

"In my first week here in Singapore, I had three days before I started work. I came here, caught a cab, and told the driver to take me to the hotel. OK, now how do I go about finding an apartment?

"I got my apartment finally after a week. But then getting from the Mass Rapid Transit trains to the apartment was a challenge. I didn't know the majority of the bus drivers didn't speak English. So I was trying to communicate with hand signals and trying to say Bedok Reservoir Road.

"Three times in my first week I got on the wrong bus. One time I went in circles twice on the same bus. The bus drivers were trying to communicate, and they used 'Ya! Ya!' I find that the term 'Ya, Ya' or 'Yes, Yes' is used quite a lot even if they don't understand. It's like 'Yes, I hear you'— not 'Yes, I understand you.' So that took time to get used to. Things like, 'I am done talking to you'— 'Yes!'

"So language. . . . A lot of my interactions are in English, but understanding Asian English — whether it was Singlish or just very fast English — the words all come out together. That was quite challenging.

"So what do I think of my cultural intelligence?

"In terms of cognitive cultural intelligence, I do not know as much of other cultures as I would like to. I had not learned any facts nor developed deep knowledge on any specific country. I should probably trace this back to my mother; in fact she is not very aware of other cultures or other people.

"However, I like to read philosophy books, which is where I picked up my cultural strategic thinking, I suppose. I use much of my cultural strategic thinking to compensate for the lack of cognitive CQ. I understand that being comfortable with yourself, doing what you want without hurting other people — I could reason that, doing what other people like — I think all the work I did in corporate immigration helped me understand the various nuances of the cultures, and I found it very fascinating. So when I went to Thailand, I go into a restaurant or a shop, and I see shoes lined up outside, I often ask, 'Would you like me to take off my shoes?' More often than not they say no because it is a tourist area, but just to make sure I ask. If there is nobody in there I will ask; if there are people in there with shoes on, I usually just go in.

"That, to me, is holding on to a strong mental cultural mindset — the ability to be mindful and perceptive in picking up cues, clues, nuances, and behaviors of another culture, and to suspend judgment of what is perceived until enough information is gathered.

"It's just being aware of surroundings. For example, when I first came to Singapore and was looking for my apartment, if I walked up and saw apartments with the shoes outside, even surrounding areas, I am like, OK, I may need to take my shoes off. When the person answers the door — were they wearing shoes or not? If I saw that they were not wearing shoes or if I saw many shoes left by the door outside of their homes, off came my shoes. If they were wearing shoes in the house, I would have probably left them on or would have asked. It is a sort of being aware.

"I also believe I am high in motivational CQ. I am curious, and I like to travel to other countries. I am confident in what I can and want to do in the world. When I say, 'I am going to travel here all by myself,' some of my peers at work say, 'You cannot go by yourself.' I am like, 'Yes I can!'

"Besides, I can have a great time by myself. If I want to go spend money on something, some people might say 'Oh! No, you can't do this, shouldn't you ask your significant others?' I am like, 'No! Why can't I do it? I want to do it. It's OK for me.' It's OK to not check with somebody for validation. For example, I go bungee jumping. Some people would say, 'Oh! My gosh! Won't that upset your family, your mother?' And I am like, 'But I don't care, I want to do it. It's going to hurt her, but it's OK.' There's nobody who's going to be hurt by this.

"I find behavioral CQ, the actual performance of appropriate verbal and nonverbal gestures and actions, the most challenging. Behavioral CQ comes from changing existing habits and creating new habits so that you are able to present yourself in a certain culture without offending the locals of that culture. I find that one way of reducing stress in intercultural encounters is to develop new habits of appropriate actions and performance by conscious behavior modification. Behavior modification simply means practicing over and over until it becomes automatic. So for example, if you are Indian and plan to go to a culture that frowns on eating with the fingers, you may present yourself better by learning to switch to using a fork and knife, or chopsticks and spoon, until it becomes automatic and you can eat with ease with the locals in public.

"Language barriers pose one of my biggest headaches in my behavioral CQ. Either they lapse into Malay or Chinese, or when they speak Asian English, I have a hard time understanding what they are saying.

"Nonverbal behaviors are even harder to cope with. I spent the last few days sitting next to someone in a conference room and having to duck because of the wild arm movements. I know I have to be very careful, as I can be very casual. I am sitting with one arm on the chair and I have to be careful that I am not too casual — that I don't give the appearance of being uninterested.

"It brings up the whole thing about personal space. In America personal space is a big issue. Give me my space around me. I notice that here, and actually all over Asia, that's not an issue. So I find that I have to be careful that if somebody comes and stands right next to me, that I don't just back off as I am accustomed to doing. I know that would be a personal affront. To me that's quite uncomfortable. It seems that in Asia that people aren't necessarily aware of other people, and so I have been walked through more than once. It's like, 'Excuse me! I am standing here.' Good example: In the supermarket, I would be standing there looking at items on the shelf and somebody would stop right in front of me. I am like, 'Excuse me! I am looking at stuff on the shelf. Do you mind!'"

Carol is a case study of a person who may not possess high levels in all three facets of cultural intelligence but is sufficiently aware of her own cultural strengths and weaknesses that she can leverage her cultural strategic thinking and motivational CQ strengths to compensate for her lack of cultural knowledge and low behavioral CQ. However, we are only as strong as our weakest links. Shoring up our weakness changes the odds dramatically for successfully living overseas.

Strategy No. 4: Assessing and Developing Your Spouse's and Children's Cultural Intelligence

Finally, it is not sufficient for a person to possess high CQ. If an employee's spouse and family leave with him or her on an overseas work assignment, the entire family must possess high CQ as a unit if it is to survive a global work assignment. In fact, past research has shown that the spouse's and/or family's inability to adjust to living in the host country is the single biggest reason for failure among American expatriates.

The phenomenon is not confined to American expatriates. The spouses and other family members of expatriates from Japan and Europe also experience adjustment difficulties, which, again, are cited as the number 1 reason expatriates terminate their global work assignments. Therefore, we expect that even if an individual has a high level of CQ and is personally able to adjust well to the sociocultural and general environment of the host nation, unless his or her spouse and family members are also able to adjust effectively, the spouse's and/or family's maladjustment can affect the individual's personal adjustment and, in turn, work performance.

Unlike a domestic work assignment, global work assignment is particularly vulnerable to spillovers of family to work life. Spillover theory suggests that an individual's experiences with home life have psychological effects that carry over into his or her work life, and vice versa. One can imagine greater spillover in global work assignments simply because such an assignment frequently involves the entire family. New family stresses arise because in almost all circumstances, all family members are displaced as a result of global work assignments.

Spouses may disrupt their careers to follow their spouses to the new host nations. And, especially in dual-career families where work is the "central life interest" or core of their identity in the spouse's life, such disruptions do induce adverse effects on his or her self-worth and self-identity. Initially, the idea of a life of leisure and luxury with maids and butlers who would attend to every whim may sound attractive to a trailing spouse. But reality quickly settles in — upon arrival, confusion and fatigue take over. All of a sudden, one finds that none of the basics so taken for granted in one's home country are in place. One needs to find housing, a car, a school for the kids to settle in, laundry facilities, food, and clothing, and to learn the social obligations of a corporate spouse.

Even if trailing spouses were not in the workforce in the host nation, their social networks are disrupted in any cross-cultural movement. The expatriate immediately needs to be totally absorbed by the challenges at the new work environment and therefore works longer hours than ever. Without emotional support from extended families or a network of intimate friends and community, adjustments may be especially difficult for spouses in foreign nations in coping with an alien culture and unfamiliar living environments. Sometimes, spouses may find "expatriate ghettos" where they hang out. But the meaningless daily drudgery of an unemployed expatriate spouse quickly wears down an otherwise career-oriented individual.

Children, too, face discontinuities in their lives. Education may be interrupted, and children lose their friends and classmates. Stripped of culturally familiar peers, they may feel culturally and socially isolated.

The spouse and family members experience completely new surroundings in their daily lives. Unless family members make special efforts to reach out to the local community to create new networks, the sojourner or expatriate may find himself or herself facing greater demands from family members living in the foreign nation when he or she is off the job. For example, a child's maladjustment to his or her new school or a spouse's dissatisfaction with living conditions, such as lack of proper child care, difficulty with securing spousal employment, difficulty in getting specific kinds of food or daily necessities, transportation, or language difficulty, and social isolation, often affects every individual family member, thereby adversely affecting the sojourner's own adjustment to the host nation, and consequently, his or her work performance in the local unit organization.

As a strategy for assessing and developing the cultural intelligence of your family, make sure to fill out the cultural intelligence profile to reflect their own ability to adapt to other cultures. More details about how to assess your and your family's cultural intelligence are included in the appendix. You should make sure your family members identify their own culture-shock profile as they perceive them in their pending or current global relocation. Ask them for the truth about how they feel. Collect all the profiles of your family. Look out for (a) areas where you think your family members' assessment of you is inaccurate and (b) areas you think could present conflicts off the job. This information is invaluable for helping you understand how you and your family differ on their thoughts and feelings about the global relocation.

FOUR STRATEGIES FOR WORKING SUCCESSFULLY IN A FOREIGN COUNTRY

Strategy No. 1: Anticipating Organizational Culture Shock

Table 6.3 is a tool to help you anticipate or evaluate the symptoms that may contribute to the degree of organizational culture shock you will experience as a result of working in a foreign country. With this tool, you rate yourself on ten factors, on a scale of 1 (lowest) to ten (highest). Each of the factors listed contributes to your overall organizational culture shock in some specific way. Keep your self-rating within the context of how you typically respond or would respond when living in a foreign country. Be as honest and accurate with your answers as you can. There are no right or wrong answers. Fill in one circle in each horizontal row.

After you have completed the profile, go back and rank the factors contributing to organizational culture shock that are most problematic for you. This information is invaluable for helping you anticipate the aspects of working in a foreign country that need special attention.

Strategy No. 2: Developing Cross-Border Technical and Managerial Competencies

If you want to be successful in your global work assignment, make sure you upgrade your technical skills in your key results areas. Technical skills and knowledge can rapidly become obsolete. Especially when you are currently holding a managerial position and are less in touch with the actual production tasks that require technical skills, you may have feelings of inadequacy or a lack of confidence in a key area of the task, or in fact actually unable to perform it. Technical skills are often essential for global work assignment (GWA) success, since a major reason for sending expatriates abroad is the scarcity of technical skills among locals in the host nation.

To get better at your key tasks in your global work assignment, you must broaden your technical knowledge over and above what is required of a job in your home country. Because of differing technological developments and legal and

TABLE 6.3
Organizational culture shock profile

Organizational culture shock symptoms	1 Low	2	3	4	5 Average	6	7	8	9	10 High
1. Problems defining role in foreign organization	O	O	O	O	O	O	O	O	O	O
2. Problems fitting socially into the foreign organization	O	O	O	O	O	O	O	O	O	O
3. Problems understanding business norms and practices of the foreign country	O	O	O	O	O	O	O	O	O	O
4. Problems understanding locals who speak slang or a different language	O	O	O	O	O	O	O	O	O	O
5. Problems juggling the conflicting demands from headquarters and foreign operations	O	O	O	O	O	O	O	O	O	O
6. Problems understanding the technologies used in the foreign operations	O	O	O	O	O	O	O	O	O	O
7. Problems in working in teams with diverse workforce	O	O	O	O	O	O	O	O	O	O
8. Feeling a loss of professional status	O	O	O	O	O	O	O	O	O	O
9. Feeling a loss of control at work	O	O	O	O	O	O	O	O	O	O
10. Problems adjusting to pace of work that is too slow or too fast	O	O	O	O	O	O	O	O	O	O

regulatory frameworks across nations, a technical expatriate must demonstrate cognitive cultural intelligence in terms of understanding how to operate across a greater range of technological platforms, and of functioning in a different legal environment from that of a domestic technical specialist.

For example, a domestic human-resource director of an MNC will need to acquire new knowledge and understand local employment laws in order to operate effectively as a regional or global human-resource director. Similarly, a chief information officer will need to appreciate and operate with different technological standards, and sometimes with an older generation of technology, when crossing cultures.

In addition to filling technical positions that locals are unable to fill, expatriates are also sent abroad to fill high-level managerial jobs such as managing directors or heads of departments of the local unit, thereby making managerial skills the other critical competency required of them. In fact, even if expatriates are assigned purely technical positions in host nations, they are typically required to manage people effectively because part of their mandate is to transfer technical knowledge to co-workers from the host nation.

Therefore, compared to technical specialists in domestic positions, technical expatriates need to possess managerial or people skills because their job often requires them to start a new production operation with the aid of local nationals. It is thus critical that technically competent global workers increase their level of behavioral CQ so that they possess the requisite cross-cultural managerial skills to facilitate the transfer of knowledge and to train host nationals in new technologies.

We continue with our story of Carol Jones, whom we introduced earlier. Her story serves as a typical example of the importance of behavioral CQ in daily intercultural encounters at work.

INTERCULTURAL ENCOUNTERS AT WORK

Carol had to develop her behavioral CQ by learning to understand the intonation, pace of speech, and accent of locals, even though they were speaking English.

"So the first day I started work and there were four or five different people all in HR explaining how Singapore worked, the organizational structure, benefits, and so on. Each of the people at some point in the conversation referred to 'Vincent.' There was an explicit reference several times. And I kept thinking, I have to make sure that I am introduced to Vincent. I should know who Vincent is because everybody is talking about him. Finally, at the end of the day, the woman I was talking to must have said it slowly or something. Then it finally hit me that it wasn't Vincent but they were saying 'For instance.'

"Four different people! And I had been so convinced that they were talking about Vincent! At one point I even made a deliberate note on my notepad to 'Talk to Vincent!' On hindsight, 'For instance' makes so much more sense!

"It still happens even months after being in this country. My common mantra is: 'I am sorry; I still didn't catch that word — what was that?' In Singapore, people throw the word 'lah' into the end of sentences. That makes it very hard to pick out a particular word when it is followed by something that you don't understand. That took another few months — to understand that 'lah' was thrown into words. Now I can usually pick it up. Or if I don't understand, I assume it had 'lah' at the end.

"People talk fairly fast. It can be very frustrating. Also, at times, people still "launch" into Mandarin. So if you are talking with someone and their phone rings, they talk in Mandarin. That I could understand, because they could be having a personal conversation and I do not want me to eavesdrop. In which case, I would just walk away rather than have somebody speaking in a different language. However, when people start to launch into Mandarin at a meeting, I am frankly frustrated. I am like, 'Hello!!! . . . I don't speak Mandarin!!!'

"How does one cope proactively with people talking in Mandarin? A lot of this happens just peripherally, so I can just go back to my own thing. I turn back to my desk and start work.

"If it is in a meeting, I will say, 'Excuse me, I don't understand. Can you speak English?' And I don't mind saying, 'Can you speak English?' because as a U.S.-based company, that's our language. There are few Malays that I work with. I just cannot understand them at all. Even when they speak English. I don't know if it is the difference in the tonalities and I am just not picking up the tone of their voice, but — it is very difficult. My manager in Malaysia is actually from India. I hear him fine, but the two Malaysians I have a very difficult time understanding.

"It is very frustrating for both of us, because I just have to keep saying, 'I am sorry, I didn't understand. Could you please speak slower?' I try to paraphrase most of what they say. But it is very frustrating for everybody. I lean forward and turn my ears towards them trying to catch bits and pieces.

"Nonverbal behavioral CQ in terms of long pauses and silence just kills me. I hear a long pause and assume that they are done. So I am constantly interrupting people, not on purpose but because I honestly think that they are done. Especially this gentleman from Malaysia. Really cannot understand. His words are very, very slow and to me it seems like listening to Morse code. That's how his words come across — machine-gun type. So he gives a pause after talking, and he is frustrated with me, I know, because I don't understand him, and so when I start talking, he is like, 'Wait!' I am like, 'Oh! I thought you were done.' That can also cause some tension among peers. We get along fine, but when there is conversation, there is some tension."

USING CQ TO BUILD TRUST AMONG LOCALS

"I can't really think of where there was a problem, but I always feel like an outsider, by being a foreigner.

"I think it took about four months, though, for people around me to trust me, even though I came with very good credentials. I came in and showed that I knew what I was talking about, laid out plans and ground-work. There is still a distance and not an openness to want to . . . until I guess that they could see for themselves that the credentials were right. That I wasn't there to take over their jobs. They definitely had a feeling of, 'An American coming in, I am going to lose my job,' or something. It took about four months before people started feeling comfortable.

"In trying to build trust, I just try to be myself! I guess I was relying sub-consciously on my cultural strategic thinking part of CQ. Regardless of where I am, whether I am traveling for pleasure or something, I try to be aware of cultures. I am open, I care about people, and I do what I say I am going to do. So I was just myself. I didn't address it, I hadn't been here long enough to know whether it was OK to say, 'I am sorry! Why is there this ten-sion? Why do you not trust me?' I did not feel comfortable addressing that.

"Well, I try to be. Not that I am always. But I try. What words to use, body language. Knowing that I can't just back up when somebody stands right up to me and starts talking, because that immediately puts up a bar-rier. Trying to look people in the eye, not shake people's hands too hard. So just trying to be comfortable with how you do that and knowing not to shake with my left hand. Not that I would, but know things like that.

"Trying to spend more time and not saying, 'Oh! In the United States, we do things this way.' Who cares what we do in the United States? What do we need to do *here*? I was very conscious of that. This is all basic cultural strate-gic thinking — being very culturally aware. Especially coming to a new working environment, the idea that 'we always do it this way' doesn't make it right. Who cares what we did there? It may not work here.

"I think what helped break down the barrier was for them to see that I was one of them. Once I got here, I realized that things work very differently here. So they heard me and saw me actually spending a lot of time talking with people back in the United States and telling them, 'We can't do that here! It doesn't work here.' So I think that once people really saw that I was interested in Asia and what was right for Asia, I think that really helped make a difference as well. I am high in my motivational CQ. I like and enjoy being part of them. So I demonstrated that I was a part of them."

Strategy No. 3: Managing and Minimizing Cross-National Mixed Identities and Role Conflicts

It is difficult for any expatriate to succeed in global work assignments if the organization is not expatriate friendly. How does an organization create a work environment than can best leverage the special expertise and experiences of an expatriate so that the expatriate can become a valuable asset to the company and to the locals? Here we focus on how an organization itself can develop its cultural intelligence in its approach toward managing the increasing globalization of employees.

Job Design. An organization with a high cultural intelligence will deliberately and consciously design a job that leverages the special talents of the expatriates or global workers. A well-designed job is one that has certain essential criteria: role clarity, reduced role conflict, and greater autonomy or job discretion. Role clarity will minimize the uncertainty faced by the expatriate, who is already overwhelmed with uncertainty derived from non-work sources such as sociocultural shocks and the general living environment of the host nation. With role clarity, an expatriate is likely to minimize role shock, thus making less painful his or her transitions to the new work environment. The company should spell out clearly the basic roles and responsibilities to be met by the expatriate. The job should lay out the performance standards required of the expatriate, and it should state clearly the authority and corresponding accountability granted to the expatriate.

An expatriate job should also minimize role conflict. A primary source of role conflict is the potentially conflicting dual allegiance required of an expatriate. In the tension between goals of local differentiation and global integration, an expatriate will often need to balance between allegiance to the local unit and allegiance to the parent organization. Unless the GWA clearly spells out the expectations of the manager and resolves potentially conflicting demands, role conflict could have detrimental effects on work performance.

Finally, an expatriate job should include job discretion and autonomy. Role discretion allows the expatriate the flexibility to determine how work is to be accomplished. With greater latitude, the expatriate can absorb the uncertainty of role novelty and craft his or her strategies to get the work accomplished.

Designing a More Culturally Intelligent Global Organization. In the field of international business, global organizations are seen to organize and design themselves in one of three dominant modes:

1. An *ethnocentric* mode, with the parent organization operating as a central hub, and overseas subsidiaries operating as spokes. A company uses people from the home country to run things regardless of the location, so, for example, an English company has English managers running its operations in Thailand, Brazil, or Spain. The parent company dominates the strategy and direction of the multinational corporation; subsidiaries are given minimal autonomy, because decisions are highly centralized in the parent organization. An ethnocentric MNC design focuses on global integration and minimizes local responsiveness.

2. A *polycentric* mode, where the strategy is based on responsiveness to local markets and the structure comprises a portfolio of relatively independent national companies in host nations. A company uses, for example, the very best Indonesian for Indonesia, the best Ghanaian for Ghana, and so on, even though the parent company may be a Canadian company headquartered in Montreal. In such an arrangement, the parent organization typically exerts some minimal central control of technology and management systems, but much decision-making authority resides with individual subsidiary companies.

3. A *geocentric* mode, where attempts are made to ensure both global integration and local differentiation. A company uses the very best it has regardless of where it comes from — for example, a French manager may be working for an English company but assigned to Indonesia because she is the best person the company has for the job. The strategy is based on balancing the complex paradox of responsiveness and scale, and the structure reflects interdependent subsidiaries differentiated by roles and capabilities, all interrelated in a complex integrated network of national organizations globally.

The organizing mode of the MNC can have a significant impact on the work systems of local units. Therefore, a culturally intelligent organization will have to consider the various cultural strengths and weaknesses associated with each model.

The dominant mode seems to be the ethnocentric arrangement. Ethnocentric modes have few problems within but face major cultural problems outside the corporation; the polycentric and geocentric have fewer cultural problems relating to the social environment.

In an ethnocentric design, expatriates transferred from the parent organization to the local unit can expect greater standardization of work systems and therefore face less novelty in the work environment than an expatriate who is transferred from an MNC that is polycentric or geocentric in nature. An expatriate with low CQ may find it easier to perform and work in a local unit where the parent organization has an orientation toward ethnocentrism. With an ethnocentric focus, the parent organization will have streamlined and created globally standardized local units in work processes, systems, and organizational culture, therefore reducing uncertainty at the workplace. This situation presents a lower level of role shock or culture shock for the incoming expatriate.

However, an ethnocentric organizational design has its own severe drawbacks in the long run. A U.S. senior executive described the practices of an ethnocentric U.S. corporation.

A U.S.-centric organization tends to make U.S. executives less culturally sensitive. They feel as though everything must fit into the U.S. view. And that is wrong. We grow more due to globalization. Globalization does not mean U.S. based. We can't make it U.S. based going outward. It has to be a triangle — Europe, the United States, and Asia. The triangle joins and jells together for something that works.

Several years ago, we did something called "Copy exactly." I know that a lot of companies did that. You will have a process and everybody will copy it exactly. It does not always work. Businesses in Asia have different needs from those in the United States. I subscribe to the "copy exactly with modifications" philosophy. You have got to adapt this to specifics. You need to understand where the differences are.

Asia is growing — one of our big growth areas. We have done a lot of good work here in Asia. I think our Asian leaders have felt so unappreciated for so long that, now that they are one of the top regions, they have very strong arrogance. You see this in how they talk to us in meetings, how they send out their messages. It's like, "We are now the number 1 group — we can influence change back in the United States or back in Europe." Just as the United States has come to Asia, now the Asian managers have started to come after the United States and Europe in the same way. Influence by bullying — and it is what we used to see from the United States.

The ethnocentric values of an MNC can backfire. I hear phrases from Asia such as, "We will now tell them this! We will make them do it our way. We will make them adopt our practices." That was one thing someone said in one of our big Asian meetings: "We are now on top. We can make them [in Europe and the United States] do it our way. Now they will listen to us." We saw a similar thing happen in Europe a few years ago when companies were merging and acquiring all over the place. Europe was a heavy merger and acquisition area, and so Europe was king a few years ago.

A parent organization that has an orientation toward polycentrism or geocentrism may push the expatriate to greater heights in cultural intelligence. Such organizations will allow expatriates to learn new ways of working rather than simply applying their existing knowledge and skills in another part of the world.

Strategy No. 4: Providing Local Mentoring and Formal CQ Training and Support

Once an expatriate arrives at the local unit, how effective he or she is at the workplace depends on how much his or her co-workers from the host nation are willing to orient or familiarize the expatriate with the local work environment. An expatriate arriving at a local unit in a host nation is akin to a newcomer employed in a domestic position. Just as with the experiences of a newcomer in a domestic position, an expatriate will be able to contribute and work more effectively if the expatriate undergoes some socialization and acculturation program at the local unit, where the individual is told and taught and learns what behaviors and perspectives are desired or appropriate within the local work setting. Hence, some formal training on cultural intelligence in that specific country and organization is critical.

For expatriates with career spouses, some local units also actively undertake spousal assistance programs that provide assistance in obtaining a visa or work permit for the spouse in order for him or her to obtain local employment, as well as assistance in working with the spouse on producing a résumé and submitting it to the appropriate local employment agencies.

Sometimes even simple, somewhat mundane work details — such as getting an employment visa or work permit, opening a local bank account, setting up a well-furnished and well-equipped office space, or providing the expatriate with support staff such as administrative assistants, secretarial support, and computer technicians — can alleviate the initial hassles the expatriate experiences when settling into a work routine. Assigning lunch buddies from local nationals can also facilitate faster learning of the local work norms, values, and practices and prevent isolation and alienation. Social support from co-workers from the host nation also acts as a buffer against work stress, since expatriates are made to feel that their presence is valued rather than resented.

NAVIGATING REENTRY AND REPATRIATION

Thus far, we have focused our attention on expatriation in global work assignments. Because global work assignments are temporary and short term, typically lasting three to five years, most employees sent overseas eventually return to their home country and parent organization. Surprisingly, expatriates often find returning to the parent organization as challenging as being sent on an overseas work assignment, if not more so.

Contrary to received wisdom, expatriates do indeed face very real and serious reentry culture shock. Research shows that 60 percent of American, 80 percent of Japanese, and 71 percent of Finnish expatriates find repatriation even more difficult than expatriation. A primary reason for the difficulty in adjusting back is that expatriates underestimated the changes that will have occurred at home and are therefore ill prepared mentally to face reentry culture shock. After all, they were returning to their home country and parent company — presumably more familiar territory than a foreign assignment. Yet, the degree and types of changes that occurred in their home country or parent organization can be significant, to the extent that an expatriate may lose his or her identity during repatriation and feel like an alien in his or her home country.

As critical as cultural intelligence is for expatriation, it is even more necessary in repatriation, because global workers are not as mindful of the living and work changes that may have taken place in their home environment in their absence. Because of the significant parallel problems expatriates face on repatriation, repatriation should be thought of as another overseas assignment. We can expect that the cultural intelligence that served the global workers so well in expatriation will play a significant role in that repatriation success — that is, in adjusting effectively back to living in the home country and working in the parent organization.

In adjusting back to living in the home country, spousal, family, and country factors matter. For example, how well spouses and family members can adjust to repatriation will depend on the extent to which their original home country's social networks have remained intact or have disintegrated during the time the expatriate family was overseas. In dual-career situations, whether the spouse is able to find meaningful work in the home country after an absence also strongly affects how well an expatriate is able to adjust to being back home. With regard to the culture toughness or novelty of the home nation, a lot will depend, too, on how much the home nation has changed during the period the expatriate family has been away in terms of the political climate, housing conditions, transportation systems, crime rate, pollution, cost of living, stage of economic development, and other factors. The culture toughness of the home nation with respect to the host nation will also determine how much cultural intelligence is required of the global worker and his or her family in order for them to adapt back home.

In adapting back to working in the home country, job factors such as the job assigned to the expatriate upon repatriation are equally important. Whether the job is clear and unambiguous and utilizes the skills and expertise gained from the overseas assignment are key factors in the repatriated worker's effectiveness. In addition, organizational factors such as the extent of organizational change in structure and process, especially changes in supervisors and co-workers; any formalized reentry socialization; the assignment of a sponsor or mentor for each expatriate; and cultural orientation or training for returned expatriates will determine how quickly the repatriated worker can perform at the level he or she is capable of.

SUMMARY: DEVELOPING CULTURALLY INTELLIGENT GLOBAL WORKERS

Working overseas is the central feature of today's careers. In some companies, having prior overseas work experience is a prerequisite for career promotion and advancement.

Have you ever taken an overseas or global work assignment? If you have, how has the experience turned out for you? If you were to reflect on your overseas assignments, how would you rate your ability to adapt to the whole gamut of cross-cultural experiences in the host country? In other words, how would you rate your success as an expatriate?

Successful expatriates are invariably those who have taken the time to plan and prepare thoroughly before they begin. Refuse to allow any lack of confidence in your ability to work abroad to hold you back. The key is to render more and better service than is expected of you, no matter what situation you face. The key is to bolster your cultural intelligence (and your family's CQ) before embarking on your intercultural work assignment. Consciously developing your personal and family's cultural intelligence will give you a competitive edge as a global worker.

7 | BUILDING HIGH-PERFORMING GLOBAL TEAMS

A key challenge facing modern organizations is how best to use and integrate the various talents brought forth by members coming from diverse backgrounds and experiences. How can organizations best make use of the diversity that exists in their companies? How do managers use their own knowledge and skills about dealing with others to avoid potential pitfalls in work encounters? Most importantly, what role might CQ play in helping us understand why some people seem much more capable than others of integrating their interests with those of other people?

Companies rely increasingly on teams made up of people with highly diverse backgrounds. Employees face the challenge of working with people very different from themselves. People working in multinational or multicultural teams (ones made up of people coming from many different countries or ethnic or cultural backgrounds) must rely on their own personal sense of identity as an anchor in dealing with others.

A highly diverse workforce means that many possible identities exist for team members; team members rely on many different identities as they work with each other. I (an American) may be working on a team with two Japanese, one German, three French, and one British manager. I carry with me my identity as an American, just as the other team members have their own national identity. At the same time, I have other role identities, as discussed earlier — my identity as a husband, a university professor, a man, a scuba diver, and so on. When I relate to my fellow teammates and they to me, I use a combination of my various roles. For example, the German manager might happen to be a scuba diver also, so we now talk about our most recent dive trips to the South Atoll of the Maldives and having spotted some hammerhead sharks. The Japanese managers relate to me based on my company affiliation, and the British manager makes a connection based on our common language and heritage. To complicate matters, how I see myself and how others see me may be shaped by their own culture, so the French manager, coming from a culture that stresses formal education and technical qualifications, views me in terms of my Ph.D. rather than my role as a husband or my gender. So working on a multinational team means understanding not only how we differ; the traits we focus on in thinking about ourselves and others change on the basis of our own culture and personal experiences. Having high CQ is critical to identifying similarities among team members because it reflects our ability to understand these nuances of self-image.

Agreement among team members regarding personal identity is of great consequence to what unfolds over the life span of a team. Many management scientists suggest that establishing the identities of others in a situation is a necessary prerequisite to getting work done and that establishing roles and personal identities is a critical feature of effective multinational teams. Team members who share a common perspective achieve better performance because of their mutual trust and their positive feelings about one another. Despite the seemingly obvious importance of accurate views about one another, little is known about how and why we come to develop our views of each other.

When people join various groups (such as a golf or tennis club), they naturally try to understand who they are dealing with. One general way to do this is to classify people into two simple categories — the in-group (people who are similar to me) and out-group (people who are different from me). What constitutes similar or different? The characteristics you use are those that are most salient based on your background and experiences. Recall that you may use more than one characteristic in deciding whether another person is in an in-group or an out-group. You may view other people based on their functional background (e.g., a marketing or finance person) and secondarily on race or gender.

This point is nicely illustrated by the sociologist Everett Hughes (1971), who distinguished between primary and secondary "status-determining characteristics" (traits that we use to determine a person's worthiness), and he argued that these should be considered together in determining a person's power and status. That is, our various identities are linked. Hughes illustrated this point by describing the status of an African American doctor to a white patient and suggested that the primary status characteristic of profession (physician being high status) was interpreted by the patient in terms of the secondary characteristic (black being lower status in the mind of the white patient). Profession alone was inadequate to understand the status afforded to this person by his patient. Describing a person's identity using multiple characteristics implies a hierarchy of identities.

It should be clear that the definition and understanding of others who are from diverse backgrounds requires a very elaborate and subtle examination. Our categorization of others is based on a personal hierarchy of importance that is largely unique and idiosyncratic. My trait identity hierarchy may vary a great deal from yours even if we are from the same country and culture. We may share a common culture, but our individual experiences may make some traits personally more important to me than they are to you.

This idea may be applied to other personal differences, such as knowledge, skills, likes and dislikes, and so on. Understanding people from a common culture but whose backgrounds are diverse may be as difficult as understanding people from entirely different countries. For example, people in the United States may well agree that race is a key characteristic of diversity, although people in Brazil may focus on socioeconomic status. Within the United States, people will generally agree that race is an important feature of people, although they differ in their views of what race means (e.g., when the first author lived in southern California, he noticed that many people focused on differences between the Anglo and Latino communities, whereas when he lived in the Midwest, the emphasis seemed to shift to the differences between "white" and African American communities).

We return to our initial question of this chapter: how do people in a community and nation understand one another as they work together?

In the next section, we talk about diversity in three different ways — personal, team, and organizational. Within each subsection we discuss the important aspects of diversity and apply CQ to show various ways in which people may work together better.

LINKING CQ WITH WORKPLACE DIVERSITY

In this section, we will explore the links between CQ and three levels of workplace diversity: the individual or personal level, the team level, and the organizational level.

Individual Diversity and Your Sense of Identity

The importance of cultural intelligence, in the context of the diversity of individuals, is best understood by thinking about what constitutes our answer to the question "Who am I?" We talked about issues of self-image and role identity earlier (see chapters 1 and 3), so we will briefly expand on this earlier discussion and talk about how we can use CQ to link personal identity and personal action.

The psychologists Hazel Markus and Shinobu Kitayama have suggested that our self-concept is a composite formed through direct experience and evaluations from people important to us. In a very general form, self-concept is a reflection of what you think it means to be a human being in your own culture. Information about our self is processed, stored, and organized in our minds in a logical structure that we can dip into as the situation demands. For example, Johann Pieters, a German global manager working in Thailand for a large engineering firm, commented:

> When I work with Thai employees, I often find myself thinking about how my own background at university and working at my company leads me to think about work differently than do the Thai employees. I mean for me the work is a challenge to create a building or bridge that is elegant and enduring as an engineer. For the Thais, it's completing a project and getting onto the next one while showing proper respect to me as their boss. I just wish that this respect wouldn't get in the way of building a proper bridge.

Your self-concept is a collection of features including your experiences, traits, goals, and ideas about how things work. It's a collection of ideas and images concerning the state of an idealized and real world; most important, it acts as a filter for incoming information. We actively regulate our self-image as the situation demands using personal motives such as the ones we discussed in chapter 1. We talked about the self-motives taken from work by Miriam Erez and Chris Earley — self-enhancement, or seeking and maintaining a positive self-image; self-growth, a desire to think about yourself as competent and confident as well as to grow and challenge yourself; and self-consistency, a desire to sense and experience coherence and continuity in your life. They suggest that one's self-concept is regulated by culture as well as by features of one's work. For example, people living in a high-power-differential culture such as Thailand have a self-image that endorses respect for authority, deference to seniors, and so on. A Thai manager satisfies his self-motives by culturally acceptable methods, so he maintains high self-enhancement by being shown proper respect by people who are subordinate to him — that is, he will seek out situations that provide opportunities for recognition. However, a manager who has a strong self-growth motivation will take on new challenges to expand his or her accomplishments and learning opportunities.

It's the first motive of wanting to feel good that is critical during the early stages of when people from diverse backgrounds meet. When people first encounter others who are different, a comparison process takes place. Part of this comparison is based on people's desire to feel good about themselves. When you meet strangers who have a background dissimilar to yours, you naturally (sometimes unconsciously) compare yourself with them and try to determine your own status relative to them. If you find them to be similar to you on issues (or characteristics) that you personally find important, then you are attracted to them, since this strengthens your own sense of self-worth. Imagine going to a party where everyone is strongly opposed to all your political views (for instance, you approve of President George Bush's decision to support the Americans in the Iraq war, and the party happens to be made up of a group of French and German managers who are against the war). How does this make you feel? Defensive, like an outsider, isolated, and a bit unpopular, we suspect (perhaps confrontational as well). This encounter may weaken your self-image, particularly if there are people at the party whom you respect and like. But suppose that, instead of this party, you walk into a party at which the guests are people who endorse your views of the Iraq war and Bush's decision to intervene. You feel more comfortable and at ease in this case and more positively about yourself. This effect is very important for understanding how diversity in groups (or teams) may impact members at the early stages of team interaction.

In this view, personal-level diversity reflects what can be called your personal role identity, or the self-image that individuals have for themselves. We sometimes refer to this image as "face," or the self you present to others around you. A person's face reflects an inner sense of self-worth as well as one that is projected for the public, and the two do not necessarily overlap. (Quite the contrary, it seems that these inner- and outer-directed selves are often very distinct from one another, which can be a problem. For example, an employee who has a strong inner sense of ethical conduct but who is asked by his company to falsify an environmental cleanup report faces a dilemma.) The sociologist Irving Goffman referred to these inner and outer selves as front stage (what is shown to others) and backstage (what is revealed only to yourself or to people with whom you have very intimate relations). A key point here is that people actively try and maintain a strong and respected face to the outside world — but how they do this depends largely on their cultural background.

For CQ, it's important to remember that a person's reaction to a work situation reflects many influences. It can reveal how a person is trying to maintain face and what they reveal to the outside. Take, for example, a person who has just entered a new country and observes a person engaging in a lot of posturing and outward demonstrations of self-importance and status (bragging, emphasizing personal titles, etc.). Is this a characteristic of a highly power-focused culture, as one might guess? Or is this particular person just overly concerned about status? Much of what people think are cultural influences may just be an individual's quirkiness and idiosyncrasy. A personal action may be cultural, or it may just be unique and odd to the person. For example, a global manager working for General Motors in a project with the Opel division in Germany said that when he first worked with his German counterpart (a fellow design engineer), he noticed she would not begin meetings promptly (contrary to how he had been advised) and wouldn't finish meetings at scheduled times. How could this be? German engineers had a reputation of nearly obsessive timekeeping and promptness. He decided that Germans weren't nearly as strict about time as he had been told by his American colleagues. However, in his next encounter, he was assigned to work with a team of five other German engineers. With this group, meetings not only began promptly according to schedule, but they finished at their scheduled point even if more work was still waiting. This variation in timekeeping and schedules is the type of difference we find among different people in all countries. The trick for CQ is separating out one person's quirks from most people's general tendencies.

The generalization of personal idiosyncrasy to cultural values and norms is one of the most common pitfalls facing a global manager. Someone with high CQ is able to distinguish between a person's idiosyncratic actions and general cultural patterns. However, this is one of the most difficult aspects of understanding — separating personal eccentricity from cultural norms for appropriate behavior. A person with high CQ looks for stable patterns of actions across people and situations to infer what is personal and what is general for a given culture. This may require the development of new strategies for action or the adaptation of existing ones. For example, our GM engineer needs to think about time and schedules in Germany outside of the Opel plant. Do Germans keep accurate and tight schedules for the train system? Shops? Theater events? Parades? It's important to consider various kinds of settings and to understand whether timekeeping is important everywhere and across most people or, perhaps, just at work, or just for engineers, or just for GM engineers at work!

When you watch people from other cultures, you are likely to make generalizations of unique actions to an entire group — this is what we mean by reverse stereotyping (imposing the characteristics of an individual onto his or her group). A high-CQ person separates quirkiness from culture. This same point can be made in a diversity context. When people from diverse backgrounds come together they may interpret a person's actions in terms of preexisting ideas concerning the person's groups. The difference between distinctions among various nations and diversity (different groups in a single country) is that you are probably better able to understand the various groups of people living in your own country than groups from another country. So understanding individual diversity means that we have something to build from — we share national culture imperfectly, but at least we do share some of it. High CQ provides additional benefits for figuring out what is going on in another group within your own culture, and furthermore, you're got a head start when dealing with your own culture than when working with a completely new one.

Team-Level Diversity

A natural extension of individual-level diversity is that of a person's identity in a work team. Here we refer to diversity in a team as the various roles people perform when they work with others. From the perspective of diversity, a work team has a number of important features. Team members who are similar to one another often report stronger affinity for their team than do dissimilar team members. Attitude similarity and demographic similarity are generally positively related to group cohesiveness. People on teams who share similar backgrounds such as age, gender, or occupational background are often more satisfied and have lower absenteeism than those with dissimilar backgrounds, and their teams have lower turnover.

These findings are consistent with the well-established principle that we talked about in the last section: people are attracted to others who are like them. Indeed, research suggests that cultural diversity generates conflict, which in turn reduces the ability of a group to maintain itself over time and to provide satisfying experiences for its members. In addition, team heterogeneity has certain administrative costs, such as increasing coordination costs, as people try to understand and work with each other.

This sounds as if team diversity is a negative thing. However, work by scientists studying top management teams has demonstrated some positive effects on performance. For example, based on a study of nearly two hundred banks, researchers found that both diversity of education and diversity of work function were positively related to innovation. The management professor Donald Hambrick and his colleagues looked at thirty-two major U.S. airlines over eight years. Top management teams that were diverse, in terms of functional backgrounds, education, and company tenure, showed a greater propensity to take action. But they were also slower in their actions and responses and less likely than similar teams to respond to competitors' initiatives.

Diversity is not necessarily a simple thing that employees either like or dislike. The first author's work with Amy Randel shows that people working in diverse teams have a mixed reaction to diversity. As we might expect, people are most identified with and attached to their team if other team members are similar to them (low-diversity team) in traits or characteristics that are very important to them personally (perhaps political beliefs or religious views). That is, there is a negative relationship of diversity to a person's sense of group identity and team membership. However, if these characteristics or traits aren't central to how a person thinks (perhaps views of local sports teams or a person's hair color), then diversity is beneficial and group identification is enhanced. That is, more diversity on traits that aren't very important is related positively to group identity and team membership. Why is this? Given that people have a general belief that diversity is beneficial and desirable (true for most cultures), they think that a diverse team is a good one. However, if the areas in which the team is diverse are those that are personally important to the team member, then diversity is actually ego-threatening and takes away from a person's attachment to their team.

As we described earlier, at least one way to understand team diversity is through the roles and identities that members assume when they work together. The roles we adopt are based on our work situation. For example, a worker from a highly universalistic culture (where everyone and everything is treated the same regardless of who you are) is committed to an identity where people follow standard procedures, regulations, and rules regardless of the situation. If a team has a member who has a strongly universalist perspective along with members who are more particularistic in their views (rules are applied according to the situation, such as giving hiring preference to family members), the resulting conflict may be significant.

For our purposes, we focus on CQ from the point of view of someone within a diverse team and what this might imply about team functioning. Because people generally seek to strengthen their personal identity, they tend to be attracted to others of similar background and views. However, this doesn't necessarily mean that the Singaporeans will group together, the French will group together, and so on. This is because national identity isn't always all that important to every person. The traits and characteristics we consider important are influenced by our culture — but only in part. Thus, a Singaporean team member may find himself wanting to talk with others with a similar functional background, or a French team member may be attracted to others with whom he or she shares a common educational background. This might lead a Singaporean to group with team members who have different nationalities but a common functional experience. These idiosyncratic identities are keys for understanding who will work well with others on a team.

Cultural intelligence from a team-diversity perspective can be dealt with as "outside-in" or "inside" the team. That is, we can view CQ from the perspective of an outsider who is trying to understand a team (outside-in) or just from the viewpoint of an insider trying to understand her own team (inside). From an outsider's viewpoint, CQ works as described in chapter 1 (individual-level diversity), but with the added challenge of understanding how several people work together. A high-CQ person observes how team members work together, looking for each team member's dominant characteristics and actions, how these identities lead members to work together, and how the work situation of the team might make certain roles more important than others. This is a daunting task for even the keenest of observers, since there are myriad ways people might work together and explanations for why they work this way. What distinguishes a high-CQ person is effectively observing, cataloging, and analyzing team members' actions.

From an insider's view (that of a team member), CQ not only provides the benefit of enabling one to understand through figuring things out (thinking CQ) but it also helps a member keep going when confronted with the difficulties of dealing in multiple cultures and subcultures (motivational CQ). Not only do one-on-one meetings present difficulties, but a person must interpret a number of actions as team members interact with one another.

What distinguishes a diverse team of people from the same country from an internationally diverse team? The general actions of team members are likely to be interpreted using your pre-existing ideas from your own culture. Although the practices and views of people from diverse backgrounds and experiences may be highly variable, we are still talking about actions within a single nation. Does this mean that the reasons people act as they do are obvious and transparent? No.

However, in highly diverse teams with people from the same country there is still a common understanding of actions and rules that aid people as they deal with one another. Take as an example the expression of "political correctness" (avoiding offending various subgroups of people through your words chosen) across nations. Within the United States there is a strong norm of political correctness (respecting one another's differences in personal characteristics such as age, race, religion, etc.) in the business environment. This does not imply that all U.S. Americans believe in equality and are unbiased; however, there is a general taboo against expressing bias in the workplace. In a team of Americans, a general norm for political correctness exists. If this norm is broken there are formal and informal mechanisms that regulate behavior. (The former can involve legal sanctions, the latter ostracization of the offender.) A high-CQ person recognizes that, in addition to individual differences, there are common influences on action as well.

In addition to general cultural norms, there are norms and rules that teams develop to run themselves. A person with high CQ can discover these norms so as to comply with them. A high-CQ team member does not merely react passively to these rules and practices; he uses the existing rules as a way of furthering his personal agenda. The leadership scholar Manfred Kets de Vries described the process of leading people from a psychoanalytic perspective, capturing ideas of transference and attachment. A charismatic leader instills within his or her followers a sense that his or her problems are their problems. Such a leader does not merely react to the challenges facing his or her followers; rather, a charismatic leader creates a sense of urgency within them concerning the problems he or she finds most critical. Thus, a charismatic leader transfers followers' identities onto him or her to create a sense of urgency in their actions. If leaders are to be effective, they must align their personal concerns with those of their followers.

Charismatic leaders transform their personal struggles into a shared, or universal, concern that team members try to solve. For example, in an individual-focused country, such as the United States, a leader must struggle against the situation as an autonomous agent. An effective leader creates a feeling of being the underdog so that his or her followers will take on the leader's struggle as their own. In a group-focused country, such as China, the group-focused leader must struggle to confront challenges as a group rather than as an individual. In both examples, a leader needs to transfer personal challenges to the team; however, a leader's personal struggles are transferred to followers through very different methods. In the United States, a leader relies on images of the struggling individual — the single brave person going up against an unmerciful system. In China, a leader relies on images of common fate and challenge with the work unit (*danwei*) as the basis for action. It comes down to a rallying cry of "Join me" versus "Join us."

As we discuss in our chapter on leadership, one of the most effective ways for charismatic leaders to transfer these struggles to their followers is through myths and symbols. For example, a paternalistic leader will assume the role of a father figure in a society that endorses parents having a strong and controlling relationship with children. From a cultural viewpoint, it becomes clear that the charismatic trait reflects different characteristics, or themes, across cultures. The struggles of Gandhi capture relevant facets of Indian culture, but not necessarily of Italian or Swedish culture.

Similarly, a high-CQ person does not merely observe passively and analyze a situation and context. He or she promotes his or her interests and goals by using the dominant cultural themes to solidify support. As a team insider, he or she acts like a charismatic leader by drawing upon existing norms and symbols of the team as a way of moving them in the desired direction.

But what impact does our organization play in understanding CQ in multinational and diverse teams? We now turn to a discussion of the organization situation and its implications for CQ.

Organization-Level Diversity and Change

The general background for work organizations is what we refer to as organizational culture. It provides a backdrop, much in the way that national culture provides a backdrop for people's ordinary lives. It provides employees with a general frame of reference concerning the world of work around them and is a critical element for a manager seeking to understand how diversity operates across an organization.

Culture can be thought of operating on different levels, ranging from a group level to an organizational level to a national level. Edgar Schein of MIT describes culture as "what a group learns over a period of time as that group solves its problems of survival in an external environment" (Schein, 1990: 111). This suggests that any group with a set of shared experiences has a culture, and so within one nation or one organization there can be many subcultures. Once a group has created a common set of assumptions about the proper way to deal with the environment around them, its members will respond similarly with a shared pattern of thoughts and beliefs.

The perspective taken by Robert Goffee and Gareth Jones in understanding organizational culture is a very useful one. Goffee and Jones developed their approach to organizational culture and change in response to a number of changes they witnessed in modern organizations such as Royal Dutch Shell, Heineken, and Unilever. They observed that what held organizations together was not reporting relationships, functions, or departments, but more fluid, shifting relationships of collaboration and interdependence. An organization's social glue was not its formal structure, but the relationships among its employees — how they viewed the organization itself as well as one another. In the early 1990s companies such as Unilever had fiercely loyal employees who nonetheless tended to protect one another when challenged from the outside. In contrast, a company such as General Electric, with Jack Welch's "number 1, 2, or out" policy (a business unit that wasn't first or second in its business area would not be sustained), reflected a strong priority on working together for the survival of the firm.

Goffee and Jones offer a way of viewing how these social architectures were related to organizational change. Their focus is on the way values, attitudes, and behaviors are shared within organizations and how they are shaped by various organizational relationships. Their model is based on two general principles of why people interact with one another — sociability and solidarity. Sociability refers to emotional and personal relationships between people who see one another as friends or companions. Friends share certain ideas, attitudes, interests, and values and are inclined to associate on equal terms. So defined, friendship represents a type of social interaction valued for its own sake. You maintain sociability through face-to-face relations typically characterized by high levels of loyalty with no expectation of deals or obligation. Solidarity, by contrast, describes work-focused cooperation between people who may be very different from one another — and who may not like one another, for that matter. It doesn't depend on close friendship or even personal acquaintance, nor is it necessarily sustained by continuous social relations. In a work environment where solidarity is high, people work together to get the job done, not because they like each other. This distinction between sociability and solidarity is an important one, because people often assume that the coincident pursuit of goals by employees means that they're working cooperatively and socially as if goal pursuit were a unifying social bond. However, employees may doggedly pursue common goals even when they do not bond to one another socially. Similarly, just because employees have common social activities (e.g., weekend picnics for the company or company-based vacations or retreats) outside of work doesn't necessarily mean they have high solidarity.

Sociability and solidarity vary independently. Considering each factor as having high and low levels, Goffee and Jones formed a 2 × 2 typology of organizational cultures: fragmented (low sociability, low solidarity), mercenary (low sociability, high solidarity), networked (high sociability, low solidarity), and communal (high sociability, high solidarity). A fragmented organization lacks both sociability and solidarity. It might seem that such an organization is unlikely to survive, since it appears neither goal focused nor pleasant to work in. However, there is some reason to believe that fragmented organizations may be able to maintain themselves. For example, organizations that rely heavily on outsourcing and those that rely largely upon the unique contributions of individuals, such as business or law partnerships, consultancies, and the like may be predominantly fragmented. Fragmented organizations derive benefit from the autonomy and freedom granted to members. Partners in professional firms, for example, possess considerable discretion to set their own work agendas and develop their professional talents without external intervention. Likewise, entrepreneurial companies may largely succeed on the basis of one or two individuals who act somewhat independently. An entrepreneurial environment may provide the dynamic conditions that allow individual creativity to flourish. Employees who fit a fragmented work culture tend to be introverted, learning best through self-contained reflection; motivated by autonomy and independence; and capable of managing their own development. Of course, the difficulty of a fragmented work culture is that a focus on the individual may result in people pursuing their own agendas at the expense of the company. Individual freedoms may be abused, and excessive selfish actions leading to infighting. Jealousy may surface as well. Lacking some coordinated efforts, it seems unlikely that fragmented organizations will remain stable or flourish over time. It is much more likely that these organizations will succumb to the disunity that characterizes them.

In mercenary organizations, a heightened sense of competition and a strong desire for success is a central feature. The dominant value is a focus on competitiveness through personal goals and action. However, a mercenary culture differs from a fragmentary one in that personal goals are aligned with company goals. People cooperate with one another to produce benefits for themselves and their organization. Day-to-day activities are rarely cooperative because employees pursue their personal goals with great focus and direction. In a mercenary culture, if you help me achieve my goals, then I am attracted to you; if you interfere with my goal pursuits, then you aren't any damn good. So what attracts someone to a mercenary culture? People are often attracted to mercenary cultures by their meritocracy and intolerance of poor performance, their willingness to openly address conflict, and a drive to measurably improve standards. Take Jack Welch's program at General Electric concerning the bottom 10 percent redundancy action. According to this approach, each year the bottom 10 percent of employees appraised lose their jobs. This created a very strong incentive to perform, and people who are attracted to this environment strongly believe in performance and getting ahead by virtue of their personal accomplishments. Although you might expect that such a challenging environment would lead to backbiting and employees' sabotaging one another's job performance, it doesn't seem to. One manager working at GE commented to us, "It really is a great place to work because you know that if you perform well it will be recognized and rewarded — there isn't any game playing going on."

The benefits of a mercenary culture for companies operating in competitive markets are clear. Organizations with a strong focus on goals consistently outperform their counterparts. However, high solidarity is not always beneficial, since a mercenary environment is one of independent action, and much work in a modern world requires teams and interdependence. Further, a strong focus on specific goals may not be as useful as you might imagine in a dynamic and turbulent work environment: it can also result in goal myopia, which may lead a company to miss out on unexpected business opportunities. Imagine a company such as 3M with a research scientist who develops a solvent or adhesive to help him keep notes attached to papers (as was the case for what became the company's highly successful "Post-It Notes"), but is left undiscovered because such a product is unrelated to the core business goals of employees and the company. Alignment of management goals may be a problem if it means that employees overlook new products and product markets because they are overly concerned with existing ones.

Another type of organizational culture is the networked organization. Networked companies exhibit high levels of sociability with relatively low levels of solidarity and are often characterized by great loyalty and a family or clublike atmosphere, with a strong emphasis on social events and rituals that reinforce the sense of community within the organization. These rituals and social events serve to sustain a strong sense of intimacy, loyalty, and friendship, and they often extend beyond the boundary of the company, with employees engaging in various social activities and networks outside of work. However, these strong relationships and friendships don't translate into a productive work environment. Employees of such a company belong to very specific and defined networks that can best be thought of as cliques and niches that are exclusive and not inclusive. In a recent executive short course that the first author taught for Unilever, he asked an audience of thirty-five middle managers (coming from all parts of the world and of the Unilever organization) who among them might take on the duties of the new CEO of Unilever in the future. Several non-European managers quickly commented that it would never be them because "It always ends up being a European and usually Dutch or British." This view of a European clique running Unilever reflects a networked culture — it's not what you can do but who you know and where you are that matter most. In all fairness to Unilever, this assessment is not really accurate, since many senior executives come from outside Europe and one of the current co-chairmen, Niall Fitzgerald, is neither British nor Dutch (he's Irish). However, even after a decade of programs that have attempted to move Unilever from a networked to a more mercenary and communal environment, these views of cliques and in-groups persist.

Friendships may constrain the open expression of differences necessary for developing and maintaining a shared sense of purpose. People from a networked organization are extroverted and motivated by relationships; they possess good social skills and empathy; they are tolerant of ambiguity; they are friendly, likable, and loyal to their friends; they have patience; and they are prepared to build long-term relationships. However, this doesn't mean that employees from a networked culture cooperate across their in-groups. Take, for example, the idea of the Chinese social groups often referred to as *guanxi*. *Guanxi* reflects social networks dependent on norms of reciprocity and interdependence. However, *guanxi* networks may actually reduce cooperation and coordination across networks, even if such cooperation would be mutually beneficial for all parties. In looking at business negotiations, one researcher actually found that, in strong *guanxi* networks, some people would actually harm themselves in a negotiation just to make certain that the other party (out-group) didn't get ahead of them!

The final form of organizational culture is the communal form. Although it's possible for companies lacking either sociability or solidarity to survive and prosper, it seems intuitively appealing that an organization with high levels of both factors is ideal. High solidarity means that members within the organization are goal and performance focused, with a strong sense of organization welfare. High sociability means that members are interpersonally attracted to one another, share information, help one another, and so on. The combination of both factors seems ideal. However, there is good reason to argue that although a communal arrangement is ideal, it is inherently unstable. Imagine an organization with a communal atmosphere. Employees are productive, the organization achieves its goals, and people like working at the company. What might happen over time? As friendships and networks solidify, there is a shift toward a networked culture, and people start to protect and cover for one another. As this happens, it strengthens the idea that there are in-groups and out-groups. Next, resentment grows as more productive out-group employees see select in-group employees protected even if they aren't performing well. As the in-group and out-group become more polarized, people from the threatened in-group will seek to support and protect their weak members and lash out against the out-group. Very quickly, a destructive cycle occurs: from protection → sanction → protection → counterattack, and the existing environment breaks down into one of high sociability, political infighting, and reduced productivity.

Even within a single team we may see a breakdown of a communal environment. As a member of a winning team, I may be offended if you come to me and claim that I am not fulfilling my obligations. Rather than responding by attempting to work harder or more effectively, I use my political connections to protect myself and to lash back at you. Very quickly our once communal team breaks down into a fragmented group of individuals.

A communal organization has much appeal. At some point, organizations with communal cultures become somewhat cultlike: witness Anita Roddick's Body Shop or Southwest Airlines in the United States. Members tend to be passionate about their organization and so, to support it, are able to expend high levels of energy over long periods. Communal cultures can often sustain complex teams apparently divided by geography, nationality, and function, for example, but united in a common purpose and close ties between espoused values and embedded practices. Individuals who fit best in communal cultures exhibit several traits, including idealism; a willingness to make sacrifices for the greater good; attraction to teams; the ability to fully identify and commit themselves to their organization; and a desire to place their organization above all others.

The Goffee and Jones framework is a very useful one for understanding how organizational diversity and CQ interact. Organizational culture is an important backdrop for a person's adjustment. Just as with national culture, the local atmosphere or culture within an organization places a large burden on an individual as he or she attempts to work successfully within a new organization. Take, for example, a Unilever manager moving from Hindustan Lever in Mumbai to the European foods group, with its strongly networked atmosphere. His assignment is to shape the foods group into a more competitive and "leaner" business unit. (The European foods group is relatively networked, whereas Hindustan Lever is highly competitive and mercenary [borderline with communal].) What happens to this global manager as he joins a highly networked part of the organization? Upon assuming his new job responsibilities, he very quickly immerses himself in the organization's goals and direction, being ambitious to get ahead quickly. This type of manager is referred to as a "rate buster" and often experiences a strong backlash from his subordinates and co-workers, who resent his high performance.

A manager with high CQ enters into this new work culture and focuses on determining the dominant practices of the business unit as well as those relevant to his local circumstance. In a networked culture, he realizes that he must spend a significant amount of his efforts socializing and getting to know his new colleagues. Further, it's not enough for him to be productive, since members in a networked organization will shun him unless he is "one of the gang." However, it doesn't end at this point. The manager must understand not only the existing company culture, but also how to effect change in this group. How best to move a networked culture forward to a more communal or mercenary one? What are legitimate ways to create change at the European foods group while not alienating employees? CQ here doesn't simply mean understanding the current situation and adjusting to it. The task is much more challenging, since the manager has been brought in to effect change.

A person with low CQ coming from a mercenary culture is likely to misunderstand the new, networked culture. Without a proper way to comprehend how organizational cultures may differ, a low-CQ person may assume incorrectly that the cliquish atmosphere of the networked organization (in which, perhaps, little attention is paid to the new person) reflects his prior work environment, in which people avoided social distractions and focused on their work. He doesn't realize that the reason he isn't included in lots of social events is that he is an outsider; he assumes it's because everyone is busy working and doesn't have time for socializing. The Goffee and Jones approach is just one way that someone might think about these organizational cultures. In chapters 1 and 2 we referred to this as a cultural strategic thinking framework.

Another way of thinking about diversity in organizations and CQ is to think about a company's structure, rules, and practices. We sometimes refer the practice of analyzing a company by studying its institutionalized practices and structure as an institutional analysis. Think of it as studying a new country by focusing on its institutions and practices, such as political structure (democracy versus socialism), economic structure (free market or centrally controlled), marriage institution (who gets married and under what conditions), educational institution (how people are educated and what they learn), and the like. In its simplest form, an institutional analysis can be thought of as understanding a company through its persistent rules and procedures.

Companies can be thought of as a collection of rational and nonrational impulses and an organizing function. That is, they develop and perpetuate policies and rules, ideas and beliefs, myths and rituals, just as they do business. The specific nature of a given organization, with the identity and activity patterns peculiar to it, exists as a product of institutional forces. For example, General Electric has developed an institutional set of practices reflecting competition, performance, and achievement. The "fix, sell, or close" policy of the 1990s (if your business unit isn't the top 1 or 2 in its area, you get a chance to fix it, sell it, or close it) is a practice that characterizes GE's mercenary environment. Does it really make sense to continue the "fix, sell, or close" rule year after year? Isn't there some point at which GE is simply closing effective business units?

An institutional approach includes several features. Norms and values are emphasized in shaping employees' actions in their company. People are influenced by company culture through a socialization process as they join the company and learn its ways. Take, as an example, the McKinsey "boot camp," or training program. When new consultants are brought in, they are subjected to a very rigorous training regime, presenting them with a number of pressures and challenges. They are taught not only how to handle this pressure, but how to handle it with the McKinsey style. Companies create informal practices based on powerful cliques and coalitions that have formed. These structures may detract from the efficient functioning of the organization. Some of these structures arise because of what is called "isomorphism," meaning that something is imitated because people think it works. If GE has success with the 10 percent program of appraisal, then perhaps I should use it in my own company. In fact, by adopting a 10 percent program like GE's, I send out a signal to my customers and competitors that I'm as legitimate as GE! As it turns out, a number of company practices exist simply because one company has imitated another in hopes of copying their success (or avoiding their failures — look at the proliferation of golden parachute packages for senior executives in large companies during the takeover frenzy of the 1980s and 1990s).

Employees' actions in their companies reflect these sometimes subtle rituals and practices. Outside forces may lead to the adoption of certain odd rituals. For example, many aspects of product labeling reflect this concern, including ladders with labels warning the consumer not to climb on them! (One manufacturer of ladders recommends not climbing above the second rung from the bottom on a ladder with eight rungs.) Although some product labeling has clear benefits for consumers (and protection for their producers), what gets labeled and how it's labeled often becomes a political and legal concern for companies. These patterns (rules) influence the behavior of organizational members as they interact with one another. They reflect a set of mechanisms through which people's actions are guided and shaped. Diversity awareness and motivational seminars have become widespread in many Western countries even though they have no demonstrable relationship to corporate performance.

Institutional influences related to CQ come from two general directions: within a company and outside it. The rules for social interaction, expectations for a person's proper conduct, and relationships are best thought of as rituals, ceremonies, and so on that come from institutional forces. Institutions influence an employee in several ways, such as socialization, forming an identity with your company, and sanctions (avoiding them). Socialization reflects the most direct means through which organizational members are taught a company's practices and rules. It's through daily actions and activities that the situation in which we act is interpreted and changed. This is one way a single employee's actions give rise to collective practices and rituals.

Cultural intelligence, from an institutional point of view, reflects a person's ability to determine how an organization functions and its impact on the people working within it. In a sense, the various diversity levels we have discussed in this chapter build upon one another, with the individual level feeding into the team level feeding into the organization level. In the next section, we discuss how these various levels interact and what role CQ plays in understanding this interaction.

CONNECTING CULTURAL INTELLIGENCE TO VARIOUS LEVELS OF DIVERSITY

We can think of cultural intelligence as operating within a diversity context consisting of at least three layers — individual, team, and organization. To integrate these three, we look at how organizational culture and institutional practices might be related to one another. Imagine a situation in which a new person joins a company. He brings with him various experiences and ideas shaped by his old company through socialization and early experiences meeting his new colleagues. He finds himself assigned to a particular division in the company and perhaps a team within his department and division. From an individual perspective, he's motivated to maintain and present a strong "face" or self-image to others. Making a good impression on others is a central feature of these early encounters. His desire to establish and maintain his image requires that he understand what constitutes status and position in his new company. This means he must observe others and determine the basis of their status. Further, it requires him to discover how to solidify those of his own talents that are valued in the organization. For example, if he is very good in dealing with people but joins a company that emphasizes numbers and analysis, he may need to work proactively to refocus people's attention on people-oriented contributions if he wants to attain a high status.

The primary difference between a low- and a high-CQ person in this example has to do with how active they are and how effective their influence is. A low-CQ person may lack the motivation to attempt change (or persevere when initially discouraged) or the critical thinking needed to create a new mental map of the organization. Instead, he'll apply his preexisting views, with disastrous results. Additionally, he may not be able to generate the right actions to adapt and fit in with the existing organizational culture. Most important, a person with low CQ can't distinguish what motivates others within the organization and the source of such motivation. Is a fellow worker behaving the way he does because of personal background? Team norms and goals? Organization culture?

A person with high CQ distinguishes among these various levels and types of diversity (individual, team, organization) and creates new ways of dealing with his company. For example, it might be that teams are very powerful within the new company and are the primary source of power (much like a networked organizational culture). Within these teams, people may possess comparable status with a great deal of flexibility for action, or they might be hierarchically structured. A high-CQ person addresses these differences by adapting his existing ideas of how teams work to this new company situation. Further, he maintains a high level of motivation since his way of thinking about the company and his style of working with others will likely need adjustment as he learns more about the company and work situation. It's one thing to enter into a new situation knowing that you have to work hard to understand things; it's a different strength to have the resolve to abandon old ways of thinking in favor of more useful ones.

FIVE-STEP FRAMEWORK FOR DEVELOPING
HIGH-PERFORMING GLOBAL TEAMS

Once a manager has established a diverse team, the job has really just begun. Teams are like flowers beginning to bud — they must be watered and nurtured for them to blossom. What's more, they need to be cared for if they are to see another season. We present a five-step framework for making an international team more effective based on high CQ.

Step 1: Work with the Team to Establish Useful Standards

First, *a manager must work with a team to establish useful standards for the team*. These standards can be developed in a number of ways through high CQ: (1) generating the standards through team interaction; (2) aligning team standards with the unique self-motives of team members; (3) persuading members to make individual sacrifices for the sake of the team; (4) making sanctions for violating team standards clear and strong; and (5) developing a monitoring system through which individual team members' contributions to the whole can be assessed.

Viewing a team's standards as transient, however, is an incomplete picture, since it ignores an employee's culture-based personal standards. A concrete example will demonstrate our point. A German manager was sent to run a large Chinese luxury hotel in Guangzhou. One of his first observations was that the desk clerks seemed to spend a great deal of time talking with one another and quite a bit less time helping hotel guests who approached the front desk. Interpreting this as rudeness on the part of the Chinese clerks, he fired a number of people and reprimanded others. After these actions and a great deal of employee outcry, he was told by a Chinese manager that the desk clerks' behavior reflected the view that the Chinese consider interrupting a conversation with a friend in order to "serve" a customer to be rude. Our point is that these differences in cultural practices led the German manager to view the employees as rude and unfriendly.

Step 2: Lead Productive Discussions in the Team

Second, *an effective team leader must lead productive discussions within the team*. Sometimes the way you discuss matters is dictated by your culture. In the famous *ringi-sei* system of decision making in Japan, team members gain consensual support for a decision by informally testing out a decision at increasingly higher levels of their team so that all affected team members buy into the decision. This decision process is culturally determined, and the lowest member in the chain has the role and the obligation to move the decision up through the system. This approach to communication and discussion, however, is not universally applicable to teams that have other standards and values. In the power and status hierarchy found in South Korea, this form of decision making would not be appropriate, since a subordinate would never take over a superior's authority and introduce a decision on his own. In such a culture, team members would work together in order to implement work goals given from the team's leader. The participation and cooperation comes in through how the Korean teams work together on an existing project or task, rather than the initiation of such a project.

How can team processes be adapted to reflect various forms of group discussion? This can be accomplished by choosing interesting discussion points (e.g., those that are important to team members) and posing an initial question in such a way that a simple yes-or-no answer is insufficient. For example, Bill Lindemann at Hughes Aircraft does not ask his work team, "Should we do 'Y' next?" Rather, he asks, "Now that we have finished the 'X' project, what should we do next?" The open-ended question, with the initial reference to past projects, encourages people to think about what would logically follow; it can't be answered by a simple yes-or-no response.

Another important way for a team leader to manage team communication is to allow team members time to respond. Often, team members have ideas that are somewhat underdeveloped; these ideas evolve as team discussion unfolds. A wise team leader will give key questions to team members prior to the discussion so that they can think about the issues, and the leader lets people have some silent moments during discussion so that they can gestate a bit. Even though these silent periods may seem awkward and uncomfortable, they can be invaluable in allowing team members to assemble their ideas. We might remember as well that these quiet periods (and other patterns of discourse in a team's discussion) will reflect self-knowledge and culture. For instance, it's considered quite inappropriate for a Korean worker to question a superior's statement or judgment. It's even difficult to solicit input from an employee, because the employee does not want to contradict what a superior might say. In Italy employees feel perfectly free to disagree openly with their superiors, and they will likely do so. Clearly, the rules for soliciting discussion must be adapted to cultural practices. In countries with a high power distance, discussion must be carefully led by a team leader, with an emphasis on letting people express themselves. For instance, team members might be encouraged to meet with one another without the leader present to reduce the concern that their opinions might differ from those of the leader.

In each team there may be differences among members concerning their individual status, and this will have an impact on who discusses what and how the discussion will proceed.

In Japan the very nature of the language conveys role and status as people speak with one another. Much of what is conveyed within a team is not actually said but is instead conveyed by who speaks and how something is said.

Step 3: Develop Team Goals

The third step for an effective team is to *develop goals for its own action*. Of course, an effective team does not establish unrealistically difficult goals for itself; the likely outcome of such goals is that the team will fail to achieve them, and members may in time become disillusioned with the team. How does a team set useful team goals, and how can a manager develop effective team goals for subordinates? First, the team must monitor its own performance and productivity, so that it has a sense of what it can and cannot achieve. Second, team members must buy into the goals through some means (e.g., team participation), and the importance of achieving these goals must be emphasized. For a self-focused culture, the team goals must be tied to outcomes for individual team members, whereas for a group-focused culture, the success and recognition of the group is reward enough for team members. Finally, the team needs to focus on its work practices so as to continually improve on existing practices.

Step 4: Cope with External Pressures

So far we have emphasized the way a team deals with its internal functioning. For the fourth step, we turn briefly to the way an effective team deals with the world around it. How can a team *cope with external pressures that it may face*?

To begin, we need to remember that each team faces outsiders who are themselves often members of other teams. This means that these outsiders represent their own teams and their personal interests as they place demands on others. So we begin by understanding the underlying goals and motives that represent the outsiders and their respective teams. Why are many managers within General Motors aggressive in their attitude about GM's successful Saturn car company? Perhaps Saturn is threatening to their own division because of its low sales, and this, in turn, is threatening to the managers. Another possibility is that the Saturn division represents a radical break from existing procedures, and this threatens an entrenched way of thinking — in other words, it threatens the status quo.

There are a number of things that an effective international team can do to fend off the advancements of others, such as (1) avoiding the influencer if possible; (2) determining the other person's (or persons') source of power and see if it can be eroded; (3) co-opting others to support the team's goals; (4) ingratiating team members to powerful others; and (5) becoming such an integral part of operations that other teams depend on the team for their own effectiveness. This last point is particularly useful, since it helps transform an us-versus-them attitude into one of mutual dependence and cooperation.

Step 5: Reward the Team's Work and Efforts

The fifth step concerns *the way that work and effort are rewarded in an organization.* There are a number of ways that rewards can be distributed among team members, such as equity, individual effort, equality, and need. What is relevant to our discussion is that the exchanges that occur within a team may be guided by several different rules that vary according to cultural values. For example, psychologists Kwok Leung and Michael Bond found that in group-focused cultures, such as China and Taiwan, equity (people receive rewards on the basis of their personal accomplishments) and equality (people receive an equal share of the rewards regardless of their contribution) reward systems are preferred depending on whether a person is dealing with the person's own team or another team. When dealing with their own teams, Chinese managers prefer to use an equality norm for giving out rewards, whereas in dealing with people from another team they followed a strong equity norm.

Of course, the rewards that are given out in a team must be tailored to the needs of the individual members as well. The American football coach Bill Walsh claimed that he tailored his nurturing of quarterback Joe Montana to Montana's own specific traits. He made certain that he rewarded Montana's willingness to rely on his own instincts, something that Montana seemed hesitant to do himself. In an effective team, members are rewarded according to their personal and cultural needs.

We would expect cultural variations in what people expect in terms of having a say in their team's functioning as well as their satisfaction with it. For example, in a highly group-focused culture, we might find that the chance to voice one's opinions does not give a big, incremental return, since these people already give their input. Try *not* giving a Swede or an Israeli the opportunity to express an opinion and see what happens! It may, however, have a stronger impact in a more independent culture where such opportunities emphasize the importance of each member as a unique person. Thus, the nature of exchange in teams reflects cultural differences and similarities in terms of rewards and of having a say in the team's procedures.

USING THE $GR^2 = T$ FORMULA

Putting these various pieces together, we see that there are three essential ingredients for a successful international team. We refer to this as the "Great Teams" formula:

$$GR^2 = T$$

where G = goals, R = roles, R = rules, and T = trust and commitment. That is, a team must have three essential elements to be successful: clear goals and direction, defined roles for each person on the team, and accepted and shared rules for how to operate. If these three elements are combined, then the result is trust and commitment to the team. A high-CQ manager is able to determine the right combination of goals, roles, and rules for a given team based on members' personal and cultural backgrounds.

SUMMARY

In this chapter we examined the potential contribution of cultural intelligence as a way of dealing with diversity in organizations. We analyzed diversity on three levels — individual, team, and organization — and we discussed how the core aspects of identity and diversity relate across the levels of analysis.

At the individual level, diversity reflects a person's unique and idiosyncratic aspects, including educational background, inherited traits, acquired skills and knowledge, and unique experiences. Cultural intelligence plays an important role in helping people understand one another and separating these idiosyncratic differences from more general patterns across people. Further, we looked at motives that guide a person's viewpoint as a way of understanding the type of representations that a high-CQ person must make to be an accurate observer and interpreter of others' actions.

Next we examined diversity from a team perspective by looking at various features of teams, including composition and internal dynamics. The roles that people draw from as they work with others on their team are critical for understanding their actions. A person's CQ relates to his or her ability to understand what traits and characteristics are important to a person and how to deal with people accordingly. Does my teammate value formal educational background? Work titles? Functional background? Nationality? Although the demands of figuring these issues out within a single nation are not as complicated as across nations, assessing the relevance of diversity within your own nation requires additional thoughtfulness because people's views are imperfectly shared within a single nation. Further, the complexity of team interactions makes it difficult for a person to fully appreciate the team dynamics that might be observed.

Finally, we looked at diversity as it relates to an organization's culture and structure. A person with high CQ has a greater capacity to operate within a wide variety of organizational cultures (flexible and adaptive) as well as to understand how such cultures might impact the perceptions and interactions of others in the organization.

What should be clear from our discussion is that the capabilities afforded an individual with high CQ are useful for both international and diverse settings. In the case of diversity within a country, much of the thinking and understanding will occur at an immediate level on the basis of partially shared experiences. I may not fully share a sense of American culture with all other Americans, but there is something distinctive about being American that I take with me wherever I go. As the novelist John Steinbeck suggested in his book *America and the Americans*, there is something distinctive about people's nationality that they take with them regardless of circumstance. Similarly, with respect to the action aspect of CQ, people from a single country share more. Gestures and their meanings are held in common with others in the same country even if they come from diverse backgrounds (e.g., the "thumbs up" for success in Britain or the *wai* for respect in Thailand). Motivation and a willingness to persevere are arguably the same as in an international context. However, a person who crosses international boundaries may be less persistent when faced with rejection than in his or her own country, assuming that with proper diligence he or she can understand his or her own country but not necessarily a different one. Crossing a national boundary may lower these expectations a great deal, so persistence wanes as a person is confronted with his or her own mistakes. To operate in diverse work situations, a manager must be prepared with high CQ to maneuver past the barriers of cultural misunderstanding.

8 | LEADING GLOBALLY

Effective leadership is one of the most powerful competitive advantages an organization can have. Whenever we meet a success or failure of any organization, we automatically think of its leadership.

Although leadership may transcend cultural boundaries, what constitutes *effective* leadership is nonetheless culture specific. An authoritarian and forceful leader may be very well regarded in one culture but not in another. Another leader who is getting on in years may command great respect in a culture that respects age but be seen as past his or her prime in another.

Leadership behaviors that are effective in one culture are not necessarily effective in others. While some leadership qualities or practices may be universal, other leadership qualities, styles, and principles are situational or culture specific. So if a manager leads others from different cultures, then cultural intelligence becomes indispensable for leadership success.

In this chapter, we begin by laying the basic foundation of leadership. We discuss what we mean by leadership and identify the qualities of leaders and leadership styles that apply equally well across cultures as well as those that do not. Then we present a six-stage process of leadership and examine how cultural variations in different parts of the world will guide what leadership styles and practices are effective in each stage. We end the chapter by providing questions that serve as catalysts for your own reflections to help you develop into a culturally intelligent global leader.

WHAT IS LEADERSHIP?

We estimate over 12,000 books, papers, articles, and studies on leadership, making leadership one of the most popular business ideas. Despite this abundance of material, there is no single commonly held view of what leadership is. Effective leadership is intuitively appealing but difficult to describe plainly. There are many theories about and perspectives on leadership. Some try to identify the personal qualities of an effective leader. Other theories look at leadership styles — the behaviors leaders display in leading followers. Another stream of leadership research focuses on the leadership process and how we can develop and nurture leaders. In this chapter, we examine leadership from a process perspective and define leadership as *the process whereby a person influences and inspires others toward achieving a desirable common vision, goal, or objective.*

This definition of leadership suggests three specific characteristics:

1. Leadership is a *process*, a set of activities that a leader does. Leadership is not about holding a position of power. It is a common mistake to believe that so long as someone holds a position of power in an organization, he or she is a leader. In this book, we focus on the actions and behaviors of a leader, not whether someone sits in any position of authority or status.

2. Leadership is a *relationship*; it focuses not only on leaders' behaviors, but also on the relationship between the leader and his or her followers. It makes sense only to talk about behaviors of leaders only if leaders' behaviors impact followers.

3. Leadership is *influence* — the process *of influencing and inspiring* followers toward a common vision and goal.

HOW UNIVERSAL ARE THE PERSONAL QUALITIES OF EFFECTIVE LEADERS?

Robert House, from the Wharton Business School of the University of Pennsylvania, initiated a worldwide study of global leadership styles and behaviors called the GLOBE project. It involved 170 social scientists and research scholars from sixty-three cultures around the world. The GLOBE project identified leader qualities that are admired as attributes of effective leadership in one culture but seen as impediments in others. For example, in high-power-distance cultures, where followers are expected to obey leaders unquestioningly, then "domineering" or "status conscious" can be regarded as qualities of an effective leader. In individualistic

TABLE 8.1
The six-stage process of global leadership

1. *Formulating a global vision:* Setting the future direction for the local organization that is aligned with headquarters but adapted to local conditions
↓
2. *Communicating the global vision across cultures:* Promoting and garnering buy-in among locals to the new vision
↓
3. *Planning, budgeting, and scheduling of local organizations:* Developing a local agenda, timetable, and milestones for meeting the vision
↓
4. *Designing the local organizational structure:* Creating an appropriate local organizational structure and staffing it with the appropriate individuals
↓
5. *Influencing and motivating locals:* Delegating responsibilities, setting goals, building teams, and creating incentive systems appropriate for the locals
↓
6. *Monitoring and controlling locals' performance:* Monitoring results, identifying deviations from plans, and taking corrective actions with feedback that is appropriate for the locals

cultures, where people prefer to work alone, leaders who are independent, autonomous, risk taking, and ambitious will be rated as more effective.

THE SIX-STAGE PROCESS OF GLOBAL LEADERSHIP

In the preceding section we reviewed some important ideas about leadership, looking at current research findings into the qualities and behaviors of leaders that differ across cultures. In this section, we describe six critical stages of the leadership process in a global setting. The six stages are set out in Table 8.1 as *formulating a global vision* (setting the local organization's future direction); *communicating the global vision across cultures* (communicating with locals in such a way as to create a common destiny and identity); *planning, budgeting, and scheduling of local organizations* (establishing detailed steps and milestones for achieving the vision); *designing the local organizational structure* (creating an appropriate local organizational structure for accomplishing the plans and staffing it with the appropriate individuals); *influencing and motivating locals* (delegating responsibilities and authority and developing business processes to streamline workflow and activities to get work done; and *monitoring and controlling locals' performance* (monitoring results, identifying deviations from plans, and problem solving by taking corrective and preventive actions with feedback that is appropriate for the locals).

Stages 1 and 2 in the leadership process are concerned with creating a vision, while stages 3 to 6 focus on realizing that vision.

Stage 1: Formulating a Global Vision

> Where there is no vision, the people perish.
> *Proverbs 29:18*

According to John Kotter of the Harvard Business School, a corporate vision refers to an image of the future that serves to clarify the general direction for change, motivate and challenge people to take action in the right direction, and help coordinate the actions of different people. A global vision is a dream for the future that transcends national boundaries — a dream that is attractive yet attainable. A good global vision for an organization must:

1. be future oriented;
2. transform organizations into global players;
3. appeal to worthwhile global ideals;
4. reflect achievable goals; and
5. excite and be easily communicated globally.

The process of creating a vision is not easy. Organizations typically develop very effective managers to plan and manage implementation of a vision, but managers often aren't good visionaries. Many managers think that creating a vision for the company is akin to planning. So, when a good manager is asked to create a vision, you'll likely hear an operating plan. These operating plans are neither future oriented nor transformational in nature, so they are unable to redirect or inspire action to create a vision. The case example in box 8.1 illustrates the difficulties in vision creation faced by a global leader who may be an excellent manager but is not a visionary leader.

From this episode of vision creation, we can observe that Hans Peter is an effective manager. The cultural intelligence Hans Peter showed as a leader was reflecting in his involving his divisional heads in values formulation for the firm. Although the values-creation team members were disappointed that Hans Peter did not spend more time espousing those values at the meeting, they were satisfied to have participated in such a high-level management decision-making exercise.

However, although Hans Peter may have been a culturally intelligent leader, he was not a visionary. Hans Peter's sharing of a vision that is based on money

BOX 8.1
Hans Peter, global leader

Hans Peter*, a top executive from Switzerland, was posted to India to head its regional headquarters in Mumbai. Hans Peter is quite culturally seasoned. In the beginning of his career he worked for a couple of years in Brazil, then went back in Switzerland. He didn't stay in Switzerland for long before leaving for many years for Thailand to head a small subsidiary in Bangkok. After Thailand, he was transferred to India to head its regional headquarters.

Hans Peter is quite impressive when you meet him for the first time; the clarity of his mind was obvious when he talked about a number of things. But once you get to know him better, you notice that he always tells the same stories and talks about the same things. His mind isn't actually very broad, but he is well able to push things in the direction he wants.

A year into his posting in India, Hans Peter received news that his Swiss headquarters had started a major change program that would affect all subsidiaries, including the regional headquarters in India. The change program was part of a company-wide business processing reengineering initiative to redesign all business processes to ensure a leaner management team.

As part of the change program, Hans Peter was asked by headquarters to develop the mission and the vision and values statement for his regional headquarters in Mumbai. Switzerland sent a change team to India to help out with the creation of the mission, vision and value statement for India. Hans Peter is more an action-oriented person than an "ideas" person. Broad "big picture" formulation was outside his comfort zone of "money making" and "hard facts." All he could envision is that the subsidiaries in India must be "money making."

The change team insisted that Hans Peter created a more sophisticated mission, vision and values statement for India. Hans Peter knew from his experience with Indians that the Indian work cultures tend towards vertical collectivism. In vertical collectivistic cultures, people shy away from making decisions and allow the person at the helm the authority to dictate (high power distance). However, they do like to feel that they have participated in a group and that they are part of the solution (collectivistic).

*Not his real name.

Hans Peter decided to enlist support from the division heads of the Mumbai operations. He called a meeting among the Indian division heads and proposed that they work together as a team to come up with values for the company. He told the division heads to "come up with some values for the company."

The Indian division heads undertook the task enthusiastically. They valued the opportunity to participate in such an important task, one that represented the future of their organization. They brainstormed conscientiously for four to five weeks before coming up with a comprehensive list of values that they thought would identify who they were and what the Indian regional headquarters stood for.

When the values were presented to Hans Peter, he quickly identified a few saying, "These are the three or so values that we should focus on." In the mind of Hans Peter, this exercise of identifying values was more for the benefit of meeting the requirements of the change team than for his operations in India.

making was not inspiring. He did not understand the nature of visioning. As a result, he did not give much time to both vision *and* values. He is obviously too operationally goal oriented and task focused. He is not very forward thinking and finds it difficult to develop new directions and vision for the firm.

Stage 2: Communicating the Global Vision across Cultures

Once a vision is created, it has to be communicated. Communicating is more than telling. To communicate a vision, global leaders must reach out to local followers in such a way that enables the locals to internalize the leader's dream. When a global leader is effective in communicating the global vision, followers see vivid images of the organization's brighter future and enthusiastically respond to the new ideal. Some cultures, particularly collectivistic cultures such as India's, prefer personal, face-to-face modes of communication. Box 8.2 illustrates how Hans Peter communicated his vision to the Indian locals he led.

Hans Peter again showed his culturally intelligent leadership by bringing everyone together from all over India to communicate the vision. Everyone felt important that Hans Peter had given them due respect by including them at the meeting. Hans Peter showed his CQ prowess by making the final decision on which values

---

BOX 8.2
Communicating the vision

Hans Peter invited all six hundred of the top and middle managers to Mumbai from different offices and subsidiaries all over India to share his vision and value statement as well as the company's current financial situation worldwide.

Hans Peter dominated the meeting and talked mostly about the company's financial status. Only toward the very end of the meeting did he announce that they would now discuss the new vision and values. He put up a transparency that read, "This is our vision: we want to earn $X by 2010." But before flashing the next transparency, which would have showed the values, he seemed to change his mind. Instead, he said, "This transparency with the values will be distributed, so you can all read it on your own time." He went on to dwell at length on the importance of meeting the target of $X by 2010.

---

the company ought to pursue. In a high-power-distance country such as India, it is important that the leader take responsibility and accountability for making the final decision, because that's the kind of leader Indians respect.

Hans Peter was not effective in communicating his vision. Hans Peter did not present an exciting image of the organization of the future. Instead, he concentrated too much on making operating profits in the near term. His middle and top managers in India were uninspired by his presentation and felt that it offered no change in direction.

Once a vision is created and communicated, then the real work of realizing the vision begins. Realizing the vision comprises the next four stages: planning and budgeting; organizing and staffing; influencing and motivating; and controlling and monitoring through feedback.

Stage 3: Planning, Budgeting, and Scheduling of Local Organizations

Planning, budgeting, and scheduling involve the development of both tangible and intangible organizational goals that are aligned with the vision of the company. Tangible goals are those measured in monetary terms. An example of a quantitative goal could be to make $1 million in profit per year for the next five years. Goals that are intangible in nature are not necessarily unquantifiable; however, they are measured not by a monetary yardstick, but by other criteria. An industry's most preferred employer is determined by industry benchmark studies that focus on how satisfied the employees are and how much the company invests in developing the human capital of the firm.

Stage 3 involves allocating resources, such as money, personnel, land, facilities, equipment, and others, to achieve these goals. Strategic decisions about resource allocation will include how much money and how many people are devoted to various functions of the organization, including research and development (R & D), marketing, production, operations, sales and after-sales, and general and administrative functions.

This stage also involves identifying milestones and mapping specific deadlines for various projects that further those goals by making decisions regarding what to do and who and how to do it. The milestones and deadlines serve as a blueprint focusing the actions of people in the organization on achieving its goals.

Stage 4: Designing the Local Organizational Structure

Designing the local organizational structure involves deciding how the organization is to be structured, both horizontally and vertically. By horizontal structure, we refer to the way tasks and activities performed by an organization are subdivided into smaller units or divisions in an organization. The basic building blocks for designing organizational structure are based on function, geography, products, or some combination of these.

Functional structure divides an organization into separate business functions such as marketing, production, R & D, accounting and finance, and information technology (IT). Functional structure is the simplest and most efficient way of organizing, because it reaps the benefits of an economics of scale by placing people who perform the same or similar jobs in the same location.

Product structure divides the organization by product line, and geographic structure divides it according to geographic location. Each subunit then effectively handles one product or geographic location for the larger organization. Each unit must still perform the functional tasks of a business (e.g., marketing, accounting, etc.); therefore, functions are duplicated for each product or geographic subunit.

Few organizations adopt purely functional, product, or geographical organizational structures. As organizations globalize and become more complex, they organize themselves into hybrid structures — mixtures of function, product, and geographical structures — to cope with the complexities of the external environment.

When a company first ventures overseas, it may create a separate export or international department to deal with all international orders and customers for its products. Gradually, as the business grows, it may consider adding a foreign subsidiary by locating a subunit in another country. The foreign subsidiary often resembles a smaller version of the parent company in that it uses the same technology and produces the same product as the parent company. Organizations that create smaller versions of the parent company in different geographical units are typically termed multinational corporations.

As the organization becomes more sophisticated, it may consider a transnational form of an organization structure. Originally coined by Christopher Bartlett and Sumantra Ghoshal, the term "transnational" refers to an organization design that ignores national boundaries. In a transnational organization, each subsidiary in a different country focuses on its location advantages, so that subsidiaries in different countries take advantage of the factor costs (for example, land and raw materials) or human resources (that is, knowledge, skills, and expertise) specific to the location to gain location advantages. Transnational structures therefore leverage on global economies of scale and see location advantages.

The second major decision on designing a global organization is its vertical structure. By vertical structure, we refer to the number of authority levels in an organization. We measure vertical differentiation by the number of layers of decision making or positions in the hierarchy in the highest and lowest levels of the organization. The more layers, the greater the vertical differentiation. Vertical differentiation is related to the level of centralization and decentralization of an organization. When most decision making is concentrated at the top, an organization is perceived to be highly centralized. When decisions are delegated to more people and at lower levels, the organization is said to be decentralized.

Stage 5: Influencing and Motivating Locals

The influencing and motivating stage focuses on the leader's efforts to direct the energies of their direct reports or followers toward accomplishing the organization's strategic objectives. A leader can adopt one of a number of strategies to motivate locals:

- *Set difficult and specific goals and corresponding rewards.* Goals give followers concrete objectives and help focus their energies amidst the complexities of organizational life. Goal-directed action is a universal behavior; people consistently benefit from well-defined and challenging goals.

- *Design jobs so that the tasks are challenging and significant, and allow the individual to exercise autonomy and utilize a variety of skills and abilities.* Job design should include human resource practices such as flexible work arrangements and development opportunities for training or learning new skills.

- *Recognize employees' individual motivational differences so that they can shape their own motivation effectiveness.* Each individual is motivated by different needs and sets of values. Some value monetary rewards, such as performance bonuses or stock options; others value intangibles, such as job security or status.

Stage 6: Monitoring and Controlling Locals' Performance

This stage focuses on the systems and activities that ensure that behaviors and performance of individuals in an organization conform to the organization's rules, standards, and goals. The most prevalent control mechanism used in organization is a timely performance feedback system, where behaviors of individuals that deviate from preestablished plans or standards are highlighted and brought to the attention of the employees so that corrective and preventive actions can be taken. Regular feedback in the form of information about an individual's performance compared to his or her goals is valuable, because it signals how well each employee is doing and whether his or her current behaviors are appropriate and are meeting organizational targets. Feedback generally falls into two categories: outcome or performance feedback — whether individuals are meeting their targets — and process feedback — whether individuals are working effectively or efficiently toward meeting their targets or goals.

HOW DOES CULTURE AFFECT THE SIX-STAGE MODEL OF LEADERSHIP?

The six-stage leadership model represents a generic global leadership process. However, how a leader ought to behave in each stage of the leadership process may and can differ widely across cultures. In other words, while we can expect vision creation and vision implementation to be key components of the leadership process regardless of where leadership is practiced, how effectively a vision can be created and implemented depends in large on how sensitive each leader is to the indigenous culture of his or her followers.

TABLE 8.2
Cultural markers in leadership

	Stage in leadership process	Key cultural markers
Creating the vision:	Formulating and communicating a vision	Cultural differences in time planning horizon: short- versus long-term focus Cultural differences in company orientation: profit versus people Cultural differences in power distance: low (participative) versus high (autocratic) relationships with superiors
Realizing the vision:	Planning and scheduling	Cultural differences in time: tempo and punctuality
	Organizing	Cultural differences in power distance in organizational designs: tall versus flat; formal versus informal
	Influence and motivating	Cultural differences in goal setting at work Cultural differences in work and personal time boundaries Cultural differences in motivational needs: achievement, affiliation, and security
	Controlling and monitoring through feedback	Cultural differences in low/high context: direct versus indirect communication and feedback giving

DEVELOPING CULTURALLY INTELLIGENT GLOBAL LEADERSHIP

As organizations extend their reach beyond national boundaries, leaders of global organizations need to deal with greater diversity in terms of workforce, consumers, legal systems, and institutional frameworks. A deep understanding of cultures around the world becomes imperative for effective leadership. We believe that effective leaders are those who adapt their leadership styles to the norms and culture of his or her followers. To do that, leaders must first learn their own cultural markers — markers that characterize their own leadership behaviors and styles at each of the six stage of leadership. They must then learn to modify their leadership styles and behaviors to fit to the culture of those they are leading.

In this section we explore key cultural markers that influence effective leadership. Table 8.2 lists the major cultural markers corresponding to each step of the leadership process. The cultural markers described here are by no means comprehensive, but they serve to illustrate how culture can influence the leadership process at different stages of vision creation and implementation.

Time Horizon: Short- versus Long-Term Focus

In creating a vision, one focuses on the future. However, different cultures have different ideas about how far into the future one should create a vision for. Sony uses a 125-year strategic planning horizon, compared with 5 to 10 years for most Western companies. U.S. organizations have a shorter term horizon, which focuses on short-term shareholder returns. U.S. managers' personal leadership styles emphasize short-run performance. In contrast, Chinese, Korean, and Japanese organizations have longer time horizons, which focus on growth orientation. Asian managers' personal leadership styles emphasize company survival and long-run performance. European organizations such as the French tend to have a middle-term time horizon that falls somewhere between the Americans' and the Asians'.

To illustrate the contrast in time horizons, let's take a look at Singapore Airlines (SIA), an Asian organization that thrives on long-term thinking and orientation. SIA regularly employs world-renowned experts to test and rate unmarked bottles of Champagne, Chardonnay, Cabernet, and Merlot that are sourced globally. The wines are selected but are then cellared for at least eight to nine years before SIA serves them to its passengers. This is to ensure that the wine has developed the right body and character for drinking. Such care for the details of customer service exemplifies the long-term vision and thinking of SIA.

Recall as well our discussion from chapter 4 about monochronic and polychronic cultures. In a monochronic culture, such as that of the United States, people think about time as a sequence of events ever stretching into the future. Action A is followed by action B, which is followed by action C. In a polychronic culture, such as Brazil's, people see time as more muddied, and they often engage in multiple actions at any given time (e.g., a Brazilian manager motions you to enter his office for your appointment while speaking on the phone, working on his computer, and writing a memo).

Orientation: Profit versus People

Cultures differ in the emphasis they place on financial profits and shareholder returns. Two researchers find that vision and mission statements of United Kingdom and France reflect the underlying cultural and institutional differences. Like those in the United States, U.K. organizations create visions that reflect their capitalistic economic orientation. Mission statements of U.K. and U.S. organizations focus more on profit and shareholder returns while downplaying the importance of employee and social priorities. In contrast, other European countries, notably the French, create visions that more closely reflect the country's philosophy of social democracy, by focusing more on employee welfare and service to society and less on financial profit or shareholder returns. European managers tend to be more people oriented. So, even when a certain strategy requires layoffs, they will time it so as to make it as painless as possible.

Some Asian countries tend to be more people oriented. Thai auto companies in the 1997 economic meltdown avoided laying off workers, keeping the operations minimal but alive to ride out the economic crisis. Through their dedication to their employees, Thai companies now enjoy the commitment and loyalty of their employees, with minimal union interference and demands, and are now indisputably the "Detroit of the East."

Power Distance: Participatory versus Autocratic Relationships with Superiors

Power distance refers to how far apart leaders and followers feel from each other. In high-power-distance cultures, leaders and followers do not socialize with each other regularly, followers address leaders formally, and the status of leaders is much revered by followers. In low-power-distance cultures, followers feel comfortable socializing with their leaders, addressing them as peers, and questioning their directives, and they expect to have input and decision-making rights with their bosses.

Leaders from cultures where power distance is high, such as those of Asian countries (including China, Taiwan, Korea, and India) prefer to make autocratic decisions concerning the mission and vision of the company. Strategic decisions such as setting the mission and vision of the company are made in a top-down fashion. Top-down decision making is in fact expected of the leaders, with subordinates taking a passive role in receiving the communication of vision and plans for the future. In contrast, with leaders from cultures where power distance is low, such as those of Western nations, where participatory democracy is valued, a more participatory form of vision creation is deemed a more effective style of leadership.

Subordinates in high-power-distance countries also avoid making decisions or taking on any responsibilities for making any decisions. In a high-power-distance country such as Japan or India, it is important that the leader make the final decision. Followers enjoy having input, but they like to feel that someone is in charge.

Cultural Differences in Tempo and Punctuality

Different cultures differ in their orientation toward tempo and punctuality when it comes to planning and budgeting. Robert Levine, the U.S. social psychologist who devoted his career to the study of time across cultures, found that tempo — the speed of life — tends to be positively correlated with the degree to which a society is industrialized. Industrialization promotes producing and consuming. In his fascinating book *The Geography of Time*, Levine showed that as societies promote more producing and consuming, they experience a greater scarcity of time, since any free time becomes absorbed into more production or consumption.

In cultures where people emphasize social relationships and social obligations and seek to foster harmony, time often plays a less crucial part. In these cultures, people tend to operate on what Levine labels "event time." Events begin and end by mutual consensus, when participants feel the time is right. Therefore, there is greater temporal flexibility and spontaneity in cultures that operate under event time rather than clock time.

In contrast, cultures that value greater speed and higher efficiency people also value punctuality. They plan, schedule, and budget work using clock-time metrics — of days, hours, minutes, and seconds. In these cultures, workers use the clock to schedule the beginning and ending of activities. The ticking of the clock governs the start and completion of tasks and activities. A friend from South America commented that while living in the United States he threw a birthday party for his son, inviting friends of the family from the United States, Central America, and South America. The invitation said that the party was scheduled from 2:00 to 4:00 P.M. on a Saturday. His U.S. friends showed up promptly at 2:00 P.M. and then departed promptly at 4:00 P.M. Several of his Central and South American friends were twenty to thirty minutes late; one friend came ninety minutes late. Not only did they come after the party was scheduled to begin, but they stayed on past 4:00 P.M.; a few of them didn't leave until nearly 2:00 A.M. the following morning. One Argentinean friend was a bit offended by the invitation and asked him why he was so anxious to get rid of them by posting the ending time for the party on the invitation!

What all this means is that in many countries, such as the United States, Germany, or England, people view time as a linear and finite resource. They therefore value time, seek to save time, and are concerned about not wasting time and about being timely and punctual. In these societies, where punctuality is very important, being late might be seen as being incompetent. In contrast, in other countries, such as India, Mexico, and South America, people take time as it comes, so norms of punctuality are not governed by the clock, and, hence, completing the

BOX 8.3
When is work ever going to get done?

Lawrence*, a British CFO, arrived in India and called a meeting with fifteen division heads to brainstorm the plans and milestones for the next six months. At the meeting, Lawrence was amazed at how quickly everyone was able to set a date for each plan and delivery milestone. He thought to himself, "They are so quick to establish dates for this and that, but are they really thinking about whether those dates are feasible?" It appeared as if they were not too concerned about potential contingencies that might arise to derail the milestones or deadlines set. He recalled the experiences he had at home, where much time was spent mulling over milestones, and deadlines were determined only after all the potential delays and contingencies were considered. As pleased as he was with his Indian counterparts at their apparent ease in setting deadlines, Lawrence harbored a nagging uneasiness as to whether they could actually deliver on those deadlines.

At another time, when the heads again decided on a deadline almost without deliberation, Lawrence interjected, "You can't really put a date on that now, because this really depends on how other targets will be reached, which at this point, are not yet clear!"

The division heads stared at him. Then one of them responded, "Let's put down a date — we can change it in two weeks."

Lawrence discovered that deadlines in the India time are flexible. In India one works with immense flexibility and shifting milestones. Unlike what Lawrence was accustomed with in Britain, in India it is all right not to meet deadlines and simply set up another deadline as you come close to the original one.

After a month, Lawrence discovered that none of the major milestones the division heads had established had been met. Indians do indeed operate under flexible time orientation, where deadlines and milestones are "stretchable." In India, because there are so many unforeseen circumstances and emergencies, the best way to cope with them is not to try and predict them, but to simply put down a deadline and adapt spontaneously to unexpected events as they arise.

*Not his real name.

Lawrence became very frustrated and upset with the fact that deliverables were not being met. To show that he "meant business," he started making demands for a specific report to be completed in two weeks. However, as each day passed, no one seemed to take heed of his demands, and little headway was made in completing the report.

Two days before the deadline, Lawrence became resigned to the fact that another deadline would be missed. Surprisingly, though, in those two days there was a sudden flurry of activity — the division head in charge of the project seemed miraculously to be able to garner support to meet the deadline. Employees at all levels stayed and worked overtime throughout the forty-eight-hour period to complete the report and print the number of copies the CFO needed to present to the head office. Lawrence reflected that this last-minute garnering of resources would not have occurred as easily back in his home country. He remembered one occasion on which employees needed to gather some data for a report to be presented to the board of directors the next day. Very few people were willing to stay late at the office to get the report done, saying, "You should have told us two or three days before! Now we have to go home." Individuals from Western Europe prefer to stick to original plans, and few people are willing to change their own plans and stay late at the office in order to meet a changed deadline.

On another occasion, Lawrence was upset with the non-delivery of an important component part from another subsidiary in India. He demanded an explanation from the head of operations of the subsidiary. Venki, the head of operations, was equally astounded by Lawrence's demands. In Venki's view, given that it was the monsoon season, Lawrence should have expected delays; he should never have expected timely delivery.

task on schedule may not be critical. Rather, time is perceived as more flexible and ambiguous. The emphasis is on human relationships and completion by mutual consent, and temporal flexibility is widely tolerated if not the norm in planning and budgeting in organizations. The example in box 8.3 illustrates the frustration Lawrence feels interacting and working with people with different time orientations.

Lawrence faces a culture that thinks of and deals with time differently from his own. In many countries time is thought of as infinite and plentiful. Deadlines are seen as expressions of desirable goals or intentions, not as hard commitments. Individuals prefer to keep their options open and to be free to act spontaneously, and they like to adapt to changing situations. When time is seen as scarce, individuals like to be prepared, and they expect a set plan to be followed. On the other hand, when time is seen as plentiful, then individuals with that time orientation act more spontaneously and usually adjust well to surprises. They are more casual about time and respond to opportunities as they arise.

A central issue for those with a scarce-time orientation is their need for closure. In their drive and need for closure, individuals with a scarce-time orientation find it difficult to leave what they are doing and want to complete their tasks as planned. However, individuals with a plentiful-time orientation tend to be more casual and spontaneous in style, preferring to disregard rules they think are unnecessary or restrictive.

Power Distance in Organizational Designs:
Tall versus Flat, Formal versus Informal

Different cultures adopt different organizational designs. Notably, different cultures have different shapes of hierarchies. Steep hierarchies or "tall" organizations have many vertical levels and a smaller span of control at each level. An example of a tall organization is the Bank of Tokyo-Mitsubishi, which has more than ten hierarchical layers, from clerical officer to the country head manager in overseas branches. A flat organization, in contrast, has fewer vertical layers and therefore a wider span of control. Power distance is not just a matter of formal structure or reporting lines; a family-owned business in Taiwan may be formally "flat," with few formal layers in the hierarchy, but clearly led with a top-down decision style by the company president or owner.

Countries where the national cultures are hierarchical, paternalistic, and familial in nature perceive their leader as a father. The leader in steep-pyramid structures commands great authority and power over the followers and tends to have "adult-child" power relationships with followers. Paternalistic and familial-based cultures include those of Turkey, China, Venezuela, Pakistan, India, Mexico, Hong Kong, Singapore; these nations prefer steeper hierarchies in designing organizations. In more egalitarian cultures, such as the United States, Norway, Denmark, and Canada, there is a preference for flatter organizational hierarchies. Leaders in flat organizations rely less on personal power and authority and more on explicit rules, standards, and procedures. Box 8.4 illustrates the problems a global leader faced and lessons he learned while trying to implement a

---

BOX 8.4

Flattening organizations in a high-power-distance country

We return to Hans Peter, the CEO from Switzerland who was posted to India to head its regional headquarters in Mumbai. Recall that a year into his posting in India, Hans Peter received news that his Swiss headquarters had started a major change program that would affect all subsidiaries, including the regional headquarters in India. The change program was part of a company-wide business processing reengineering initiative to redesign all business processes to ensure a leaner management team. After examining the existing structure, Hans Peter decided to reorganize from an existing highly centralized and pyramidal structure of six large divisions (with six division heads) to a flatter structure comprising fifteen smaller divisional units.

Such a change in organizational structure posed a number of problems. First, there had been very little succession planning in the organization because there had been very little change of personnel in and out of leadership positions. The heads of all six divisions had been at the helm for the past twenty years and would be retiring within the next five years. Because of the high-power-distance culture in India between the leader and his or her direct reports, executive succession planning is not commonly practiced. This made it difficult to select and appoint new leaders to head the fifteen new, smaller divisional units. Second, the issue of saving face is extremely crucial in Asia, including India. It would be deemed highly inappropriate for any of the existing six divisional heads to head any of the new division units, since restructuring the six bigger divisions into fifteen smaller divisions would mean a step down in terms of status for these division heads. Therefore, finding six replacements for the existing heads, let alone finding another nine to head the fifteen new divisional units, posed a major restructuring challenge.

Hans Peter had to decide how he could restructure the existing six large divisions into fifteen smaller divisions, find the appropriate new heads for these divisions, and yet save the face of the six existing top executives.

Hans Peter restructured by promoting the six division heads to directors of the organization. In a meeting with the new directors, Hans Peter emphasized that they would be responsible for mentoring new heads of divisions but not be required to manage their individual division's daily operations. Hans Peter also stressed that as directors, they would serve as coaches for the incoming new heads of the fifteen divisions. By creating new director positions for these six division heads and designating them as coaches for the new incumbents, Hans Peter managed to remove them as division heads and yet "saved their face."

Some of the directors embraced the role of the coach enthusiastically. They served as advisors to the newer heads but did not interfere with daily decision making. Other directors, especially those who had previously been more influential and hands-on, found it more difficult to adapt to their new role. This group continued to make decisions for the divisions rather than offer advice to heads.

Hans Peter next brought in an internal senior human resource consultant to assess the selection of new senior management staff.

Hans Peter wanted to make sure the new division heads he selected fulfilled three criteria: they had to be technically competent to perform their role, they had to be able to work cooperatively with peers and direct reports, and they had to be able to assert influence over others.

Hans Peter called in a human resource consultant from the Swiss headquarters to develop a center for selecting Indian executives for the new critical roles. Hans Peter realized that assessments used in Switzerland might need to be modified to adapt to the Asian and specifically the Indian context. For example, in one assessment center exercise, participants had to make a decision about buying a plot of land to accommodate the company's demands for employee parking. Participants were given two options: to choose a piece of land with virgin forest or to choose a piece of land that was adjacent to a hospital and a grade school. An initial pilot of the exercise showed that Indian executives did not hesitate to choose the plot of virgin forest over the piece of land near the hospital and grade school. Because environmental activists are not strong in India, the choice of cutting down trees in virgin forests did not pose the ethical dilemma that the decision-making exercise was supposed to present. Eventually, they had to change the exercise, making the choice not a virgin forest but a slum, so that the choices would appear more equal.

In selecting executives, Hans Peter found out that just as the manner in which one influences others differs across cultures, how leaders are selected differs as well. In Western cultures, those who spoke up frequently tended to be the ones seen as having greater influence over other members in the group. In Asia, including India, those who tended to be silent or passive in the group but who, when they spoke, commanded attention seemed to have greater influence.

Hans Peter learned that although the criteria for selecting top executives may remain the same across cultures, selection strategies and the behavioral cues for the fulfillment of those criteria can and do differ across cultures.

headquarters-mandated initiative for business process reengineering by flattening the organizational design of a local organization that preferred a steeper and taller design.

Cultural Differences in Work and Personal Time Boundaries

In some cultures, such as Denmark and other Scandinavian countries, there is a distinction between work time and social or home time. Workers draw very clear boundaries between work time and personal time, and they expect to have their weekends free and to take their lunch breaks and vacation judiciously. These individuals expect to work hard during their scheduled forty-hour work week; they do not find it reasonable to take time away from family life by working sixty to seventy hours per week, as is common in the United States and Asian countries, where the distinction between work time and personal time is not as stark.

As a case in point, a German professional working in a Singapore head-hunting agency refused to answer the phone during lunch breaks. Although she was a very conscientious and committed employee, in her view, lunch was her personal time, and it was not reasonable to expect her to work through lunch.

In one major conference held in Norway, the general conference chair, a Norwegian, was absent from the opening ceremony of the conference because the function was scheduled on a Sunday. On Sundays, with no exceptions, he dons the uniform of a scoutmaster and spends quality time with his ten-year-old son on scouting expeditions and activities. Norwegians pride themselves in balancing work and family life and drawing clear work life boundaries.

A Hong Kong manager working at an investment firm related a story of some relevance on this topic. It seems that his company installed a very nice shower facility for the convenience of its employees. A number of the managers, however, were unhappy with this addition. When asked what the problem was with the showers and locker rooms, one manager commented, "Now all they need to do is put in some cots and we won't ever be able to go home." Prior to introducing the showers, employees always had an excuse to go home (for at least a short visit) and have some time with their families, even if they had to return to work later. This provided them with some separation of work and family that was now largely absent.

Cultural Differences in Motivational Needs for Achievement, Affiliation, and Security

> If Maslow was an Asian, the apex of human needs will be social harmony, not self-actualization.
>
> *Musings of a Taiwanese social psychologist*

People are motivated, energized, and driven to perform by different needs. The nature of these needs and the relative value placed on each of them reflect our underlying hierarchy of cultural values and therefore differ from culture to culture.

Collective cultures value social needs for harmonious relationships over more individualized needs for personal achievement or self-actualization. In Nepal, the McDonald's employee-of-the-month award is rotated amongst all employees and not identified by individual productivity or performance, so that the employees' need for social harmony within the group at the workplace is stressed over individual achievement. If incentive and reward systems conflict with the inherent culture of your followers, you may reap the form of the reward system but lose its meaning, purpose, and substance.

In some cases rewards may be used to motivate future performance rather than compensate for the past. In some small computer companies in Japan, the employee who performs worst receives the largest individual annual bonus! Why? Japanese business culture uses shame as a motivational tool, and the presentation of the bonus is made in public. The person who receives the large bonus is thus made to realize that he hasn't performed at all well. He then works much harder to ensure he doesn't receive such a public distinction the next year.

In countries that are high in rule orientation, such as Japan and Greece, intangibles such as job security are valued more highly than self-actualization. In countries high in power distance, intangibles such as position and status are valued more than tangible financial rewards such as bonuses or stock options.

Direct versus Indirect Communication of Feedback in Low- and High-Context Cultures

The greatest challenge in the controlling and monitoring stage of the leadership process is in giving feedback to subordinates.

Box 8.5
Providing negative feedback across cultures

Providing negative feedback is tricky because feedback is evaluative and can therefore lead to hurt feelings. Warren*, an American, learned that the manner in which he gave feedback to employees appear to work well in the United States but not as well in India. People in a low-context culture such as the United States are more direct and efficient in their communication style. They focus on results and outcomes rather than on effort or process. For instance, Warren would go through a report prepared by an American subordinate, point the flaws out directly to the subordinate, and direct the subordinate to "correct it and come back tomorrow."

When giving feedback in Asian countries such as India, one must recognize and respect the effort the employee has put into his or her work and not focus simply on the work's outcome. Giving negative feedback is especially tricky in Asia because Asians tend to experience greater loss of face when feedback is too confrontational. For example, in Thailand one must think very carefully and be extremely polite when giving negative feedback. If negative feedback is given too directly, it may backfire on the feedback giver or the boss. The boss may be accused of being highly ineffective for not giving adequate or clear instructions to his or her subordinates in the first place.

In India, which is a high-context culture, Warren had to modify his communicative style to be more indirect and to recognize effort explicitly. When Warren said to an Indian employee, "I appreciate the effort that you have put in, but why did you not think about doing it this way?" the Indian employee understood that he or she had to correct the work.

*Not his real name.

Collectivist cultures value what psychologists call self-effacement because they place the group before the self. Self-effacement means downplaying rather than promoting oneself, making oneself "invisible," and not taking credit for one's success. Individualistic cultures, in contrast, value self-promotion. Self-promotion means promoting oneself, making oneself "visible" to others, and taking personal credit for one's success. This isn't to suggest that managers in an individually oriented culture such as the United States wish to take undue credit for work; however, they do wish to have appropriate recognition for their accomplishments. Such recognition is celebrated and shared publicly; in group-oriented cultures, it is kept more private.

As a result, we find that American managers who have individualistic orientations tend to use much more positive feedback to motivate individual followers; however, in Asian cultures, giving positive feedback to individuals is less prevalent, as the act tends to embarrass rather than motivate the individual. Compliments and criticisms in Asian cultures are usually not conveyed openly, or, if they are, they're directed at a group and not an individual.

Indirect ways of giving feedback are therefore deemed more tactful in high-context cultures. Asian cultures such as Japan and Hong Kong also prefer indirect communication of negative feedback, rather than the direct feedback that some cultures, such as the United States, are used to. American managers are more likely to provide directions to subordinates on a face-to-face basis, whereas Japanese managers are likely to use written memos. Furthermore, when it comes to negative feedback, U.S. managers will deliver negative feedback in face-to-face interactions, while Japanese managers may ask a peer of the subordinate to deliver the feedback. Box 8.5 illustrates the intricacies of providing negative feedback across cultures.

SUMMARY

The ability to carry out global leadership is a reality in today's business environment. Effective global leaders are able to lead in culturally diverse work settings. How has your experience been when you have had to lead a global company made up of individuals from different cultures? Of the six stages of global leadership development we presented in this chapter, which one reflects your strength, and which one reflects an area you need to develop further?

In this chapter we introduced our six-stage process of global leadership and explained each stage in detail. The six stages are (1) formulating a global vision, (2) communicating a global vision, (3) planning, budgeting, and scheduling of local organizations, (4) designing the local organization structure, (5) influencing and motivating locals, and (6) controlling and monitoring locals' performance.

We identified key cultural markers in each of the six stages. In formulating and communicating a global vision, the key cultural markers are time horizon: short term versus long term, orientation: profit versus people, and cultural difference in power distance: low versus high. In planning, budgeting, and scheduling of local organizations, the key cultural marker is cultural differences in tempo and punctuality. In organizing, the key cultural marker is power distance in organizational designs (tall versus flat, formal versus informal). In influencing and motivating locals, there are three key cultural markers: cultural differences in goal setting at work, cultural differences in work and personal time boundaries, and cultural differences in motivational needs. In controlling and monitoring locals' performance, the key cultural marker is direct versus indirect feedback in low- and high-context cultures.

Build your cultural intelligence by using the six-stage global leadership development model, and you will become a culturally intelligent global leader.

SUMMARY AND CONCLUDING THOUGHTS

Where has our cultural journey taken us? Our discussion of cultural intelligence and its importance in dynamic, global work environments is illustrated nicely with the case of BP-Amoco described by the business professor Manfred Kets de Vries of INSEAD. When Robert Horton became CEO of BP-Amoco, he confronted a number of challenges. The company was in financial difficulties, and he drew upon his experiences of living in the United States for a number of years (though he was born and raised in Great Britain) to provide a directive and aggressive style of dealing with his executives and board. He believed in calling people out and facing them down if they weren't performing. Unfortunately, his tenure was relatively short-lived: he rubbed too many people the wrong way and was replaced by a more traditional British manager, David Simon.

Simon's style of operating reflected his upper-class British origins, including an education at Oxford and a graduate degree in business from INSEAD. He dealt with subordinates in a direct but personable fashion, emphasizing a dignified but directly operational approach to the business. At a time when the business was in turmoil, he provided continuity with this traditional British company's cultural past while giving ample direction to his senior staff for day-to-day operations. More recently, Simon became the chairman of the board and put John Browne in the position of CEO. Browne has moved ahead with an emphasis on vision and forward thinking. His characterization of BP-Amoco as a "learning organization" is a critical reflection of his approach.

What's interesting about the BP-Amoco transition of these three leaders is that as the company and global culture of the company has moved forward, so has its need for different types of leaders. During a time of great corporate complacency, Horton's roughshod approach was useful in unfreezing people's views, although the thaw came at a cost. After creating an environment of uncertainty and competition, some structure and attendance to people's needs were critical, and David Simon provided a needed balance. But daily success and status quo can't position a company for the future, and so John Browne's visionary emphasis has complemented David Simon's tactical and operational emphasis. However, why couldn't BP-Amoco have had a single leader competent to direct the company during these transitional phases?

Horton appears to have had very strong motivational CQ but was perhaps lacking in cultural strategic thinking and behavioral CQ. Simon seems to have had high knowledge (cognitive) CQ as well as moderate energizing and behavioral CQ, but seems to have been lacking in cultural strategic thinking CQ. John Browne appears to have high cultural strategic thinking (visionary) CQ and modest energizing CQ. Taken as a group, these three CEOs, each of whom was successful at different periods in the life of the company, exhibited very different patterns of CQ and, we would suggest, differential potentials for success depending upon the company's corporate and global culture. Ultimately, a true global leader possesses all facets of CQ, enabling him or her to deal with changing global and company culture.

CQ can be thought of, metaphorically, as the head, heart, and body of cultural adaptation. The "head" facet of CQ captures the high-level thinking or thinking-about-thinking part of adaptation. We referred to this as cultural strategic thinking (CST), a term that encompasses the way you develop strategies and methods to learn more about a new culture. Complementary to this facet of CQ is the actual knowledge you have about a culture (cognition), which is reflected by your general knowledge about various parts of the world and how people operate in these regions. Most cultural training programs have emphasized this feature of adjustment, with a focus on lists of features to be learned concerning customs and taboos. Not using your left hand to offer someone your business card in the Middle East and not looking a superior in the eye in an Asian culture are a couple of norms that can be cited. The problem, however, is that these lists are invariably incomplete, as are our own memories!

The "heart" of CQ refers to several important features, including your self-confidence to engage others, your perseverance in the face of setbacks, your ability to maintain goal-directed and focused attention, and your evaluation of others' values and beliefs. A person's actions are generated from a reservoir of energy and commitment. If this reservoir is deep and plentiful, then even the most significant setbacks and failures are met with redoubled effort. But if these reserves are lacking, even minor setbacks may lead a manager to disengage and give up.

Our third and final element, the "body" of CQ, refers to your actions and behavior adaptation. It isn't enough to know why people act as they do, nor to simply feel motivated to deal with them. In order to increase everyone's comfort, you must adapt your actions to theirs. Take the example of a manager from a low-social-distance culture (Mexico) speaking with someone from a high-social-distance culture (Germany). The tendency of the Mexican manager is to get physically close to his German counterpart (typically twelve to eighteen inches) while his German colleague moves away (typically twenty-four to thirty inches). Do they notice the resulting tension from this tango of cultures? Perhaps. But it is just as likely that they will not notice; the encounter will simply feel uncomfortable or odd to them. This discomfort translates into problems of communication and the potential for distrust. Often, if someone is uncomfortable with another person but doesn't know why, he or she will infer that the other person is untrustworthy or unreliable. Avoiding eye contact is a sign of respect for your boss in Indonesia but signals dishonesty in Canada. Action or behavioral CQ refers to your capacity to adapt your actions and generate new ones that are useful in a new culture. It may involve changing speaking distances, engaging in or avoiding eye contact, or changing your style of speech. These actions facilitate cross-cultural encounters by creating an environment of trust and comfort between people.

Taken together, the head, heart, and body of CQ provide for effective adaptation across cultures and countries. As we've stated throughout the book, it isn't enough to be strong in a single dimension, although various facets seem to complement one another better than others depending on the work-related topic (e.g., multinational teams versus leadership); these facets of CQ always operate better in concert than alone. Ultimately, we hope that you will take your CQ results and use them in several ways. First, you should identify your strengths and use them accordingly, because nothing enhances adaptation like successful encounters in a new culture. Second, use your weaknesses as a focus for your efforts in the future. If you know you've got a low action CQ score, then it will serve you well to focus attention on adjusting your behaviors according to those of people in a new culture. Some managers find it useful to seek advice and experience from acting coaches. Remember, you are not acting to fool someone; you are acting and mimicking behaviors to help others (as well as yourself) feel more comfortable in encounters, which results in improved communication, understanding, and trust.

In the next section, we revisit and discuss a developmental guide (see chapter 2) that you can follow to implement the CQ program we've presented here.

DEVELOPING YOUR CQ USING THE PRISM MODEL

In chapter 1 we introduced an approach that we call the PRISM model of using CQ in your own work environment. After a brief review of this approach, we'll describe several work situations in which we've used the CQ method. The reader will recall that we described the PRISM model as consisting of five core components:

- *Preparing your mind* (how you acquire knowledge and how you think). Goal: acquiring the rules or cultural knowledge for effective adaptation to different cultures.

- *Reviewing and learning* (how you think about your thinking; how you plan, monitor and review; and how you learn). Goal: knowing how and when to reconfigure the rules for effective adaptation to different cultures.

- *Identifying your strengths and weaknesses* (knowing your strengths and weaknesses by having your CQ profiled—e.g., are you weak or strong in cultural strategic thinking, motivation, and/or behavior?). Goal: increasing self-awareness of your CQ and developing a road map for training and development to enhance effective adaptation to different cultures.

- *Setting goals and targets* (knowing what you want to achieve and exerting energy and drive to achieve your goals and targets). Goal: establishing the *Reasons* for effective adaptation to different cultures.

- *Mobilizing your resources* (displaying appropriate behaviors and actions for adapting to different cultures). Goal: ability to use appropriate behaviors and actions, or repertoires, for effective adaptation to different cultures.

Now that you've completed this book, you're ready to develop your CQ using the PRISM model in a new assignment or work situation.

The first fundamental component is "Prepare your mind." Preparation is a key first step. You need to prepare and plan well for new cultural experiences. If you fail to plan, you plan to fail.

The central component in the PRISM model is "Identifying Your Strengths and Weaknesses." This component focuses on your plan for developing and enhancing your CQ. It's important to focus on your relative strengths and not to dwell on your lowest scores. Our experience is that if you leverage your natural strengths, you'll have much better success than if you focus on your weaknesses and simply attempt to overcome them. This isn't to say you should ignore your problem areas; a global manager needs a full and accurate account of relative strengths so that he or she can do a proper job of overcoming limitations. However, it's our belief that overcoming

and so on. Information is the key resource for the manager who scores high in the cultural strategic thinking aspect of CQ. It's this information that provides a basis for developing and testing out your ideas about the new workplace culture. However, once this information is gathered, you actually gain your insights through an internal process. This outside-to-inside sequence is critical for this type of manager. Once brought inside, information becomes the fuel for the fire of insight and, subsequently, the knowledge aspect of CQ (cultural knowledge). In a parallel fashion, a person with very high cognitive CQ has a vast knowledge of world cultures in general. This type of manager needs to learn as much as possible about a new culture so that he or she can then draw upon this learning directly. The key resource for the manager with high knowledge CQ is to gain access to information that tells him or her directly about a given culture. It is this type of manager who's best suited for traditional methods of cultural training, which stresses the lists of cultural dos and don'ts in a given country.

Finally, a manager with high behavioral CQ must gather resources from observation of other people's actions. It is through acting and interacting with others that he or she will be able to work effectively. Social mimicry is one of the key talents here, and this obviously requires direct observation of others. We've found that at least modest levels of direct contact and interaction are needed to optimize one's adjustment to the new culture. Observations may be made by watching others on television, but the most powerful lessons are learned by direct contact and socializing. For the manager with high behavioral CQ, key resources are other people, simply acting as they normally do.

In all likelihood, you will have several facets of CQ in your favor as you approach new work challenges. A strong combination (as we discussed earlier in the book) is a manager who has high cultural strategic thinking along with high behavioral CQ. The key resources for this type of manager are, ironically, a bit at odds. The cultural strategic thinker wants to gather data and digest it in a careful, well-reasoned fashion, while the behavioral manager needs to get into the thick of things and walk his or her own path. If the two resources are well balanced, the cultural strategic thinking and behavioral CQ manager uses his or her strategic plans as a way of gathering alternative ways of acting in a new setting. He or she asks himself or herself not only what's being done (acting) but also why it's being done (cultural strategic thinking). A combination of high cultural strategic thinking CQ and high energizing CQ is a formidable pair as well. This manager takes his or her self-confidence and motivation and channels it into a systematic discovery of new ways in which people conduct themselves. Lacking either element would be limiting — having cultural strategic thinking without goals and confidence means you'll become discouraged quickly and give up, while having energizing CQ without cultural strategic thinking is unguided and potentially fruitless.

In our PRISM framework, it is important to review and learn from each cultural encounter and experience and to evaluate and judge the successes of your adaptation and adjustment. Here you need to rely on a variety of sources:

- Work colleagues (perhaps through a 360-degree feedback session, where appropriate);
- Company evaluation through your supervisor;
- Reactions from casual encounters in shops, stores, restaurants, theaters, subways, and buses;
- Personal assessment of adjustment and comfort in dealing with others;
- Personal assessment of knowledge and awareness of the new culture; and
- Reassessment of your CQ after working on improving areas of deficiency.

Just as you were systematic in developing your plan for determining the best way to integrate yourself in your new work culture, you need a systematic way of judging your success in doing so. Adaptation to a new culture is the heart of what we mean by cultural intelligence, so the critical question is, "Have I adjusted and adapted?" How do you answer this question? You begin by looking at our sources for evaluation listed above and compare these with your successes in a variety of situations, such as at the office, at the market, in social settings, and at home as you deal with friends and colleagues as well as strangers. Importantly, another key person to ask about this success is yourself. Do you feel more comfortable dealing with others in this culture than you did when you first joined it? Do people seem to "get" you? Are people comfortable around you, and do they seek you out and enjoy dealing with you? When you go to the market or a shop, can people figure out what you want to buy, or do you continue to have trouble communicating your ideas? Has your family made the transition as well? How are things going for your spouse? In reality, your spouse's adjustment will be a key factor in whether you'll complete your work assignment. If you can answer yes to each of these questions, then it's very likely that your adjustment has been a great success. We've found it useful, as a final check, for a manager using the CQ method to reassess the CQ facets after being in an assignment for roughly six months and to check for improvement in previously weak areas. If you focus your efforts, there is no reason that you shouldn't improve your CQ scores substantially within six to twelve months.

NEW DIRECTIONS AND SAMPLE PROGRAMS BASED ON THE CULTURAL INTELLIGENCE FRAMEWORK

Although work on cultural intelligence is in its infancy, we have implemented several corporate and educational interventions based on our framework. These programs include a specialty seminar developed for Deutsche Bank in India and Russia as well as full-time MBA programs at the Nanyang Business School and the London Business School. In this section, we describe these programs as examples of how managers can make use of CQ in various types of companies.

Deutsche Bank Smart Sourcing Program

Our program at Deutsche Bank was developed to complement an ongoing training program that had been developed by the London Business School for Deutsche Bank's outsourcing activities. Like many companies in the financial industry, Deutsche Bank has made a move to outsource a number of its corporate needs to foreign locales, including India, Russia, and the Philippines. The bank's work in India represents a significant new effort to provide superior service for its clients while reducing its operating costs.

India has emerged as a key area for outsourcing, particularly in the area of information technology and software programming, with Bangalore and Hyderabad being key cities. Companies in India dealing with software solutions for global companies include Infosys, DSL, and Intelliapp Solutions. Many global financial institutions such as Citicorp, Bank of America, and Deutsche Bank rely more and more on these companies for their software development needs.

In 2003 the London Business School was contacted by Deutsche Bank to expand upon an ongoing and successful outsourcing program already in place (which Deutsche Bank refers to as the company's "smart sourcing initiative"). The bank's needs were both specific and general, with a focus on developing the most effective relationship possible with its outsource partner, a fully owned subsidiary that was in the process of being separated out. Of course, the real challenge facing Deutsche Bank's employees was to make their interactions and team activities with their Indian partners as effective as possible. To this end, we developed a two-and-a-half-day seminar for their mid-level and senior managers from the GTO (Global Technology Organization) group.

The Deutsche Bank seminar was designed around the theme of outsourcing to India, and the bank sought to enhance their employees' effectiveness in working globally. Our design consisted of several modules capturing various aspects of CQ.

First, the design philosophy was not teaching the dos and don'ts of doing business and working with Indians. Our emphasis was not on the cognitive aspects of CQ; rather, we emphasized the thinking-about-thinking and energizing elements. The program began with general cultural issues surrounding expatriate and global work assignments using an exercise developed by Nigel Nicholson at the London Business School, in which participants rank order fifteen key characteristics of a candidate for an expatriate work assignment. This type of brainstorming activity is parallel to exercises such as "survival in the desert [or on the moon]," with an important difference — it stimulates the participants to think strategically about traits that are important in various cultural circumstances. After this exercise, the participants had a nice Indian meal and an evening presentation concerning Indian business practices and etiquette in the IT sector. Our intention was to provide some specific rules and practices that might complement the earlier exercise, thus combining a high level of cultural strategic thinking with some specific content for India.

On the following day, the participants went through a series of cultural training exercises, including a formal discussion of the elements of CQ, and they were provided their specific CQ results based on a survey they completed prior to the start of the program. In addition to their CQ scores, they were provided with some analyses of their emotional and social intelligence as a basis for comparison with their CQ. After discussing the meaning of their scores, the Deutsche Bank managers broke into small groups to discuss more specifically how they might use their CQ strengths to improve their current outsourcing projects. The purpose of this exercise was to get them to learn new strategies and methods for dealing with people from another culture.

The CQ brief was used as a springboard for an afternoon discussion concerning multinational teams and how to run them more effectively using a culturally intelligent approach. We focused on four basic questions:

1. Who are we as a team?
2. Who am I as a member of this team?
3. How do we go about the work of teams?
4. How can we maintain and improve upon our team successes?

These questions were addressed using a variety of methods, including self-assessment surveys, role playing, and small-group discussions.

The most effective multinational teams have at least three core elements that we refer to as the "$GR^2 = T$" or "Great" teams formula (where G = goals, R = roles, R = rules, and T = trust and commitment). The three elements are goals × roles × rules, meaning that a multinational team needs to have a focus or purpose through common goals, clearly defined and integrated roles, and agreed-upon rules and procedures for dealing with one another. If these three elements are in place, then a team is very likely to experience high trust and commitment. The critical question that arises when multinational teams are formed is how to create and agree upon goals, roles, and rules using CQ knowledge.

As we discussed in chapter 7 on global teams, two elements of CQ are critical at this formative stage of a multinational team: thinking about thinking and energizing. The energizing aspect of CQ is the most straightforward, because developing a common and shared team view is very difficult for highly diverse multinational teams. Perseverance and confidence are needed if teams are to overcome their differences and focus on their similarities. High-level strategizing is also required, because members of the team must discover what they have in common — a kind of lowest common denominator of the multinational team.

The Deutsche Bank program next focused on information specific to India about the general IT business environment, the industrial structure, and general knowledge. This was not intended as some kind of crash course on India. Rather, this information provided a general context for the following day's presentation by a professor of business strategy who focused on outsourcing with IT companies in India. His presentation, which also focused on cultural strategic thinking about India, provided a broad context for understanding the use of outsourcing as a way for businesses to gain a competitive advantage. He emphasized the general role that outsourcing may play for achieving business strategies and enumerated the key elements in finding good outsource partners.

An important focus of this program was to work on the cultural strategic thinking aspect of CQ so that not only did participants learn how better to deal with their Indian outsource partners, but also they would be helped in developing future outsourcing relationships in different countries. Our emphasis was on specific team building and communication in India using a set of general skills that might be as easily applied to Russia, the Philippines, or Malaysia.

We have also used CQ as a guide for MBA education at the Nanyang Business School and the London Business School. We describe our efforts at the Nanyang Business School because it is, to the best of our knowledge, the most comprehensive cultural training program of its type.

Nanyang Business School

At the Nanyang Business School at Nanyang Technological University in Singapore, all MBA students go through a rigorous and systematic assessment of their CQ. CQ is a central component of both the undergraduate and MBA programs.

The world's first academic training program on cultural intelligence was launched at Nanyang Business School in July 2003. The program was exclusively designed and developed by the Center for Cultural Intelligence (CCI) at Nanyang Technological University. A group of fifty-eight managers and executives from twelve different countries in all parts of the world congregated in Singapore to undergo a unique and innovative cross-cultural experience anchored in cultural intelligence. Participants were profiled using the cultural intelligence assessment instrument, and they received detailed feedback on all facets of cultural intelligence. They also knew how their scores compared to the managerial norms of representative groups.

Participants were placed in cross-cultural dyads throughout the training to enable them to develop strategies for interacting, communicating, and collaborating with people from different cultures, as well as to assess their effectiveness in cross-cultural adjustment and adaptation. One highlight of the multisensory and multimodal training program was a visit to one of Singapore's most famous cultural sites, Little India, where participants, in their cross-cultural dyads, were asked to take pictures or snapshots of different cultural activities (e.g., fortune telling using cards or parrots, henna tattoos, a spice processing plant, temples, restaurants, street vendors, etc.). Although some of the managers and executives were from India, they found the experience of trying to discover the subtle and nuanced cultural differences between the Indian culture in Singapore and the Indian culture in their home country refreshing and challenging. They realized they had to activate their cultural strategic thinking to deal with the task, as did the non-Indian participants.

Another highlight was the one-day training program that was jointly developed by CCI and a team of theater performers from a local avant-garde theater group. The theater experience really challenged participants to develop their behavioral repertoires for effective cross-cultural adaptation. They were put through a gamut of highly interactive and behaviorally challenging activities that helped them gain deeper insights into the behavioral aspects of CQ.

London Business School

At the London Business School we implemented a scaled-down version of the ambitious program run at Nanyang. All MBA students at the London Business School work in internationally diverse teams ranging from five to seven people. This diversity is reflected by a student body that is approximately 85 percent of non-U.K. origin, coming from over forty countries throughout the world. Team-based activities are central to success in the school environment throughout the two-year program, which includes coursework, study groups, and field project activities. Effective functioning in an internationally and interculturally diverse work setting is critical for these students.

The MBA students undergo a four-day leadership skills orientation program that includes 360-degree feedback sessions, role playing and case study exercises, team building, and team process exercises, as well as cultural intelligence training. The CQ training begins with the MBAs completing the CQ inventory prior to their matriculation at the university. Next, they are provided with a half-day discussion of culture and the work environment, along with a debriefing of the CQ assessment tool. In addition, they receive extensive information about their personality structure (through an assessment using the NEO "Big Five" survey revealing their personality in five dimensions) as well as the team roles they preferred and measures of their emotional and social intelligence. They are debriefed during the course of their skills week concerning these various assessments. We emphasize a number of skills during the debriefing session such as cultural thinking strategies for learning about other peoples' cultures and behavior styles. There is a strong emphasis on the MBAs' sharing with one another their own version of best practices to discover new cultures and to explore which of these strategies might best suit each participant. Another critical and somewhat unusual point for these students is their extremely high energizing CQ scores. (Perhaps this should be expected, given that students come to a school like the London Business School because of its international environment.) The problem from which many of our students suffer is overconfidence concerning adjustment. Just as overconfidence in work might lead a person to take on challenges that result in failure, it may, in a cultural context, cause someone to just push his or her way through difficult situations without paying enough attention to the nuances of the challenge. Just as too little confidence may be a problem (one that can lead to the person's withdrawing from the situation), too much confidence may tempt someone to do too much too soon.

The CQ briefing is followed up with a mid-year meeting with each of the teams to see how their team dynamics are progressing. This mid-year discussion includes a 360-degree assessment by the team members within each team, focusing on cultural and personal adjustment issues. Although this program has only recently been introduced into the MBA program, the results appear very promising for identifying those individuals who are adept at adjusting to and working in highly diverse teams.

WHAT ARE THE NEXT STEPS FOR CULTURAL INTELLIGENCE?

In this book we have provided a new way of thinking about clashes of cultures and values and of operating as a global manager. The challenges that face managers working in an intercultural environment (whether they are leading a diverse team within a country, leading a diverse international team, or managing a facility overseas) are numerous. Past approaches using country- or culture-specific training fail to capture the complexities facing the modern global manager. Lists of the top ten things to do or not to do in a country, details about a country from a geopolitical viewpoint, and so on are a useful starting point for cultural training, but they are grossly incomplete. Even methods such as cultural assimilators using vignettes and scenarios to teach people the general rules for operating in a given country are incomplete. One useful method is being pioneered by Professors Dharm Bhawuk and Richard Brislin. Rather than focusing on a particular target country, the emphasis is on a target cultural value that can be shared across countries. For example, they have produced a cultural assimilator drawing from the culture theory of individualism to create critical incidents that apply across countries, rather than emphasizing any single nation. Critical incidents are drawn from individualism-collectivism theory and cover a wide range of social behaviors based on the self, goal prioritization, and motivation.

This general values–based assimilator has some drawbacks. Cultural values–based assimilators can be costly to design and time consuming for participants. More important, however, it remains unclear how the knowledge gained in cultural values–based assimilator training might transfer to similar (but new) circumstances with dissimilar surface features within the target culture, given the documented poor transfer of learning associated with teaching by analogy. That is, it remains unclear whether cultural assimilators provide any more cultural strategic thinking benefits for participants than their traditional country-based counterparts. Further, the focus on a particular cultural value in this approach may inadvertently lead global managers to overemphasize one aspect of culture over more significant ones for a particular country. For example, although Thailand may be characterized by a certain level of individualism, power and hierarchy are more central to people's actions. If people are trained with a specific cultural value assimilator, they may use this "lens" to interpret everything that they see around them, even if it isn't the right lens to use. Despite this limitation, the Bhawuk and Brislin approach represents an important advancement in training methods because it taps into the thinking-about-thinking part of cultural intelligence we've emphasized so much in this book.

So in the end, what we are left with is a very different way to think about how managers adjust to a multicultural and international environment. Our emphasis has been on the head, heart, and body of adjustment — thinking about thinking and knowledge, energy and confidence, action adaptation and mimicry — as a way to understand and predict a person's ability to adjust to new and dynamic environments. Although we've emphasized international adjustment, it should be apparent that our approach improves people's ability to adjust to diverse environments based on other kinds of characteristics such as gender, race, and age, as well as occupation and profession. Cultural differences exist all around us — in our companies, across business units or departments. For example, we do some consulting work for Unilever. This large, global company provides a good example of the layers of diversity that a global manager faces. Unilever has international diversity, with operations in over forty countries worldwide: business group diversity in areas such as personal care products, foods, and chemicals; occupational diversity in areas such as marketing, R & D, or production; personal diversity such as age and gender differences; and so on. These layers of diversity (woven together much like a spiderweb) are not easily addressed through a traditional approach to diversity based on cultural awareness. There is just too much diversity to capture in an awareness program! Our alternative is to set aside the specific learning of facts in favor of a coordinated integration using cultural strategic thinking, energy, and focus, as well as effective action.

The world is immensely complex, and the challenges faced by a global manager may seem insurmountable. However, a full appreciation of your cultural intelligence and how to leverage it to your advantage is an important first step in tackling this complexity. The culturally intelligent manager is someone who can grapple with global challenges and prevail.

FURTHER READINGS

GENERAL COUNTRY-SPECIFIC INFORMATION

Microsoft Encarta
Baedeker's guides
Foreign embassies and travel bureaus
Local country interest groups
Country chambers of commerce

BUSINESS INFORMATION

Adler, N. J. (1991). *International dimensions of organizational behavior* (2nd ed.). Boston: PWS-Kent.

Adler, N. J. (2002). *International dimensions of organizational behavior* (4th ed.). Cincinnati, OH: South-Western.

Bandura, A. (1997). *Self-efficacy: The exercise of control.* New York: W. H. Freeman.

Bond, M. (1988). *Beyond the Chinese face.* Hong Kong: Oxford University Press.

Dowling, P. J., Welch, D. E., & Schuler, R. S. (1999). *International human resource management: Managing people in a multinational context* (3rd ed.). Cincinnati, OH: South-Western.

Earley, P. C., & Ang, S. (2003). *Cultural intelligence: Individual interactions across cultures.* Palo Alto: Stanford University Press.

Earley, P. C., & Erez, M. (1997). *The transplanted executive.* New York: Oxford University Press.

Earley, P. C., & Mosakowski, E. (2004). Cultural intelligence. *Harvard Business Review.* October.

England, G. W. (1975). *The manager and his values: An international perspective from the United States, Japan, Korea, India, and Australia.* Cambridge, MA: Ballinger Press.

Erez, M., & Earley, P. C. (1993). *Culture, self-identity, and work.* New York: Oxford University Press.

Gannon, M. J. (1994). *Understanding global cultures: Metaphorical journeys through seventeen countries.* Thousand Oaks, CA: Sage Publications.

Graham, J. L., & Sano, Y. (1989). *Smart bargaining: Doing business with the Japanese.* Los Angeles: Sano Management.

Hall, E. T. (1966). *The hidden dimension.* New York: Doubleday.

Hampden-Turner, C., & Trompenaars, A. (1993). *The seven cultures of capitalism: Value systems for creating wealth in the United States, Japan, Germany, France, Britain, Sweden, and the Netherlands.* New York: Currency Doubleday.

Harris, P. R., & Moran, R. T. (1979). *Managing cultural differences.* Houston, TX: Gulf.

Hofstede, G. (1991). *Culture and organizations: Software of the mind.* London: McGraw-Hill.

Martin, J. (1993). *Cultures in organizations: Three perspectives.* New York: Oxford University Press.

Mitsubishi Corporation (1988). Tatemae *and* honne: *Distinguishing between good form and real intention in Japanese business culture.* New York: Free Press.

Moran, R. T., & Harris, P. R. (1981). *Managing cultural synergy.* Houston, TX: Gulf.

Schein, E. (1985). *Organizational culture and leadership.* San Francisco: Jossey Bass.

Schneider, S. C., & Barsoux, J. L. (1997). *Managing across cultures.* London: Prentice-Hall.

Thomas, D. C., & Inkson, K. (2004). *Cultural intelligence: People skills for global business.* England: Berrett-Koehler.

Ting-Toomey, S., & Korzenny, F. (1991). *Cross-cultural interpersonal communication.* Newbury Park, CA: Sage Publications.

Triandis, H. C. (1994). *Culture and social behavior.* New York: McGraw-Hill.

Whyte, D. (1994). *The heart aroused: Poetry and the preservation of the soul in corporate America.* New York: Currency Doubleday.

Yip, G. S. (1992). *Total global strategy: Managing for worldwide competitive advantage.* Englewood Cliffs, NJ: Prentice-Hall.

APPENDIX: A SELF-ASSESSMENT OF YOUR CQ*

OVERVIEW

The following questions are about dealing with cultural diversity. There are no right or wrong answers. Instead, the questions simply allow you to assess your preferences, desires, and habits. Thinking about these questions can help you understand your unique strengths and how you relate to people with different cultural backgrounds that you meet both in your own country and in other societies.

Read each question carefully and choose either *a* or *b*. Do not think too long about any question. If you cannot decide on a particular answer, skip the question and come back and answer it at the end.

SECTION A

Instructions

Which of the following choices best describes you when you are in situations characterized by cultural diversity? Circle either *a* or *b* (not both) for each question to indicate which better describes you as you are most of the time.

1. Would you rather work with someone who is from
   a. the same or a similar culture, or
   b. a very different culture?

2. When you are with a person from a different culture, do you
   a. plan what you say, or
   b. act spontaneously?

3. Do you like to
   a. travel in your home country, or
   b. travel to faraway places?

4. When you know you will be meeting someone from a different culture, do you
   a. script what you want to say before you start, or
   b. treat them as you would any other person from your own culture?

*© Linn Van Dyne and Soon Ang

5. Do you typically
   a. assume many roles, or
   b. adopt one primary role?

6. At parties with people from diverse cultural backgrounds, do you
   a. mimic other people, or
   b. maintain your own style?

7. In your daily work, would you prefer a job in a culture that is
   a. similar to your own, or
   b. different from your own?

8. When thinking about understanding people from different cultures, are you
   a. an expert, or
   b. a novice?

9. Do you view yourself as
   a. beginning to learn more about culture, or
   b. having lots of cultural expertise?

10. When speaking to people from diverse cultures, do you use a
    a. consistent speaking style, or
    b. variety of accents?

11. Would you say you are
    a. not really aware when people are from other cultures, or
    b. very aware when people are from other cultures?

12. Which best describes you?
    a. I read more than two languages, or
    b. I read one or two languages.

13. Are you
    a. alert to the possibility that someone might be from a different culture, or
    b. indifferent that someone might be from a different culture?

14. When you are in groups of people who have diverse backgrounds, do you
    a. usually stick to your normal way of speaking, or
    b. change the way you speak depending on the group?

15. When you work on a project, do you find you prefer to work with
    a. people from similar cultures, or
    b. people from different cultures?

16. When you are with people who have a different cultural background, do you
    a. think about the differences, or
    b. forget they are different?

17. In getting a job done, which describes you better?
    a. I am indifferent to working with people from other cultures.
    b. I celebrate cultural differences.

18. When it comes to knowing how to cope with cultural diversity, would others say you are
    a. very knowledgeable, or
    b. a neophyte?

19. In your spare time, would you choose to
    a. upgrade your technical skills, or
    b. learn about cultural differences?

20. Given the choice, would you select working with people who are
    a. not that competent technically, but are from similar cultures, or
    b. technically *very* competent, but from *very* different cultures?

21. In terms of knowing how to navigate new cultures, do you see yourself as
    a. highly experienced, or
    b. at the entry level?

22. Do you tend to
    a. be aware that people from another culture are different, or
    b. pay very little attention to whether or not they are different?

23. Is it your habit
    a. not to plan in advance when interacting with those from different cultures, or
    b. to take charge of your interactions when with those from different cultures?

24. Do you typically
    a. stick to our own mannerisms, or
    b. modify your mannerisms when you talk with people from different cultures?

25. Would you rank working with people from different cultures as
    a. one of your many interests, or
    b. a top interest?

26. Do you
    a. eat what is familiar to you, or
    b. try what others eat when having meals with people from other cultures?

27. Are you more likely to
    a. set clear goals before you start working with others from different cultures, or
    b. work with them as if they were your regular colleagues?

28. When you have to meet strangers from another culture, do you
    a. go with the flow and according to the situation, or
    b. carefully plan your conversation in advance?

29. Would you say that you enjoy
    a. striking up conversations with culturally diverse people, or
    b. having conversations with those who are more similar?

30. In your work, do you
    a. use a uniform style of interacting with everyone in the group, or
    b. change the way you interact depending on the cultural backgrounds of those in the group?

31. In business situations that require cross-cultural negotiations, do you have
    a. deep knowledge, or
    b. basic knowledge?

32. When visiting different cultures, do you
    a. modify the way you dress, or
    b. dress the way you do in your home country?

33. When conflicts arise with those from other cultures, do you
    a. learn from failures and build on successes, or
    b. pay little attention to cultural sources of failures and successes?

34. In keeping a conversation going with someone from another culture, do you
    a. have difficulty dealing with ambiguity and differences, or
    b. deal successfully with ambiguity and differences?

SECTION B

Instructions

Imagine that you are in a situation where you are interacting with people from different cultural backgrounds. Circle the answer (*a* or *b*) that best describes you.

35. In culturally diverse situations, you are
    a. spontaneous
    b. planful.

36. In culturally diverse situations, you are
    a. predictable
    b. flexible.

37. In culturally diverse situations, you feel
    a. involved
    b. indifferent.

38. In culturally diverse situations, you are
    a. systematic
    b. casual.

39. In culturally diverse situations, you are
    a. neutral
    b. engaged.

40. In culturally diverse situations, you have
    a. cultural knowledge
    b. technical knowledge.

41. In culturally diverse situations, you
    a. anticipate
    b. react.

42. In culturally diverse situations, you are a
    a. learner
    b. professional.

43. In culturally diverse situations, you feel
    a. highly interested
    b. somewhat interested.

44. In culturally diverse situations, you
    a. go with the flow
    b. prepare in advance.

45. In culturally diverse situations, you are
    a. reserved
    b. a good actor.

46. In culturally diverse situations, you are
    a. broad
    b. narrow.

47. In culturally diverse situations, you are
    a. excited
    b. neutral.

48. In culturally diverse situations, you are
    a. current
    b. dated.

49. In culturally diverse situations, you are
    a. unsure
    b. energized.

50. In culturally diverse situations, you are
    a. confident
    b. uncertain.

51. In culturally diverse situations, you
    a. speak one language
    b. speak many languages.

52. In culturally diverse situations, you are
    a. experienced
    b. a novice.

53. In culturally diverse situations, you view interaction as
    a. an activity
    b. a priority.

54. In culturally diverse situations, you are
    a. conscious
    b. unaware.

SCORING INSTRUCTIONS

Section A

For each item, score a 3 in the box to the right of the item if your answer corresponds to the letter shown in the answer column. Add up the columns at the bottom of the page to get your cultural strategic thinking (CST), cultural motivation (MOT), and cultural behavior (BEH) scores.

Question/item	Answer	CST	MOT	BEH
1	b		☐	
2	a	☐		
3	b		☐	
4	a	☐		
5	a			☐
6	a			☐
7	b		☐	
8	a	☐		
9	b	☐		
10	b			☐
11	b	☐		
12	a			☐
13	a	☐		
14	b			☐
15	b		☐	
16	a	☐		
17	b		☐	
18	a	☐		
19	b		☐	
20	b		☐	
21	a	☐		
22	a	☐		
23	b	☐		
24	b			☐
25	b		☐	
26	b			☐
27	a	☐		
28	b	☐		
29	a		☐	
30	b			☐
31	a	☐		
32	a			☐
33	a	☐		
34	b			☐

Section A subtotals for

CST	MOT	BEH
_____	_____	_____

Section B

For each item, score a 3 in the box to the right of the item if your answer corresponds to the letter in the answer column. Add up the columns at the bottom of the page to get your cultural strategic thinking (CST), cultural motivation (MOT), and cultural behavior (BEH) scores.

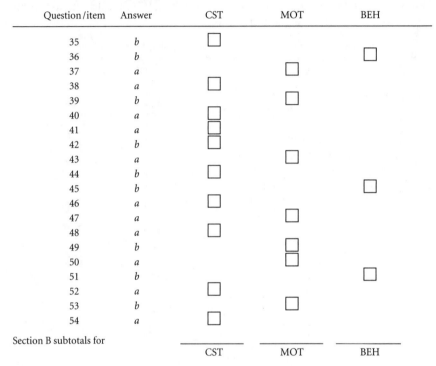

Question/item	Answer	CST	MOT	BEH
35	b	☐		
36	b			☐
37	a		☐	
38	a	☐		
39	b		☐	
40	a	☐		
41	a	☐		
42	b	☐		
43	a		☐	
44	b	☐		
45	b			☐
46	a	☐		
47	a		☐	
48	a	☐		
49	b		☐	
50	a		☐	
51	b			☐
52	a	☐		
53	b		☐	
54	a	☐		

Section B subtotals for

——————— ——————— ———————
     CST   MOT   BEH

Worksheet

	Cultural Strategic Thinking (CST)	Cultural Motivation (MOT)	Cultural Behavior (BEH)
Subtotal from Section A			
Subtotal from Section B			
Total (Sections A + B)			

OVERALL CULTURAL INTELLIGENCE

Overall Cultural Intelligence (CQ™) = Total CST + Total MOT + Total BEH

Write your overall Cultural Intelligence (CQ™) score here: _____

Interpretation of Your Overall CQ™ Score

Your score	Interpretation
126 and above	You have **excellent** overall CQ in your ability to work in diverse cultural settings (domestic and/or international).
95–125	You have **average** overall CQ in your ability to work in diverse cultural settings (domestic and/or international).
94 and below	You **need to develop** your overall CQ to be able to work more effectively in diverse cultural settings (domestic and/or international).

Interpretation of Your Cultural Strategic Thinking Score

Your score	Interpretation
51 and above	You are **excellent** in your cultural strategic thinking.
38–50	You are **moderate** in your cultural strategic thinking.
37 or less	Your cultural strategic thinking indicates a **red alert**. This indicates that you need to work on your cultural strategic thinking — especially if your work and life activities put you in situations with people who have different cultural backgrounds.

Interpretation of Your Cultural Motivation Score

Your score	Interpretation
45 and above	You are **excellent** in your cultural motivation.
38–44	You are **moderate** in your cultural motivation.
37 and below	Your cultural motivation indicates a **red alert**. This indicates that you need to work on your cultural motivation — especially if your work and life activities put you in situations with people who have different cultural backgrounds.

Interpretation of Your Cultural Behavior Score

Your score	Interpretation
30 and above	You are **excellent** in your cultural behavior.
21–29	You are **moderate** in your cultural behavior.
20 and below	Your cultural behavior indicates a **red alert**. This indicates that you need to work on your cultural behavior — especially if your work and life activities put you in situations with people who have different cultural backgrounds.

VARIABILITY IN YOUR SCORES

If your scores vary ("excellent"; "moderate"; "red alert") across the three facets of cultural intelligence, you should think of ways that you can capitalize on your strong areas ("excellent") and ways that you can improve in areas where your scores are "moderate" or "red alert."

For more information about the assessment of cultural intelligence, please contact Professor Linn Van Dyne at Michigan State University (vandyne@msu.edu) or Professor Soon Ang at Nanyang Business School, Nanyang Technological University, Singapore (asang@ntu.edu.sg).

INDEX

Italic page numbers indicate material in tables or figures.

DATE DUE

DEMCO 38-296